# Manufacturing
# Casebook

# World Class Manufacturing Casebook

## Implementing JIT and TQC

# Richard J. Schonberger

THE FREE PRESS
*A Division of Macmillan, Inc.*
NEW YORK

Collier Macmillan Publishers
LONDON

The Free Press
A Division of Macmillan, Inc.
866 Third Avenue, New York, N.Y. 10022

Collier Macmillan Canada, Inc.

Printed in the United States of America

printing number

5   6   7   8   9   10

**Library of Congress Cataloging-in-Publication Data**

Schonberger, Richard.
  World class manufacturing casebook.

  Bibliography: p.
  1. Industrial management—Case studies.
2. Production management—Case studies.
3. Manufacturing processes—Case Studies.   I. Title.
HD31.S3386   1987           658           86-25822
ISBN 0-02-929340-5
ISBN 0-02-929350-2 (pbk.)

# Contents

*Preface*                                                                    *vii*

*Introduction*                                                                *xi*

*About the Cases*                                                            *xxv*

1. HyGain-Telex: Analysis for JIT Production                                    1

2. Implementing Kanban at Hewlett-Packard,
   Fort Collins (A)                                                            7

3. Hewlett-Packard, Fort Collins (B): Keeping
   Operators Busy—and Productive                                             15

4. Double A Products: JIT Implementation
   at a Small Plant                                                          18

5. American Ceramic and Glass Products
   Corporation: Quality Philosophy                                           26

6. Omark Industries: Top Management–Driven JIT                               31

7. JIT Beginnings at Burlington Industries                                   41

8. Toyondu Company: Developing a Small
   Average Supplier into a Top-Notch Supplier                                49

9. JIT at Intel—Penang, Malaysia                                            57

10. JIT at Intel—Manila, Philippines                                        61

11. Just-in-Time Production at Hewlett-Packard,
    Personal Office Computer Division                                        65

12.  In-Line Manufacturing (Alias JIT) at Heatilator         77

13.  H-P—Computer Systems Division                           95

14.  Toyota Auto Body, Inc., of California                  107

15.  3M Videocassettes—Hutchinson, Minnesota               116

16.  Getting Ready for Mixed-Model Production
     at Kawasaki Motors in Lincoln, Nebraska                120

17.  Ultrix Corporation                                     124

18.  JIT in Premanufacturing, North American
     Gear, Inc.: Part A—Detail Engineering                  130

19.  JIT in Premanufacturing, North American
     Gear, Inc.: Part B—Purchasing and Order Entry          140

20.  TQC/JIT at Tennant Company                             152

21.  Goodstone Tire Company: Creating
     Responsibility Centers                                 165

22.  Land and Sky Waterbed Company                          173

23.  Lincoln Electric Company                               181

24.  JIT Beginnings—Hewlett-Packard, Greeley
     Division                                               199

25.  JIT in Purchasing at GE, Erie                          212

26.  St. E's Hospital                                       234

     *Bibliography*                                         *251*

# Preface

This case book contains twenty-six cases illustrating the implementation of world-class manufacturing (WCM) concepts. One case concerns a small Japanese company, two involve American-owned plants in the Pacific basin, and the rest involve North American manufacturers.

Most of the cases are based on my own experiences in the last three or four years in helping companies to implement just-in-time (JIT) production with total quality control (TQC). A few are older than that, a few others are based on interview data rather than my personal visit to the site, and still others have been written by someone else. In most of the cases, names and dates are not disguised.

## JIT Case Method

Each case includes questions on issues that companies commonly face in their attempts to implement WCM concepts, particularly JIT manufacturing and TQC. The case questions are embedded in the discussion, which is at variance with the usual case format. The idea is to read some material—perhaps a page—and then to read and answer a JIT/TQC question pertaining to that material. A student (or instructor) in this way can treat the issues in the case in less time than it takes for a case in the usual format.

Most casebooks either place the questions at the end of each case or do not include questions at all. Furthermore, in the case study approach used in U.S. business schools (the Harvard case method) there are no correct answers. The case studies focus on the method of analysis, which tends to cast out very bad solutions but leave several, sometimes contradictory, acceptable solutions.

The WCM cases, on the other hand, all have quite definite correct answers. Students who have read their lessons in WCM or JIT/TQC (from other books) usually will converge on the right answers when the case is discussed. That means that case discussions are not long and drawn out.

Since the new case method takes students through cases rapidly, it might be thought of as the "just-in-time case method."

## Philosophy

How can cases rich in real data have just one set of correct answers? Is the conventional method wrong?

The traditional case method was right for the past era in manufacturing, when plants were so full of waste and manufacturing systems so complicated that any single set of right ways to manage them was impossible to discover. JIT/TQC does away with much of the waste and complexity; in fact, one rule of thumb (there are others) in arriving at the right answers in the cases is, "If it does not reduce waste and complexity, you have the wrong answer."

Much of the conventional method also revolved around tradeoff analysis: If you make quality better, cost goes up; if you respond faster to the customer, quality goes down—and so forth. Today the JIT/TQC community believes, with only slight overstatement, that "there are no tradeoffs." When quality improves, costs do, too; when lead times go down (faster response), they go down because quality has improved, and costs drop at the same time.

Today's books on JIT and quality are all preaching the same concepts and philosophies. We seem to have entered an era of universals—a set of concepts and answers that are good in all cases. It appears even to apply to office and customer-service work, but those applications are not as well developed.

We may call that set of concepts *principles of manufacturing.* (I have read or scanned most of the books in print on manufacturing and have found that the word *principle* has rarely been used before in connection with manufacturing.) Elsewhere I have provided a seventeen-point list of principles of manufacturing (see Chapter 13 of *World Class Manufacturing: The Lessons of Simplicity Applied,* Free Press, 1986). That list may evolve a bit over time, but it will serve dependably right now for any manufacturer wanting to follow the WCM path.

## Use of Casebook and Target Readership

The concepts and techniques of JIT/TQC or, more broadly, WCM may be found in existing books and booklets. Next comes implementation. That is where this casebook, along with the companion book, *World Class Manufacturing,* fits in. Each case tells something about a company's implementation experiences. (The companion book imbeds implementation narrative—real company examples—in discussion of what WCM is about and the implementation concepts.)

This casebook is intended for company training classes, for college and technical classes, and for any individual employed in the manufacturing sector who cares about industrial improvement.

# Introduction

Each case in this book relates how a plant or a company put itself on a course of continual and rapid improvement. Some readers will be satisfied with what they can glean from the narrative in the cases; others will take a more formal training approach, including answering the case questions. The questions steer you toward the issues that companies tend to face in their own implementation efforts. Arriving at "correct" answers to the questions should not be difficult, as long as there has been advance (or concurrent) study of the basic concepts of world-class manufacturing.

Most of those basic concepts are presented elsewhere (see bibliography). The purpose of this introductory section is to present a few additional concepts—ideas not previously published. The concepts center on ratio analysis of shop-floor conditions and the "naturalistic" approach to quality improvement. With understanding of the ratios—a sort of JIT litmus test—you should find it even easier to answer the case questions correctly. Awareness of naturalistic quality, a concept, not an analysis technique, will also help you with the questions.

## Micro-JIT: Ratio Analysis

Just-in-time is usually associated with the production lead time for a *product*. Similarly we used to think of quality assurance (QA) in terms of a product. Now in QA we speak as often of control of a process. Let's extend that view to JIT. That is, how can JIT be applied to a single process or machine, or to a sequential set of processes?

The best way to focus JIT on processes—call it *micro-JIT*—is through JIT ratio analysis. Exhibit I-1 provides three kinds of ratios to use to assess how bad the process is currently and what the opportunities are to improve it through JIT.

## *Lead Time to Work Content*

The first ratio is production lead time to work content. The ideal is 1 to 1: one hour of elapsed time—the lead time—to one hour of actual work content. More practically, the ideal is 1 or 2 to 1. A good ratio, which is not often achieved, is 2 or 3 to 1. Bad, and typical, is a ratio of 5, 10, 20, 100, 1,000, or more to 1. The world's piece-goods producers manufacture tens of thousands of components in which the lead time exceeds five weeks, but the actual "under-tool" time, in which value is being added and work is being done, is only five hours—or, sometimes, five minutes.

Exhibits I-2 and I-3 are actual cases from two divisions of a large U.S. company. The company has a vigorous JIT campaign in progress, and the exhibits—and others like them—were developed

---

*Apply ratios to each machine, process, or production line*

- LT to work content:

  | | |
  |---|---|
  | Ideal | = 1 or 2 to 1 |
  | Good | = 2 or 3 to 1 |
  | Bad (typical) | = 5, 10, 20, 100 to 1 |

- Process speed (assumes 10 shifts/week) to sales rate:

  | | |
  |---|---|
  | Ideal | = 1 or 2 to 1 |
  | Good | = 2 or 3 to 1 |
  | Bad (typical) | = 5, 10, 20, 100, 1,000 to 1 |

- No. of pieces to no. of work stations/operators in a production line:

  | | |
  |---|---|
  | Ideal | = 1 or 2 to 1 |
  | Good | = 2 or 3 to 1 |
  | Bad (typical) | = 5, 10, 20, 100, 500 to 1 |

**Exhibit I-1.** Micro-JIT Ratio Analysis

by the company's JIT planners to identify where the opportunities are and what the baseline for improvement is.

Exhibit I-2 includes a photo and a schematic of what is in the photo. The scene is of a sprocket-boring operation. Four pallet boxes, each holding ten sprockets, are "on deck." Those forty sprockets are worth $11,000. It takes twelve minutes to bore each sprocket, which totals eight hours, or 480 minutes, to process all forty. The lead time for the fortieth one, therefore, is 480 minutes for twelve minutes of work. Since the sprocket currently on the machine once was way back in the queue as the fortieth unit, it, too, took 480 minutes for twelve minutes of work; that is a ratio of 40 to 1. And so it is for all of the sprockets, day in and day out. The 40 to 1 ratio is the average for all units.

The ideal ratio is twelve minutes of lead time for twelve minutes of boring time. That would be achieved if each sprocket arrived from the prior work center just in time to be bored—zero queue time.

The boring machine operator, the operator at the prior station, and the supervisors have the task of reducing the ratio. They must solve transport, setup, down time, raw material, machine variation, operator methods, and other problems in order to reduce the ratio.

**Exhibit I-2(a).** Sprocket Boring

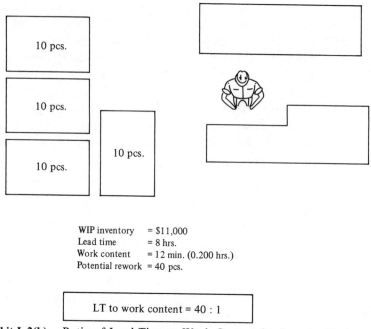

WIP inventory   = $11,000
Lead time       = 8 hrs.
Work content    = 12 min. (0.200 hrs.)
Potential rework = 40 pcs.

LT to work content = 40 : 1

**Exhibit I-2(b).**   Ratio of Lead Time to Work Content for Sprocket Boring

Exhibit I-3 is a more striking example. There are 14,000 plastic handles in the two wooden pallet boxes. The handles are valued at $3,220, and they await their turn on the handle-printing machine. Printing time is just 0.05 minutes, but it takes thirty hours to print the last of the 14,000 handles. The ratio is 14,000 to 1, a whopping opportunity for improvement.

As it happens, in this particular case, there is nothing to prevent moving the handle-printing machine right next to the extruder to permit printing one right after it is extruded. That would lower the ratio from 14,0000 to 1 down to 1 or 2 to 1; in addition, the need for pallet boxes and fork trucks would disappear.

## Process Speed to Sales Rate

The second ratio in Exhibit I-1 is process speed to sales rate; or, instead of sales rate for the final product, it could be the use of a component at the next process. The ideal ratio is 1 or 2 to 1. (Theoretically, the ratio could be less than 1 to 1; that could happen for a product that sells or is used day and night but is made only one

**Exhibit I-3(a).** Handle Printing

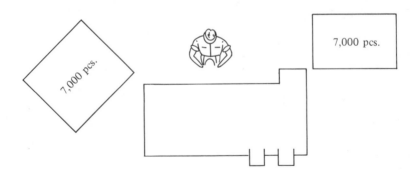

WIP inventory     = $3,220
Lead time         = 30 hrs.
Work content      = 0.05 min. (0.001 hrs.)
Potential rework = 14,000 pcs.

LT to work content = 14,000 : 1

**Exhibit I-3(b).** Ratio of Lead Time to Work Content for Handle Printing

shift a day.) Good is 2 or 3 to 1. Bad (and typical) is 5, 10, 20, 100, 1,000, or more to 1.

Note that process speed means exactly that; in other words, we are not talking about average output rate, which would include stops for setups, down time, and breaks. Furthermore, the ratio applies to a single part number, not to several different part numbers processed through the same work center.

For example, a saw may be cutting table tops to size at a speed of one every three minutes, or a rate of twenty an hour. The saw cuts table tops at that rate for fifteen minutes out of each hour and cuts legs, arms, support members, and other parts the other forty-five minutes.

Our targets for ratio analysis are the process that saws the table tops and the process that uses them. To find the ratio, we need the use rate of the table tops at the next process, belt sanding. The belt sander sands table tops steadily all day long at a rate of one every twelve minutes, or five per hour. Thus, the saw cuts at a rate (twenty per hour) four times faster than the use rate (five per hour). The ratio is 20 to 5, or 4 to 1, which is bad.

Exhibit I–4 shows the mismatch between the saw's rate of production of table tops and the use rate at sanding. Five tops are sawed in fifteen minutes; this builds the inventory before the belt sander, as is shown in the middle of the schematic. Then, as the saw performs other work, the inventory is reduced by one unit every 12 minutes, which is the continuous rate of sanding at the belt sander.

The inventory that builds in front of the sander once every hour is wasteful. The challenge to the saw operator, the supervisor, and others involved is to decrease the ratio. The solution may be as simple as dusting off an old, slower saw and dedicating it to sawing table tops at the use rate of 1 every 12 minutes. If the saws are inclined to jam, keep a few sawed tops on hand as buffer stock.

## Pieces to Work Stations or to Operators

The third ratio is number of pieces to number of work stations or to operators in a production line or line segment. The ideal is 1 or 2 to 1. Good is 2 or 3 to 1. Bad and typical is 5, 10, 20, 100, 500, or much more to 1. Every idle job, every idle piece, every container in transit or in queue between processes raises the ratio.

This ratio is an excellent way to analyze office work, including

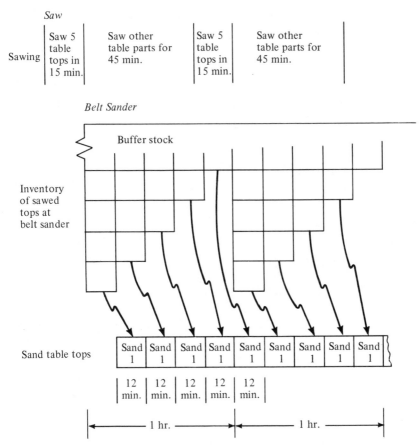

**Exhibit I–4.** Mismatch Between Production Rate and Use Rate


order entry, purchase ordering, engineering, and design. An engineering example will illustrate:

If there are one hundred engineering jobs in process, and ten engineers to work on them, ninety are idle at any given time. The ratio is 10 to 1, and it needs to come down. If the average engineering job takes five weeks when the ratio is 10, the average would be only about 1 week if the ratio were down to 2 to 1—two jobs for each engineer. At that ratio, each job would take the same amount of engineering time but would spend only one-fifth as much time in a state of delay.

A simple means of driving the ratio down to 2 to 1 and keeping it there is to employ a version of kanban: Allow exactly twenty jobs in process at a time, and add a job only as one is completed—or, since engineering jobs take a variable amount of time to complete, allow no more than twenty-two and no less than eighteen jobs in process at a time. (Be sure to have "other work" to do in case the number of projects falls below eighteen.)

This example, the ratio applied to engineering, works about the same way in the factory. It is an especially potent tool for analyzing job shops and model shops.

## Pieces in "Capture"

In some kinds of manufacturing, sizable amounts of lead time and pieces resist extinction, because a bake or burn-in oven "captures" the piece for hours or days. In those cases it may be useful to express the lead-time-to-work-content and pieces-to-work-stations ratios with and without capture time.

An example would be the baking of the varnish on the armatures in an electric motor plant. Assume that the bake oven holds fifty armatures, while the rest of the armature line, twenty-four stations, contains just seventy-five other armatures. With capture time, the pieces-to-work-stations ratio is 125 to 25, or 5 to 1—not very good. Without capture, it is 75 to 25, or 3 to 1—not too bad. The difference between the 5 to 1 and 3 to 1 ratios is glaring; it's message is that engineers need to place high emphasis on achieving a process break-through to reduce the bake time.

## Macro Effects of Micro-JIT

When the three ratios are drawn down into the "good" zone, a remarkable transformation begins. I refer to what happens to the people tending the processes, be they direct labor, technicians, chemists, or maintenance people.

The effect is most pronounced when people along the product flow path are already geographically quite close together; then, by drawing down one of the ratios, they become closely linked *in time* as well as geography. An example of that follows. A second example will introduce the additional problem of spatial separation between processes. A third will add, on top of distance, the problem of trips in and out of a stockroom between processes.

## *Taking Out Pieces*

One U.S. plant, a leader in implementing JIT, had reduced its production lead time from weeks to about one shift. Work centers that formerly were isolated from each other, often in separate rooms, had been linked into long production lines. Work-in-process inventory dropped about the same degree as lead time. Still, there were thousands of pieces in plastic tubs, on wheeled racks, and on lengths of conveyor along each production line. Compared with those thousands of pieces, there were perhaps fifteen machines and ten operators. The pieces-to-operators ratio was in the hundreds to one.

The plant also was a leader in implementing quality circles, and the budget for training had been increased to the point where operators spend 6 to 7 percent of their time in classes learning about process improvement. The rate of employee suggestions, or quality circle suggestions, was up to about 1.5 per operator per year, which is nearly ten times as many as the typical U.S. suggestion program yields. Still, when compared with the hundred or more suggestions per employee that have been achieved in some years at companies like Hitachi and Toyota in Japan, 1.5 a year is not very good. The plant manager was frustrated, because most of the operators still were reluctant to "take ownership" of their processes or their machines. He continually coaxed and cajoled people to eliminate the "DMZs" (demilitarized zones) between one process and the next along the flow lines.

The DMZs, of course, are where idle pieces pile up in the tubs and carts. The piles of idle pieces insulated one process from the next. The effect is a bit like the real DMZ that separates the North Koreans from the South Koreans, hence the metaphor. Lowering the ratio of pieces to people couples the processes together so that they are more like a bucket brigade. The processes, which still have separate identities, start to behave more like a single machine. As a single machine, everything must work dependably, and the people's actions must be carefully coordinated. Every disturbance is visible and demands the attention of the operators and their supporting cast.

In other words, micro-JIT—pulling down the ratios one process at a time—unleashes the desired macro effects: problem diagnosis and problem-solving as a way of life. It's something like an extended spring thaw breaking up the ice jam on the river, when the ice chunks begin to flow downstream.

## *Taking Out Pallets and Forklift Trucks*

Where processes are separated by distance, manufacturers often resort to a bulk handling device to reduce the number of material transfers between processes. Where the bulk handling device is a forklift truck, a special opportunity for improvement is often available.

Let us say that a lift truck moves pallets between machine A and machine B, and the quantity per pallet is nine pieces. Let's ignore the pallet at machine B from which the operator is taking work. The operator of machine B sees one piece in the machine and nine in transit; the ratio of pieces to work station is 10 to 1.

Reducing the ratio to 2 to 1 is simple: Replace the lift truck by a hand cart or dolly moving a quantity of one. All of the JIT benefits obtain: About a ninefold reduction in inventory, scrap or rework, and lead time. The two machine operators become aware of each other and of things amiss in the two-machine process. Those advantages are likely to exceed the extra labor of making nine times more trips between A and B. (And the extra labor to push the cart creates its own incentive to take the next step: Move the machines closer together.)

Regardless of that, there is a large bonus: A costly lift truck is taken out, and its batteries, battery charging, maintenance, trained driver, and wide aisles cease to be needed. Furthermore, lift trucks in factories are dangerous, they run into things and cause damage, and they track at least some dirt, oil, and chips and release some air pollutants. The pallet, too, is eliminated, along with maintenance on it and the dirt that attaches to it.

In view of the very high use of forklift trucks in industry, the potential for savings is staggering. There are only a small percentage of present factory uses of lift trucks where the truck cannot be eliminated: cases where the item weighs 70 or 200 or 2,000 lbs. Since the 2,000-lb. item is probably moved one at a time anyway, there are no JIT advantages in the offing, so let the truck stay. The 200-lb. item requires some way to lift it onto a conveyance. A crane could lift it onto a wheeled dolly—if a crane is handy. If not, perhaps the lift truck, doing both the lifting and the moving, is justified. The 70-lb. item can be lifted by one or two people onto a wheeled cart, but there is some cause for concern about back strain; the choice of best handling method is not clear-cut. In some cases heavy loads can be moved in special wheeled containers, tiltable for dumping or with bearing bases for easy sliding of the load.

In short, we must draw this conclusion: In most cases, the world-class factory will not have forklift trucks, except on receiving and shipping docks. I'll put it differently: For the most part, lift trucks don't belong in our production areas.

## Taking the Stockrooms Out of the Flow

In still other cases, the problem is compounded by an extra handling step into a stockroom and out again days or weeks later. Some of our computer-based systems include a stockroom step between every pair of consecutive operations in the manufacture of a component part. The lead-time-to-work-content ratio and the pieces-to-work-stations ratio are enormous, usually in the thousands to one.

It is now a well-understood tenet of JIT that the stockroom steps have to be taken out of the flow. In some cases, no one even gets nervous about the prospect of eliminating some or all of the buffer stock in the stockrooms. In most cases, however, there is genuine concern, even alarm. Someone will tell why: "We may not need that buffer stock this week or next. But before too long, a serious problem will crop up, and lack of the buffer stock will shut down the whole factory."

Here is the simple solution: Keep the buffer stock, but let it gather dust. Have the normal flow of the product be direct from work center to work center. Tap the buffer stock in storage only when the occasional severe problem demands it.

This solution eliminates many load and unload steps, cuts travel distances, may allow simpler, lighter types of handling conveyances, and slashes production lead time. The much closer time linkage of the people in the flow—minus the stockroom delays—is equally important. Other gains: Since two handling steps are eliminated, the items incur less damage; a large amount of inventory transactions, stocktaking, and move tickets are wiped out.

The pieces-to-work-stations ratio drops just a little: The buffer stock is still in the stockroom, but with stockroom trips cut out, there is a bit less in transit. The sizable improvement shows up in the lead-time-to-work-content ratio, which drops sharply.

To be sure, there are some items that do not lend themselves to this approach, because they deteriorate in the stockroom; rubber O-rings, food, certain chemical compounds, intravenous pouches, and some pharmaceuticals are examples; a first-in, first-out rotation of stockroom items is required—at least once in a while.

Hundreds of thousands of other components, however, do qualify for the technique of retaining the buffer stock in the stockroom but bypassing it in the production flow: fittings, frames, and fixtures; cables, cartons, and covers; shells, sleeves, and shafts; bolts, brackets, and bearing races; and many more.

Work-in-process (WIP) stockrooms are the most offensive, but often there also is advantage in bypassing raw material stockrooms. For example, if frames, cartons, sleeves, or brackets are purchased, the JIT concept calls for delivery right to the point of use in the factory; some companies call it "dock to line" delivery. If the supplier is normally dependable but sometimes delivers a lot high in defectives or delivers late, there must be buffer-stock protection. The concept applies: Let that buffer stock gather dust in a stockroom, but make dock-to-line deliveries in the norm.

There are always some purchased items delivered in quantities too large to store on the line. Why not send *part* of the delivery quantity directly to the line—whatever there is room for on the line—thereby avoiding double handling at least for that portion? The improvement will show up in a lower *purchase* lead-time-to-work-content ratio.

The ratios used in micro-JIT analysis do not tell *how* to improve, but they do set a target. Part of the problem in the period of industrial malaise in the recent past was the lack of targets for improvement.

## Naturalistic Quality Improvement

The array of concepts and techniques available to industry to improve quality is now both well known and in vigorous use in many top companies. Only a brief additional point shall be made here. It pertains to the power of making one item and immediately inspecting it or trying it at the next process. If anything is wrong, you stop production, search out the cause, and fix it, and only then do you restart production.

Big Western companies strayed from this simple, natural, powerful approach to quality improvement for at least two reasons. One is that production lot sizes and transit lot sizes grew too large. Huge, wasteful inventories were injected between processes, making it impossible to try out the piece at the next process right away. The second reason is that production employees were not trusted to do their own inspections. A separate group of inspectors were hired to do it, and since it was not economical to hire one inspector for every process, they inspected randomly out of large lots.

One historian states that Japanese professors on the quality-control lecture circuit in 1959, including the prominent authority Dr. Kaoru Ishikawa, advised managers to have production employees do their own inspections.[1] Toyota, unlike some other companies (such as Nissan), took the advice seriously. In fact Taiichi Ohno, the Toyota vice president (who appears to have been the mastermind behind JIT), resisted the U.S. Army's insistence on use of sampling inspection for the trucks Toyota was producing for the Army's Korean War venture. Ohno agreed to it only as a secondary check—after operators had already performed in-process self-inspection. By the 1960s, Ohno states, the number of inspectors had shrunk considerably since they had "so little to do."[2] (Later Toyota, in seeking and winning the Deming Prize for quality, added the full range of TQC concepts and tools; the naturalistic way was valuable but not sufficient.)

Naturalistic quality improvement is intimately tied to the central concept of JIT: that processes should be closely linked together in time—piece-for-piece production and transit from process to process. Adherence to the naturalistic approach to quality may thus be measured by the ratio of lead time to work content, process speed to use rate, and pieces to processes.

[1]Michael A. Cusumano, *The Japanese Automobile Industry: Technology and Management at Nissan and Toyota* (Cambridge, Mass.: Harvard University Press, 1985), p. 351.
[2]*Ibid,* p. 362.

# About the Cases

A few of the cases in this book include direct questions on the ratios used in micro-JIT analysis. All of the cases in the book have questions that relate to the concepts on which the ratios are based. Many also deal with the issue of how to get people involved in data collection and problem-solving and how to bring about a sense of process ownership.

The cases are arranged more or less randomly. Heaven forbid that they be grouped by function (purchasing cases together, scheduling together, accounting together, etc.)! The issues in the cases do not belong to any specialty. In fact, one of the underpinnings of WCM thought is that strict boundary-marking between shops, trades, functions, and levels is a good part of the problem that led to industrial stagnation in the first place. World-class manufacturing requires that people and machines be organized the way the work flows, which integrates resources in the cause of product improvement; fiefdoms break up and functional distinctions blur.

Nor are the cases grouped by industry—metal working cases together, electronics together, and so forth. There would be some value in doing so. On the other hand, the various ways of implementing JIT/TQC cut across industries: Valves, motors, and hand-push industrial scrubbers all tend to have one distinct approach to JIT and TQC. Plywood making and metal bonding tend to have another. Diesel trucks and computer work stations tend to have another. Foundries and design engineering tend to have still another.

While you are thus advised not to look for a group of cases that fit your present job or industry, you can select cases by taking a peek at the lists of topics covered. The topic lists precede the text on the first page of each case.

One more thing before you begin the cases: If you haven't already read the preface, please do so. It makes a few points about what to expect of the cases and how this case study approach differs from the usual one.

# World Class Manufacturing Casebook

## Implementing JIT and TQC

# 1

# HyGain-Telex: Analysis for JIT Production

*Case topics:*

Lead-time-to-work-content ratio
Pieces-to-work-stations ratio
Distinction between preventive
    maintenance and setup
Frequency of delivery
Kanban

Statistical process control
Total preventive maintenance
Simplifying the schedule
Partnership with customer
Cellular manufacturing

The HyGain-Telex plant in Lincoln, Nebraska, manufactures antennas. It currently has a U.S. Army contract for Model X32 antennas. The contract requires a production rate of two hundred Model X32s per day. The contract quantity may be changed quarterly.

Chris Piper, the foreman, is collecting data for a JIT project. Piper has selected the X32 antenna base (not the whip part of the

---

Except where otherwise specified, all case studies were written by Richard J. Schonberger. These studies are intended for instructional use and are not necessarily accurate in all respects. The characters and some of the data in this initial case study are fictitious, but much of the process data are based on a real product at HyGain-Telex.

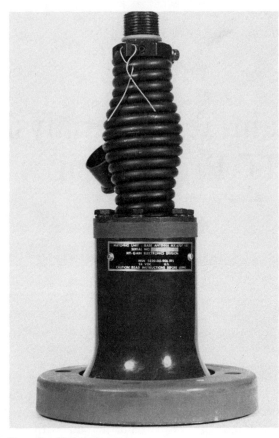

**Exhibit 1-1.** Base for X32 Antenna

antenna, which is fairly simple) for the JIT project. Exhibit 1-1 is a photograph of the base.

## Manufacture of the X32

There are several stages of manufacture for the X32 base, which is a cylinder 6 inches in diameter and 10 inches high. These are the basic production processes, and their standard times, with which Piper was concerned:

- Mold the Lexan plastic base. Some holes are molded into the base by use of core plugs. 2.50 minutes.
- Drill and tap (eight operations). A dozen more holes are drilled;

half of the drilled and molded-in holes are tapped, and half are installed with "helicoils"—self-threaded inserts (a rather old technology). Seven drill or tap operations taking from 0.12 to 1.02 minutes; installing helicoils, 1.82 minutes.

- Assemble (epoxy) as "birdcage" (ferrite core, coaxial cable, etc.) inside the Lexan base. 1.78 minutes. (Note: The birdcage is produced as a subassembly, going through twelve operations.)
- Foam the assembly. 2.61 minutes.
- Paint. 1.82 minutes.

## Flow Data

Piper felt that the place to start was between drill-and-tap and assembly. Drill-and-tap ran one shift, and assembly usually ran two shifts. Piper asked L. G. Smith, the industrial engineer, to find out the flow distance between processes, especially those two processes. Smith scaled off the distances on the factory blueprints and came up with a total flow distance of 1,296 feet, which breaks down as follows: from mold to drill-and-tap, 192 feet; from drill-and-tap to tank assembly, 144 feet; from assembly to paint, 480 feet; and from paint to final prep, 480 feet.

Piper wanted to be sure. "Are those prints current?" he asked. Smith assured him that they were. Just to make sure, Piper got a tape measure and checked some of the distances; they were indeed correct.

For flow-time data, Piper went to Raul Nieves, the scheduler. Nieves pointed out that the flow time from molding to final prep had been "as short as about five days for a few lots, but we are quoting six weeks to marketing." Piper asked Nieves to come up with some sort of average. Nieves did so by putting pieces of colored tape on a few molded bases from several lots over the space of three weeks. The average flow time, found by noting how long it took for the taped units to get to final prep, was seven weeks. One week of that was the flow time from the start of drill-and-tap to assembly.

---

*Question 1.* What is the ratio of actual production lead time (or flow-time) to work content time from the start of drill-and-tap to final prep?

---

3

Nieves also provided Piper with scheduling and unit-load data. Scheduling released work packets in lot quantities of 2,000. Drilled and tapped bases were forwarded to assembly by forklift truck, in wire-bound pallets holding about 400 bases. In other words, about five forklift trips were required to move one "packet-release" quantity to assembly.

## Problems

At this point Piper called a meeting. Smith and Nieves were there, along with Karen Jones, manager of quality assurance; Bob Crane, an inspector; Doug Atkins, a drill press operator; and Ellie Olson, an assembler. Piper announced that the purpose of the meeting was to "brainstorm what can and maybe can't be done to reduce WIP and flow time" between drill-and-tap and assembly. Piper explained that the purpose was to improve and not look for blame. In that spirit, "please speak frankly."

Piper's first question was directed to Atkins: "Doug, there's no setup time on the drill press that you use for the X32—it's a dedicated tool, right?" Atkins said that it was.

"How about up time on the drill press? Is it reliable?" asked Piper. Atkins replied that the drill press itself was fine but that the tapping head with spindles in the taps were a problem sometimes: "They break or the bushings loosen," which results in off-center taps or a marred surface around the outside. "Then I have to call maintenance to make adjustments or replace the head."

"About how many hours per month are you down waiting for them to make those adjustments or replacements, Doug?" Atkins estimated about five hours.

Ellie Olson was next. "Ellie, do you have any problems with the bases? Quality problems or running out of bases?" Ellie said that sometimes she did have to wait for the fork truck to bring another wire-bound; she estimated six hours of wait time per month.

The quality problems were the biggest headache, Olson felt, and she looked at Bob Crane, the inspector, for corroboration. Crane agreed that the defect rates were high, especially cracks and fractures around the helicoil inserts. Some, "maybe 5 percent," they thought, were minor defects that Crane or Olson let pass. Crane had figures on how many were defective but repairable and defective-scrapped: 2 percent repaired, 4 percent scrapped.

Karen Jones, quality manager, pointed out that their customer, the Army, had been rejecting an average of 7 percent in recent months. "I believe that the majority of the problems can be traced back to drill-and-tap," she stated.

Piper then asked if anyone knew what level of work-in-process (WIP) there was of bases. Nieves said he had just made a rough count; there were six wire-bounds full at drill-and-tap and eight and a half full at assembly.

---

*Question 2.* If fifteen direct labor employees are involved in the production of the Lexan base, what is the ratio of pieces in process to people who could work on them?

---

## JIT Opportunities

At this point the group began brainstorming on JIT opportunities. Some of the options they discussed:

1. Setup reduction (adjust and replace spindles/bushings) on the drill presses. To this suggestion, everyone nodded their heads, but no one commented pro or con.
2. Cut transit quantities. Nieves (scheduler) protested: "The fork truck drivers would be making more trips."
3. Adopt kanban. Nieves liked the idea.
4. Use process control charts in drill-and-tap. Everyone thought it was about time to do some of this.
5. Adopt total preventive maintenance. This was Piper's (the foreman's) idea. The others showed little reaction; they seemed not to know what that meant.
6. Put in conveyors. Smith (the I.E.) offered that one; nobody challenged the idea.
7. Slash the buffer stock. Nieves suggested this, pointing out that inventory counting was a headache anyway. Olson was indignant: "I run out of bases too often the way it is."
8. Get rid of the packet-release quantities. Smith suggested this but admitted that he did not know what kind of scheduling might replace the packet-release system.

9. Bring the design engineers in to come up with a better design of the base. Everyone smiled and nodded vigorously.
10. Expand the size of the task force (which they were calling themselves by that time), including a customer (Army) representative. This was Jones's suggestion, which was met by a couple of favorable nods.
11. Move a drill press into the assembly department. This was Smith's idea. Crane (inspector) said that "if we do that I won't have to inspect the bases—and I'm not complaining; it's a boring job."

The meeting broke up with plenty of ideas but no decisions.

---

*Question 3.* What should be done? Should all the ideas be implemented? None of them? A different set? What order? To what extent? What time period? What guidance and direction? Discuss each of the eleven options that came out in the brainstorming session.

---

# 2

# Implementing Kanban at Hewlett-Packard, Fort Collins (A)

*Case topics:*

From mechanical to manual
Extent of change to cellular
   manufacturing
Line storage of raw materials

Kanban shelving acting as
   Pareto charts
Open factory concept
Asset turnover

Hewlett-Packard's desktop computer division is in Fort Collins, Colorado. One of the division's main products is the HP-9000, Series 500 desktop computer, which can be ordered in some 6 million different configurations. The fully integrated configuration includes a keyboard, printer, display, light pen, and so forth, and some of those primary modules come in many varieties. Size of customer order varies from one unit to several units. The full computer systems are mostly for scientific and professional uses and sell for $30,000 to $80,000.

JIT production began with a pilot project in the 9000-500 manufacturing area. The pilot project was limited to subassembly of major modules and final assembly, and the JIT production procedure centered on a belt conveyor, a carousel storage unit, electric sensing platforms, and other production and inventory control technologies. The pilot project is described in the appendix to this case study. Its successor is described below.

---

*Question 1.* Some aspects of the 9000-500 product line make JIT implementation difficult. Comment on them, and offer suggestions for overcoming the obstacles.

---

## Expanded JIT

A year after the start of the pilot project, the carousel in primary storage was gone, and so were the belt conveyor and sensing platforms. Standard shelves replaced the carousel unit, and assemblers fetch their own materials rather than having them delivered by belt conveyor and off-loaded by a mechanical arm.

---

*Question 2.* What possible advantages are there in getting rid of the mechanical devices?

---

## Eliminating Work Orders

The expanded JIT project governs materials flows in eleven stages of production. Included are packaging, button-up, unit final test, and printed circuit (PC) board assembly, as well as module subassembly and unit final assembly. There are several "generic" work stations and operators in each of the eleven stages, except for one or two where an operation is done on a single expensive machine. The plant layout is shown in Exhibit 2-1.

---

*Question 3.* Is cellular manufacturing (group technology) employed in the Fort Collins JIT approach? Explain.

---

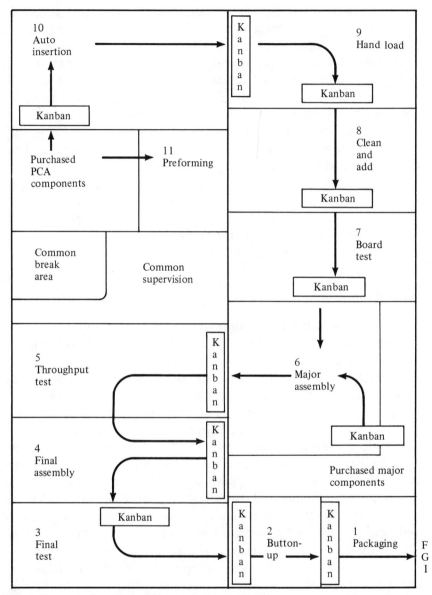

**Exhibit 2-1.** Layout, Hewlett-Packard, Fort Collins

Scheduling and production control in final assembly and test are *not* driven by work orders. Instead, the customer order, maintained in a computer file, specifies the configuration and authorizes production. Final assembly gets its components from racks located between it and the throughput test area, and the people in throughput test refill the vacated space in the rack. The throughput test people fetch untested components from a rack on the other side of their work area, and component assemblers refill the vacated space in that rack. Fetch-refill extends backward all the way to initial steps in printed circuit board assembly. The customer order accompanies the units through button-up and packaging and into finished goods inventory (FGI). Since the products are built to order, and FGI is only a "pass through operation," earlier stages of production have no use for the customer order.

---

*Question 4.* Some aspects of the 9000-500 product line favor JIT implementation. What are some of those aspects? Discuss.

---

## Primary Storage

There are now two primary storage areas on the shop floor. One is for the small components that go into PC boards; the other is for purchased parts that go in at module and final assembly stages—from cables to packaging materials to hardware. In both storage areas, when any parts are picked for issue, the stock clerk uses a computer terminal for on-line deduct of the issue quantity from computer records. Even screws and other less expensive hardware and electronic components are accounted for that way. The resulting stock balances are compared with a replenish point set for each part number; when the replenish point is reached, the kanban material system goes into action and the "overflow" or secondary stockroom replenishes the primary storage shelf space. (Pilot testing is going on with selected suppliers to replenish via kanban.) A stock clerk orders special materials that are not normally kept in the primary stockroom whenever such items show up on an "exploded" customer order. Usually materials are issued to primary stockrooms in the supplier's package quantity.

---

*Question 5.* What JIT concept is implied by the way the storage areas are named? What is the JIT goal in improving the purchased parts stores operation?

---

## Kanban Techniques

There are several types of kanban that signal a need for more parts: empty taped squares on the floor, empty spaces in racks, empty wheeled carts, plastic kanban plates, metal kanban clips, and colored cards. In work centers where the card version of kanban is used (kanban actually means card in Japanese), there are several card types:

- Green cards are recirculating kanban for normal flows of materials.
- Orange cards designate rework.
- Blue cards are attached to units that are used just for testing purposes (no customer for the unit).
- Yellow cards are for higher-than-normal accumulations of service parts.
- Red cards are used when, for some reason, there is a need to violate kanban and "push" materials for a while. The section manager must sign approval for a red card to be used and must also assign a person—e.g. a buyer—to correct the problem. (There was a need to use a red card only five times in five months, usually in order to keep labor productive in the face of a temporary material shortage.)

The cards and plastic plates are used like this: There is a shelf space for, let us say, I-O doors. An assembler who takes an I-O door from the shelf leaves a plastic plate or card imprinted with identifying information. The plate tells the stock clerk in primary storage to get another one from the primary storage rack or from overflow storage in order to replenish the shelf space. At first the usual shelf quantity was four items (and one card for each item); now it is down to one in many cases.

At one time there was a different kanban for every different keyboard type, power supply type, and so forth. Now there is just one kanban with one generic identifier printed on it for keyboard, another for power supplies, and so on. The customer order, which can be seen on computer screens, tells *which* keyboard.

---

*Question 6.* What is the advantage of this "generic" kanban approach? What is the disadvantage?

---

In PC board assembly the metal kanban clips are the main type of kanban signal. A kanban clip is like a clothespin with a 1-inch-diameter disc attached. The disc has the stock number of the PC board printed on it.

One place where the kanban clips are used is between PC assembly and PC test. The assembly and test areas are separated by shelves having separate pigeon holes for about fifty diffferent board numbers. Each pigeon hole holds one PC board, and most boards have four pigeon holes. Each board has one kanban clip attached to its edge. When a subassembler fetches a board, what happens to the kanban? It is simply clipped to a wire at the shelf opening for that staćk of four PC boards. Later another board is pulled and another clip is added. The chain of kanban clips hangs from the wire, and the longest chain of clips identifies the board that needs to be assembled next. Operators in PC test go to the shelves, grab the longest set of clips, and take them back to the shelves where untested boards are held. The right boards are selected, tested, clipped, and put into the correct pigeon hole in the shelf holding fully tested boards.

---

*Question 7.* The pigeon-hole shelving, which is like a Pareto chart, does the same job as what kind of report in an MRP system?

---

Any PC board—or keyboard, fan, or the like—that needs rework goes into a special shelf tagged with an orange kanban. A maximum of two orange—two in rework—is allowed. Operations are shut down if rework gets worse than that. If a certain part is not on the shelf, and no assembler has one in process at a work bench, is it in rework? An assembler or manager can find out simply by standing up and looking over the top of a shelf or work bench to spot the orange kanban in the rework shelf.

---

*Question 8.* The vision of the plant that is conjured up by the sentence above might be dubbed the "open-factory concept" (after the open-office concept). Should there be a JIT concept on what type of manufacturing space is best? If so, what is it?

---

# Results

For the part of the plant making the 9000-500, WIP inventory turn-over went from 7.5 to 45.6 between August, 1983, and May, 1984. In PC board assembly alone WIP fell from 30–40 days to 3–4 days' supply. In the same time period, output went up 29 percent. Asset turnover, which includes the cost of space and equipment as well as materials, improved from 4 to 13. By the end of 1985, the Ft. Collins management group expects the entire plant—not just the 9000-500 product area—to be converted to just-in-time production.

---

*Question 9.* Most manufacturing plants would have trouble measuring asset turnover accurately. What accounting steps need to be taken to be able to do this?

*Question 10.* What remains to be done to strengthen the manufacturing system in the 9000-500 area?

---

## Appendix: Pilot Kanban Project at H-P, Fort Collins
### (JIT As It Used To Be)

The pilot kanban project centered upon final assembly, module sub-assembly, and purchased parts for the modules. Kanban "pull" signals govern the flow of materials and work units through three stages:

*Stage 1.* Beside each final assembly station there is a kanban square that holds just one wheeled cart for a product. The square is outlined in yellow tape on the floor. The square empties when an assembly is completed and sent to packing. The empty square is the signal to send over another cart holding a customer order and the modules (completed subassemblies) for final assembly that are specified on the customer order.

*Stage 2.* The modules are made at generic subassembly stations. A kit of parts for one module comes to the station in a plastic tub by belt conveyor. This amounts to about thirty minutes' worth of work. The operator at a station issues a pull signal—"send another tub of parts"—by picking up the present tub from a sensing platform. While the operator goes to work on that tub of parts, a light (wired to the sensing platform) comes on in the parts control area nearby. The parts controller takes a tub of parts from a carousel storage unit and puts it on the belt. An arm extends and offloads the tub onto the platform, which shuts off the light. The tub on the platform is one unit of buffer stock "on deck."

*Stage 3.* The carousel storage unit for purchased parts is out in the midst of the subassembly and final assembly stations. The carousel unit, referred to as primary storage, holds enough kits to make modules for about four 9000-500 systems. Purchased part quantities depend on use rates and the cubic value of the part. Empty cavities in the carousel are filled from overflow or, sometimes (the ideal way), directly from a delivery truck. Empty carousel cavities are the third type of kanban signal.

# 3

# Hewlett-Packard, Fort Collins (B): Keeping Operators Busy— and Productive

*Case topics:*

Long stoppages               Labor flexibility
Supervisory oversight

As is typical of final products makers in its industry, most of the product cost at Hewlett-Packard, Fort Collins, is for overhead and purchased parts. While direct labor is only about 5 percent of the product cost, direct labor still has a central role in plant effectiveness, and managing direct labor wisely—keeping everyone busy—is a challenge. That is especially so because Hewlett-Packard is one of those companies that does not lay people off. When sales on a product tail off, people are retrained and reassigned.

## Long Stoppages

At H-P, Fort Collins, a stoppage for lack of a part is often relatively long: thirty minutes or an hour. The length of the stoppages does have a good side: a longer uninterrupted period for the operator to work on an improvement project.

---

> *Question 1.* What is there about this production situation that makes the typical stoppages for lack of parts this long?

---

The types of improvements operators have engaged in have evolved over time. At first, the focus was on training. Operators were reading Schonberger's *Japanese Manufacturing Techniques,* Hall's *Zero Inventories,* and selected other works. When they ran out of job-related reading materials and were down to crossword puzzles and *Playboy,* somebody came up with the excellent idea of redoing the assembly manuals. With input and drafting assistance from operators, engineers converted them from verbiage to exploded drawings, easier and less tedious to follow, which cuts mistakes.

Records are posted on the wall showing number of minutes of operator down time and what was done with the down time. For example, in one period a work group had 40.5 hours of down time. The chart on the wall broke these hours into:

25.25 hours cleanup, paperwork, typing, miscellaneous
1.75 hours in meetings
1.75 hours of rework
8.50 hours on TQC
3.25 hours on procedures

---

> *Question 2.* What is management's proper role in making sure that operators keep busy on meaningful activities?

---

The PC board assembly area is covered by electrostatic discharge (ESD) carpeting. Custodians are not allowed in this area. Operators are responsible for cleaning their own work areas and also for simple maintenance of their tools, fixtures, and equipment.

---

> *Question 3.* What is your assessment of the approach used at H-P, Fort Collins, to get the most

---

out of the direct labor force? How may the approach be sustained and improved?

## Labor Flexibility

In the fall of 1983, H-P, Fort Collins, had brought in John Richards to conduct a seminar on JIT/TQC. That evening at dinner the general manager raised a question having to do with labor flexibility. The G.M. pointed out that all "nonexempts" were hired on at the same wage rate.

"You mean janitors, guards, and so forth are hired at the same wage as assemblers and machine operators?" Richards asked.

"Yes, exactly," said the G.M.

Since pay raises are based on performance ("pay for performance"), a good guard could be earning more than an average operator ten years later. Thus, there aren't the usual job-wage classification barriers to labor flexibility. Without wage-class barriers, it was easy to move operators from one job to another. Still, there are status barriers. "I doubt that we could get an operator to push a broom," was the G.M.'s comment.

Richards pointed out that at Kawasaki in Nebraska job applicants are shown a page in the middle of the employee handbook. It says something like: "You are hired as a Kawasaki employee. You are not hired as an assembler, welder, painter, fork truck driver, janitor. You must understand as a condition of employment that you will do any job that needs getting done."

The G.M. thought the Kawasaki approach was excellent and immediately decided that he would try to implement it.

> *Question 4.* H-P, Fort Collins, already has a good deal of labor flexibility. Do they really need *more* labor flexibility? If so, why?

# 4

# Double A Products: JIT Implementation at a Small Plant

*Case topics:*

Focused factory
MRP-to-JIT conversion
Standard containers
Shortening change times on
  automatic screw machines
Kanban

Cutting buffer stock
Purchasing by MRP
Questioning the variance/
  efficiency counting system
Distribution inventories and
  shipping frequencies

Double A Products (DAP), headquartered in Manchester, Michigan, is a manufacturer of valves, pumps, and power units. Its products are sold to the industrial hydraulics market through a large network of distributors as well as by contract to certain customers, like the U.S. Army Tank-Automotive Command. DAP was a subsidiary of

---

The Statesville operation (being very small and therefore "portable") was moved to Searcy, Arkansas, where it was consolidated with the operations of a similar plant in another division of the parent company, Vickers, Inc.

Brown & Sharp Corporation until February 1985, when DAP was bought by Vickers, Incorporated, a Trinova Company.

DAP has manufacturing plants in Manchester and Traverse City, Michigan, and Statesville, North Carolina. The Statesville plant was started up in 1980 as a "focused factory" producing two narrow lines of valves. The following discussion concerns implementation of just-in-time production at the Statesville plant.

## Statesville Chronology

The Statesville plant employs thirty-four people, including twenty-seven hourlies, nineteen of whom are direct labor. The hourly work force is flexible and nonunion. Their jobs are covered by standard times for the purpose of efficiency reporting—by department, not by individual operator.

The plant produces the Series 3 and Series 5 directional control valves (see photo in Exhibit 4–1); these are the largest selling products among the hydraulic valves in DAP's product line. Seventy percent of Statesville's output are finished products to go to Manchester and then out to the distributors. The other 30 percent have

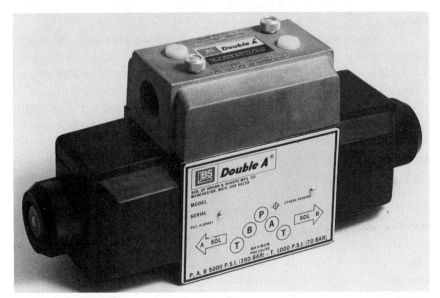

**Exhibit 4–1.**   Directional Control Valve

options attached or are used as components that go into circuit stack valves assembled in Manchester.

There are eighty-nine variations, or models, of the Series 3 and 150 of the Series 5—a total of 239 models altogether. The models are assembled from different combinations of ninety-nine part numbers. For either series there are:

- Made parts: one body, fourteen kinds of spool, five different solenoids, and three miscellaneous parts
- Purchased: fifty-eight common parts and nine raw materials

Some of the fifty-eight common purchased parts go into either series; the rest are unique to one series or the other.

By October 1981, Statesville was producing 450 valve units per week. Production scheduling was manual, and there were "tons" of inventory and a recession to cope with. Purchased materials on hand were valued at $417,000.

By April 1982, the plant was in much better shape. Production was up to 800 units per week. The A.S.K. Manman software package, a closed-loop material requirements planning (MRP) computer system, was up and running, which helped reduce inventories 21 percent in two months. Purchased materials had fallen to $330,000. Manman featured work-order generation and a full standard cost system.

By about mid-1983 Russell Copeman, vice president of manufacturing at the Michigan headquarters, was ready to take advantage of Statesville's unique capability to achieve short production lead times. That capability was based on the focused-factory concept—a narrow product line and modest number of part numbers. Statesville was capable of making any component part within one week and of assembling any mix of finished valve sets in one day. The MRP system—which scheduled work orders for component parts in weeks, eight weeks out (with a ten-week forecast via a planning bill of materials)—seemed cumbersome. Copeman decided to cross over from MRP-generated work orders to visual kanban/JIT.

The switch was made under Copeman's guidance and aided by a JIT implementation team composed of these Stateville personnel: Gene Rossbach, plant manager; Tom Zalewski, office and materials manager; Jim Walter, manufacturing services manager, and Ernie Giavedoni, quality control manager.

The cutover to JIT took place in November 1983 in the name of "austerity," "eliminating waste," and "raising productivity." By then production was up to 1,200 units per week; purchased inventories were at $450,000.

## JIT: Results and Techniques

A little over a year later, in January 1985, on a production volume of 1,400 units per week, work in process (WIP) inventories had been reduced 60 percent. (Purchased materials on hand were $500,000.) Inventory turns were at 7.3 (and rose to 9 by June, 1985), versus 4.5 to 5 under MRP and 2 to 2.5 under the manual model of plant scheduling.

---

*Question 1.* Was it worth while for Statesville to have implemented MRP first, and then JIT? Would it have been better to skip MRP and go directly to JIT? Explain.

---

## *The Shop Floor*

The initial JIT emphasis was on manufactured components, which were under Statesville's control, instead of on purchased items, which were not. According to Zalewski (who became operations manager upon Rossbach's retirement), "We felt if we could reduce WIP, it would create a cascade effect to reduce all inventory." Initial implementation steps included developing standard containers for every item and ground rules for their use, as well as rules governing work practices and job selection. The rules are as follows:

1. If a container (which holds a fixed quantity) is empty, fill it.
2. If a container will be empty on Friday, work overtime to fill it.
3. If all locations are full, don't work.
4. If the above three rules are met, work on anything in any sequence or quantity you desire.

Work orders have been eliminated, except to schedule some low-use component part numbers. Statesville also curtailed the use of economic order quantities (EOQ).

Instead of work orders and EOQs, production is driven by a two-week schedule from Manchester, updated every Monday. It works like this: On Monday of week one Manchester sends Statesville an order for that week's production; it is based on historical usage plus any specials. On the second Monday Statesville gets another firm order, and on Friday the two weeks' production is shipped.

Component parts manufacture is authorized not by a master production schedule but by kanban pull signals. That is, all components to assemble a given model are in containers in the plant, and production, authorized by kanban, merely replenishes containers.

All finished manufactured and purchased components are stored in the assembly room. They are held in specially designed standard containers that hold a fixed count of the given part. The containers reside in self-feed flow racks.

Standard containers are also used in the machine shop. A key operation in the machine shop is to produce spools on automatic screw machines. One of fourteen different kinds of spool goes into each valve body. Change times on screw machines had averaged six to seven hours, and lot sizes were in the range of 400–500 spools. The long changeovers are mostly avoided by running sequences of spools that comprise a family. Changeovers within a family take only thirty minutes, which makes it reasonable to run lots of fifty.

Screw machine operators select their jobs based on kanbans (cards) received from grinding/buffing, which is the using work center. Kanban racks show how many kanbans are accumulating for a given spool type. While running a certain part in a spool family, the operator may see kanbans building up for a different part in the family. The operator then may decide to switch to the other part, the purpose being to keep lot sizes small and production responsive to greatest needs.

In grinding/buffing, the last operation for spool manufacture, there is a rack with drawers in it that holds spools awaiting grinding. This "buffer stock" is never larger than one week's requirement for any spool. When a grinding operator empties a drawer, a card goes to the kanban rack in the screw machine area, signaling the need for production of that spool type.

---

*Question 2.* What, if anything, would need to be done to make it reasonable to reduce the buffer stock to one day's worth?

---

Grinding/buffing receives its kanbans from the assembly department in the next room. Assembly releases kanbans to grinding/buffing when a container from a flow rack has been emptied. Assemblers and machine operators, not material handlers, move the empty containers, which enhances direct communication from work center to work center about priorities or problems.

The simple visual shop floor system works partly because the machine centers were laid out the way the product flows. When the plant was conceived, Copeman envisioned the plant as a flow-through operation at the outset, and so the plant was set up that way.

At first, however, Statesville used a conventional scheduling system: Each of the three main components—valve, body, and solenoid tube—required several operations, and work flows and inventory records were tracked (inventory adjustment to computer records) at each of those operations. For example, to produce turned parts—the spools—the operations are: op. 10, screw machine; op. 20, secondary lathe; op. 30, heat treat; op. 40, center grind; op. 50, buff; and op. 60, degrease and inspect.

Now, inventory is tracked only at points of component completion—that is, through heat treat and through final inspection. (Inspection is the responsibility of the operator.)

## Data Processing and Paperwork

Purchased parts and raw materials are still ordered using the back-scheduling capability of the MRP system. A planning bill of materials for each of the two series of valve provides usage percentages, which enables the computer to calculate the quantity to order.

---

*Question 3.* Should purchased items continue to be ordered via MRP?

---

Statesville still "cuts" one work order per week for the purpose of collecting labor charges by direct labor department. (Zalewski is considering reducing this to one work order per department per month.) Weekly labor costs are then allocated by quantity of Series 3 and 5 units made that week.

Bills of material and routings determine standard costs, and actual direct labor charged against weekly (or monthly) work orders is compared against standard to arrive at a series of monthly manufacturing variances. Since manufacturing labor standards are almost identical between valve models, the allocation between Series 3 and Series 5 is simply a percentage of the total.

As an example, suppose that thirty Series 5s and forty Series 3s were produced last week and that total weekly direct labor was $4,000. Forty-three percent (30/70) of the labor expense, or $1,720, would be charged to the Series 5 valves. Fifty-seven percent (40/70), $2,280, would be charged to Series 3 valves.

---

*Question 4.* JIT companies in Japan tend to use variance from budget instead of variance from standard cost. Should Statesville convert to a variance-from-budget approach? Explain.

---

The MRP system produces an "order action—make" report and "order action—purchase" report. Since the real signal to make is a kanban, Statesville ignores the "make" report. However, Zalewski says he sometimes looks at the "make" report "just to see if Manchester may have loaded a large spare part order" into the system, which would "throw my system a curve ball."

Statesville assembles strictly to requirements from Manchester. If Manchester orders 1,400, 1,400 are made. WIP buffer stocks are small—one week's worth and dropping. (Manchester still retains four weeks of finished goods from which to fill orders from the distributors.)

Manchester runs its finished goods planning using a distribution requirements planning (DRP) system, which feeds requirements to the MRP systems at the manufacturing sites. Since Statesville can build and ship, if needed, in a shorter time period than the two-week planning cycle used in the DRP system, a simplification has been adopted: Instead of putting hundreds of purchase orders into both the DRP and MRP systems and adjusting for receipts and acknowledgements, Manchester just notes what they need on a single sheet of paper and sends it via facsimile transmission to Statesville. Manchester then simply adjusts balances on hand when shipments are received from Statesville.

As a result of the simplified scheduling and visual production control approach, paperwork at Statesville was cut 70 percent.

*Question 5.* How may the scheduling and shipment system be improved?

# 5

# American Ceramic and Glass Products Corporation: Quality Philosophy

*Case topics:*

Quality philosophy
Selection of a quality control
   department head

Role of inspectors

The American Ceramic and Glass Products Corporation employs about 13,000 people, each of its three plants having between 4,000 and 5,000 of that total. About three-quarters of its sales volume came from standard glass containers produced on highly automatic equipment; the balance of the company's sales were specialized ceramic and glass items made in batches on much less automated equipment. John Parr, production manager, had just completed a trip that cov-

Adapted from Robert C. Meier, Richard A. Johnson, William T. Newell, and Albert N. Schrieber, *Cases in Production and Operations Management*. Copyright © 1982, pp. 8–18. Reprinted by permission of Prentice-Hall, Inc., Englewood Cliffs, N.J.

ered eight states, seven universities, and three major industrial centers. The purpose was to recruit personnel for American's three plants. He felt that his trip had been extremely successful. He had made contacts that he thought would lead to hiring some good people into critical jobs.

Parr was strongly interested in hiring a capable person to head the inspection and quality control department of the Denver plant, American's largest. The position had just been vacated by George Downs, who had taken an indefinite leave of absence because of a serious illness. There was little chance that Downs would be able to resume any work duties within a year, and a substantial chance that he would never again be capable of working full time. During the ten years that Downs was chief of inspection and quality control, he had fully modernized the firm's inspection facilities and had developed a training program in the use of the most modern inspection equipment and techniques. The physical facilities of Down's inspection department were a major attraction for visitors to the plant.

## Thomas Calligan

During his trip, Parr interviewed two men whom he felt were qualified to fill Downs's position. Although each seemed more than qualified, Parr felt that a wrong choice could easily be made.

Thomas Calligan, the first of the two men, was a graduate of a reputable trade school and had eight years of experience in the inspection department of a moderately large manufacturing firm (about 800 employees). Calligan began working as a production inspector and was promoted to group leader within two years and chief inspector two years later. His work record in all three positions was extremely good.

Calligan's reason for wishing to leave the firm was "to seek better opportunities." He felt that he could not expect further promotions in his present firm in the near future. His firm was known for stability, low employee turnover, and slow but assured advancement opportunities. Calligan's superior, the head of quality control, had been recently promoted to that position and was doing a more than satisfactory job. Further, he was a young man, only thirty-two years old.

## James King

James King, the second of the two men Parr was considering, was a graduate of a large Southwestern university and had about five years of experience. King was currently head of inspection and quality control in a small manufacturing firm employing some 300 people. His abilities exceeded the requirements of his job, and he had made arrangements with his employer to do a limited amount of consulting work for noncompeting firms. King did not wish to make consulting his sole source of income, but he felt that his current position was equally unsatisfactory. He believed that by working for a large firm he would be able to use his talents fully within that firm and thus resolve conflict between his professional interests and the interests of his employer. That was his main reason for applying for the job at American Ceramic.

King's work record appeared to be good, and he recently had been granted a sizable pay increase. King, like Calligan, began his career as a bench inspector and was rapidly promoted to his current supervisory position. Unlike Calligan, King viewed his initial position of bench inspector mainly as a means of financing his education and not as the beginning of his lifetime career. King was thirty-one years old.

## Role of Inspection and Quality Control

The chief difference between the two men was in their philosophies on the role of inspection and quality control in a manufacturing organization. Calligan's philosophy:

> Quality is an essential part of every product. . . . It is the product development engineer's function to specify what constitutes quality and the function of quality control to see that the manufacturing departments maintain these specifications. Accurate and vigilant inspection is the key to controlled quality.

When asked how important process control was in the manufacture of quality products, he stated,

> Process control is achieved primarily through the worker's attitude. If a firm pays high wages and provides good working conditions, they should be able to acquire highly capable workers. . . . A well-executed and efficient inspection program will, as it has done in my firm, impress

the importance of quality on the employees and motivate high-quality production. In the few cases when quality lapses do occur, an efficient inspection program prevents defective products from leaving the plant.
. . . Any valid quality control program must hold quality equal in importance to quantity. . . . Quality records must be maintained for each employee and be made known to both the employee and his immediate superiors. Superior quality should be a major consideration in recommending individuals for promotion or merit pay increases.

---

*Question 1.* Criticize Calligan's philosophy in the light of what is known about quality assurance today.

---

King's philosophy paralleled that of Calligan only to the extent that "quality was an essential part of every product." King made the following comments on his philosophy toward inspection and quality control:

If quality is properly controlled, inspection becomes a minor function. The more effective a quality control system becomes, the less inspection is required. . . . The key to quality control is process control, and inspection serves only as a check to assure that the process controls are being properly administered. . . . An effective inspection scheme should locate and pinpoint the cause of defects rather than place the blame on an often innocent individual. A good rejection report will include the seeds from which a solution to future rejections can be developed.
. . . One sign of an unsatisfactory quality control system is a large, impressive inspection program.

King was asked what steps he would take to develop such a program if he got the job of chief of inspection and quality control in the Denver plant. He answered:

I would design and install a completely automatic inspection and process control system throughout the plant. By automatic I do not mean a mechanical or computer-directed system, but rather a completely standardized procedure for making all decisions concerning inspection and process control. The procedures would be based on a theoretically sound statistical foundation translated into laymen's terminology. The core of the program would be a detailed inspection and quality control manual.

When asked how long that might take, King continued,

I constructed a similar manual for my present employer in a period of less than twelve months and had the whole process operating smoothly within eighteen months after beginning work on the task. Since your firm is somewhat larger, and accounting for my added experience, I would estimate it to take no longer than two years and hopefully significantly less time. . . . As previously stated, I would place major emphasis on process control and would minimize inspection by applying appropriate sampling procedures wherever possible. . . . Employee quality performance should be rated on the basis of process control charts rather than on the basis of final inspection reports. The employee should be trained and encouraged to use these charts as his chief tool toward achieving quality output.

King further stated that one of his reasons for seeking a new employer was that he had developed the quality control program in his present firm to the point where it was no longer challenging to him. He further stated that he felt the same situation would recur at American Ceramic and Glass Products; but, because of the size of the firm, he thought he could direct his attention to bigger and more interesting problems rather than feel compelled to seek outside consulting work to satisfy his need for professional growth.

When asked what his real interests were, King stated, "Application of statistical concepts to the nonroutine activities of a manufacturing organization." He cited worker training, supplier performance, and troubleshooting as areas of interest. King submitted several reports that summarized projects that he had completed in those or related areas.

---

*Question 2.* Criticize King's philosophy and approach in the light of what is known today about quality assurance.

---

This was the extent of information that Parr had on the two individuals he felt might best fill the position vacated by Downs, the retiring chief of the inspection and quality control department.

---

*Question 3.* Under what conditions would you expect Calligan and King, respectively, to be more effective? For example, what kind of company or industry or level of management sophistication, etc.

*Question 4.* Which of the two candidates, if either, should be selected for the position of chief of the inspection and quality control department? Explain your choice.

---

# 6

# Omark Industries: Top Management–Driven JIT

*Case topics:*

| | |
|---|---|
| Top management & JIT | Supplier reduction |
| Quick setup | Finished goods reduction |
| Task force | Supervisory resistance |
| JIT training | Productivity improvement & |
| Corporate philosophy | staff cuts |
| Inventory carrying cost | "Least man" concept |
| Machine cells | Gain-sharing |
| Employee involvement | Financial benefits |
| Total preventive maintenance | |

In the brief history of implementing just-in-time production in Western companies, the impetus to take the JIT plunge has usually come from people somewhere below the company president. Omark Industries is one of the few exceptions. The JIT effort at Omark was led by John L. (Jack) Warne, corporate president and chief operating officer.

## Background

Omark Industries, headquartered in Portland, Oregon, is a metal fabricator with plants spread across the northern tier of states and into Canada and Brazil. Omark's principal products are, in rough order of prominence, saw chain, small-arms ammunition and allied products, log-handling apparatus, and speciality fastening devices and drill bits. Since the lumber industry has been depressed in this decade, Omark's annual sales have been static at about $300 million. Omark employs about 3,500 people, all nonunion.


## JIT Beginnings

JIT at Omark may be traced back to October 1981, when Jack Warne joined a group bound for Japan for a $5,000, two-week tour of manufacturing plants. Warne admits that relaxation and tourism were on his mind about as much as Japanese manufacturing.

One of the companies on the itinerary was Nippondenso, a Toyota supplier of starters, alternators, and other electrical components for automobiles. In a prep session before the tour, an articulate, knowledgeable Japanese engineer explained to the tour group what they would see. His description of lightning-fast model changeovers and zippy, delay-free production sounded far-fetched. The spokesman's explanation of how Nippondenso achieved the results did not sound so far-fetched. Eyebrows were raised and interest was piqued.

The plant tour confirmed that the engineer had not exaggerated. Warne recalls witnessing a changeover on a starter line. About eighty production employees were building small starters for cars. With clockwork precision the crew took just fifteen minutes to change over the line to run truck starters four times larger. The line looked to be at full speed immediately.

Warne remembers having mixed feelings of dismay and excitement: dismay because he could not continue believing that Omark, his company, was in a strong competitive position; excitement because Nippondenso's techniques looked simple to learn and not impossible to transfer to his company, which might put Omark two legs up on the masses of manufacturing companies in North America and Europe.

On his return Warne presented his findings to Omark's CEO, Edward S. (Ted) Smith, and the board of directors. A ten-person Japanese Management System Task Force was formed, first for further fact-finding and later for preparing implementation recommendations. The task force was chaired by Dr. Michael Rowney, director of productivity and technology; members were drawn from corporate officers and staff and from line managers at Omark's Oregon Saw Chain Division. Functions represented were human resources, training, communications, controller, manufacturing, and R&D. Some of the features of the implementation plan and facilitating corporate actions are as follows:

- Omark would use its own term, zero inventory production system (ZIPS).
- Warne appointed a three-person ZIPS coordinating committee: Rowney; David Pinch, corporate comptroller; and Les Jenkins, manager of personnel development. It was a well-respected, highly credible group.
- $300,000 was budgeted for training in the first year, much more in the next year.
- More than thirty employees, including CEO Smith, went to Japan in 1982.
- In August 1982 a team led by Warne presented a two-day seminar on ZIPS and people involvement at each plant location.
- Smith brought together nearly all of the corporate officers for a series of special discussions. The group hammered out, word by word, an Omark "statement of philosophy." This corporate philosophy, a commitment to people involvement, quality, and ZIPS, went out to all employees, stockholders, and others.

## Results

The $300,000 training effort in 1982 got the entire manufacturing workforce fired up about cutting inventories and delays in the production flow.

Next, the idea had to be sold to the board of directors. One concern was the cost to carry inventory for one year. Pinch, the controller, estimated the cost to be 25 percent of its value. Thus, the board was told that each $1 million in inventory reduction was a $250,000 annual cost reduction. The board approved a significant budget for moving machines and developing new tooling for quick setup.

The results of that top-down "total immersion" in ZIPS were

dramatic. The average inventory for the whole company had been static at about 179 days of sales for the ten years prior to the launching of ZIPS in 1982. By 1984, inventory was down to eighty-five days of sales.

---

*Question 1.* ZIPS/JIT was "sold" to the Omark board based on projected inventory carrying cost savings, at 25 percent. Is that a good way for other companies' officers to persuade their boards to support their own JIT efforts? Note: 25 percent—or 24 percent (2 percent per month)—is a widely used carrying cost rate in North America, and it has been for decades. (European manufacturers generally use a lower rate.)

---

While inventory is a universal measure to which corporate officers can easily relate, it does not always reflect the improvements (or lack of them) at the plant level. A truer measure of JIT, or ZIPS, performance is reduction in production lead time. (Some unwanted inventories may take years to work off or to declare as excess and sell off; also, some inventory may be finished goods retained for marketing purposes and not truly reflective of manufacturing performance.) In some Omark plants, lead time reductions were far more spectacular than the overall company inventory improvement. For example, the Guelph, Ontario, plant cut its production lead time (raw metal to finished saw chain bar) from twenty-one days to three days between November 1982, the "official" ZIPS launch date, and May 1983.

Some plants jumped the gun, starting up pilot ZIPS projects prior to November 1982. Every plant location, including those that did not jump the gun, reported sizable inventory reductions within a few weeks of the launch date.

Michael Rowney generalizes about the Omark approach:

Like most plants in the western world, we traditionally group like machines together in a department, and the product travels from one department to another with many stops along the way, a journey often of 6–12 weeks duration. Now in many plants the ZIPS teams boldly pulled machines out of these groupings and put different machines alongside each other with little or no space for WIP between them. Operators found themselves next to the person who performed the previous operation instead of out of sight, and the sequential operations took place within minutes or seconds of each other instead of being separated by days.

Furthermore, according to Rowney,

> By far the most impressive result was the involvement and enthusiasm of the people [on the shop floor]. Long lists of problems revealed by removing the cushion of inventory had been identified and were being attacked with vigor. . . . It was most encouraging . . . that we had so much involvement and idea generation by people on the shop floor even before we had the benefit of quality circles.[1]

---

*Question 2.* Would it have been better to put in quality circles first?

---

In May 1983 the corporate staff held a week-long "show-and-tell" conference in Portland. All the plants sent representatives, who crowed about their successes. The capstone event was a Friday evening dinner and awards ceremony in which plaques, bottles of wine, and other prizes were passed out for best at inventory reduction, best at setup time reduction, best at quality improvement, best overall ZIPS, and so forth. Every plant got awards for something (including humorous prizes).

Coincidentally, just before the ZIPS conference, senior Omark officers had traveled to New York to make a presentation to financial analysts on Wall Street. While inventory performance is usually not a leading topic of interest to Wall Street analysts, the Omark presenters highlighted their ZIPS effort and results. The upshot: ZIPS conference attendees in Portland watched their company's stock price climb four points, from 20 to 24.

---

[1]Michael J. Rowney, "Early Experiences with ZIPS (Zero Inventory Production System) at Omark," unpublished speech, 1984.

## Implementation Approach

Omark's ZIPS effort was badly in need of training materials, but none were available when Warne decided in 1981 that the company should proceed with ZIPS. Fortunately, an English translation of Shigeo Shingo's book on the Toyota production system came on the market "just in time."[2] Omark bought 600 copies.

The Shingo book was poorly translated; irreverently, people said it was written in "Janglish." (And no wonder. English-speaking countries had never bothered to translate the available Japanese engineering, scientific, and manufacturing books and articles—including a wealth of materials on quality and JIT. Shingo and his publisher could hardly have expected much return from their investment in translating that book into English.) At each Omark plant natural work groups worked through the Shingo book. Commonly the plant manager assigned different chapters to different people. Reports were made; implementation plans were formulated. Since the Shingo book places emphasis on quick setup (SMED, or "single-minute-exchange-of-die"), most plants focused initial ZIPS efforts on quick die-change techniques. Many machines and setup procedures were improved, cutting setup times from hours to, often, minutes. (For one example, see Exhibit 6–1.)

---

*Example from Guelph, Ontario, plant, Omark Industries*

- Dies (about 600 lb. each) on racks in L-shaped area near presses.
- Die cart with roller conveyor on top shelf brings die to press.
- Front gate on cart lowered.
- Connect compressed air hose to side of die. Air pushed through holes in bottom of die raises die slightly when slid onto flat bed of press.
- Die shoved into place—equipped to receive die in right position.
- Quick clamping mechanisms complete die change.

  Total die change time: about 2 min.
  Formerly: 2–3 hrs.

---

**Exhibit 6–1.** Air-Cushion Method of Quick Die Change

[2]Shigeo Shingo, *Study of 'Toyota' Production System from Industrial Engineering Viewpoint* (Tokyo: Japan Management Association, 1981).

In late 1982 Richard Schonberger's *Japanese Manufacturing Techniques*[3] became available, and in 1983 Robert Hall's *Zero Inventories*[4] went on the market. Omark bought several hundred of each. The books espoused the same basic concepts as Shingo's and, being easier to read, brought the full JIT message to a wider Omark audience, thus adding fuel to the ZIPS fires that were already roaring.

---

*Question 3.* At Omark, those who read the books were generally the college-graduate types of people or, if not, then at least people who had attained managerial positions. Can we expect such people in other companies to read books on manufacturing, or was Omark a unique case? Can we expect others, down to shop employees, to get their JIT/TQC training by reading books? If not, how? Consider the question from a worldwide perspective. (Note: There is still a scarcity of books and training materials on JIT/TQC in such languages as German, Italian, Chinese, and Korean. Translations from the Japanese and English materials are available in only a few languages. Thus, while college-level people in most countries can usually read the English-language materials, the majority of employees cannot.)

---

The list of JIT (and companion total quality control) techniques undertaken, and results of those techniques, at Omark's plants is too long to relate here. Just two examples will be mentioned:

1. In the first two years the number of suppliers was cut significantly following the JIT purchasing concept of selecting and developing a "few good ones."

2. Some plants—for example, the Guelph, Ontario, saw-chain plant—got their manufacturing lead times down to about one day. That triggered talk about filling orders out of the plants and slashing finished goods in distribution warehouses. By comparison, it had

---

[3]Richard J. Schonberger, *Japanese Manufacturing Techniques: Nine Hidden Lessons in Simplicity* (New York: Free Press, 1982).

[4]Robert W. Hall, *Zero Inventories* (New York: Dow Jones–Irwin, 1983).

been taking an average of three days to fill an order out of the warehouses.

> *Question 4.* If filling orders from all of Omark's plants were reduced to three days (including order-entry and pick and pack), should *all* distribution warehouse stocks be eliminated? Discuss.

## People

The ZIPS-inspired upheaval in manufacturing practices was met with enthusiasm by many, but not by all. In Jack Warne's estimation, the supervisors were the hardest to change; marketing was next hardest, and middle management next. Warne feels that 90 percent of the supervisors did accept the changes; 10 percent continued to be more authoritarian, which does not fit well with the ZIPS *modus operandi.*

> *Question 5.* Why should authoritarian leadership be an obstacle?

It was generally understood that ZIPS would cut needs for staff support (especially materials-related staff) and drive direct labor productivity upward. Still, no one at Omark could have anticipated the degree of success ZIPS had in raising line and staff productivity. The productivity improvement rate in the *peak* ZIPS implementation period was mearly 35 percent. Attrition could not begin to absorb the excess labor. A wide variety of cleanup and fixup work, training, and quality circle activities helped temporarily with the problem of excess people.

The problem was compounded by two uncontrollable external factors: (1) no significant recovery from the slump in the lumber industry, Omark's prime market, and (2) a highly unfavorable (to U.S. exporters) currency exchange rate, which allowed foreign makers to emerge rapidly as tough competitors in the market for saw chain. Stihl Company of Germany became the toughest of those foreign competitors. Without ZIPS, Omark might have seen its high share of the world saw chain market destroyed and been faced with a crisis. As it was, ZIPS-related improvements in plant efficiencies allowed plant consolidations—much less manufacturing space was needed—and minimized the number of people who had to be layed off.

Omark's efforts to avoid layoffs and eventually to follow more of a lifetime employment policy were inspired partly by earlier widely-read books on Japanese management of *people*. The JIT/TQC books, which are concerned with management of *all* productive resources, do not discuss the lifetime employment concept. However, the Shingo book recommends the "least-man" concept: Have as the permanent work force the very least number of people that meet the lowest foreseeable sales demands; then meet all demands in excess of that through use of temporary employees.

According to David Pinch, corporate management had thought that a good approach would be to establish, subject to wage-and-hour law restrictions, a permanent cadre of trained temporaries; they could be mostly people like housewives or students who want to work and earn money at just certain times of the year.

Though there were layoffs and plant consolidations, ZIPS appears not to have earned a "black eye." A visitor recently asked one employee what he thought of ZIPS. "There is much better job security now," the employee stated. "In the past sometimes we would work twenty-four hours a day, seven days a week—then have a layoff. Too often we were working hard making parts that were not needed. Now we have more normal hours making parts that *are* needed."

Omark has also undertaken measures to build employee loyalty: (1) Under a stock ownership plan, some 75 percent of wage-earners are now stockholders. (2) A savings and investment program provides that Omark contribute $0.50 for each $1.00 the employee puts in, up to 6 percent of the employee's earnings.

In spite of all the company's efforts on behalf of the employees, there *were* some layoffs, which are always wrenching. Thinking "If I had it to do over again," Jack Warne says he would have had more contingency planning for the combined effects of a business downturn and ZIPS success.

---

*Question 6.* If Warne were able to do it all over again, could he have relieved the pain of job losses to any appreciable degree? If so, how? If not, why not?

---

## New Ownership

In 1985, Omark was bought by Blount Corporation, a construction company. Blount paid 37.5 per share, a price too attractive to resist, since the stock was trading publically at 24 at that time. Overall, Omark's officers could take pride in having their company viewed so attractively by the company that bought them out.

# 7

# JIT Beginnings at Burlington Industries

*Case topics:*

JIT in spinning and yarn
  preparation
Ratio of lead time to process
  time
Equipment replacement
Batch production and
  changeovers

Individual piece rate
Equipment mobility
Size of equipment
JIT as a competitive advantage

## Background

The 1980s have not been kind to America's textile industry. Between 1980 and 1984 about 250 textile mills were shuttered, eliminating some 110,000 jobs. A combination of strategic mistakes and tough foreign competition has plagued the U.S. industry. Tariffs in 1985 already averaged 22.3 percent on textile products, but the foreign onslaught continued. The U.S. Congress seemed in the mood to pass further protective legislation.

---

The author thanks Burlington Industries for help in providing representative data.

## Burlington Industries

Burlington Industries (BI) is a major manufacturer of fabrics for apparel, home furnishings, and industrial products. A foundation process at BI is production of greige cloth, which starts with bales of cotton, rayon, acrylic, wool, or other fibers and blends. The raw material goes through blending, carding, drafting, spinning, twisting, spring winding, dyeing, cone winding, warping, slashing, weaving, and various finishing steps.

BI was among the first U.S. textile companies to engage in a serious just-in-time production effort, with training and pilot JIT projects beginning in 1983. In 1985 JIT training, sponsored jointly by corporate and plant-level industrial engineering, was expanded, and small JIT projects were started in many plants.

Two plants were selected as good candidates for major plant reorganization following JIT concepts: the Edgeley spinning plant and the Oakes yarn preparation (package form) plant, which are in North Carolina. Gerald Irons, director of corporate IE, pointed out that comparatively large proportions of the operations at the two plants involved handling small containers of yarn through many production stages, plus several types of equipment that are fairly portable. Thus, the two plants seemed "wide open for about any type of JIT actions." On the other hand, being wide open offered so many alternatives that it was proving hard to agree on the best ways to proceed.

### Edgeley

The Edgeley plant has been in existence for several decades. Currently, owing to the depressed state of the textile industry, Edgeley operates well below peak capacity. Its equipment, while old, still works well. The plant operates in the batch mode with production lead times in the range of five or six weeks, which is at least ten times greater than actual process times of 2.5 to 3 shifts.

Cotton and cotton blends are processed at other BI spinning plants, while Edgeley sticks to synthetics, like polyesters, acetate, rayon, and acrilan. Currently the plant processes nine blends of those four fibers and six yarn "counts." The count is measured in yards per pound. (One single = 840 yards/pound, five singles = 4,200 yards/pound.) Two of their yarn blends are produced with "nubs";

the yarn goes to yarn preparation, weaving, and finishing plants for processing into nubby drapery fabrics.

---

*Question 1.* For this type of plant and range of products, is a lead time-to-process time ratio of 10 to 1 bad? Not so bad? Explain.

---

## Process and Layout

A spinning plant has four basic operations:

1. *Blending.* Fibers are blended together and rebaled.
2. *Carding.* Paralleling the fibers and combing the material into "sliver."
3. *Drafting.* Sliver is drawn out to a smaller diameter. Servo drafting further parallels the fibers while homogenizing the blend, and finish drafting prepares the sliver for spinning by further reducing the sliver diameter.
4. *Spinning.* Finished sliver is spun into yarn and onto bobbins.

Edgeley is a three-level plant. Bale stock enters at three truck receiving docks at basement level. The bale stock is stored, then later opened, blended, and rebaled. Blending is done by the "weigh-pan" blending method on two blending machines. Tints and antistat oils may be added during blending. Downtime is not a problem on the blending lines. There are about two line changeovers per shift, and changeovers average two and a half hours. Blended bales move by fork truck to carding.

Eight carding machines are located one room away from the blending lines in the basement. Setup time on a carding machine is about two hours. It takes about fifteen minutes for a carding machine to produce one 30-by-48-inch can holding 50 pounds of sliver. Machine down time, machine jam-ups, and malfunctions occur but are not major problems.

Sliver cans go by elevator to servo drafting on the first floor. Eight to twelve cans of sliver are accumulated prior to running a batch on one of the servo drafters. Eleven servo drafters draw the sliver down from 3,200 to 400 grains per yard; weight sensors control the amount of draw. Servo-drafted stock is coiled into 20-by-48-inch cans and conveyed to pin drafting. It takes fifteen to twenty minutes to fill one can.

Ten pin drafters are set to draw out the stock further—to a weight set at somewhere between 60 and 125 grains per yard.

Setup time on both the servo drafters and pin drafters averages forty-five minutes. Jamming and other manfunctioning is not much of a problem.

Fred Doyle, plant manager at Edgeley, feels that chances are good for getting corporate approval to replace the present servo and pin drafters with an advanced type of machine. Just six of the new machines, costing $67,000 each, would have the capacity of the present twenty-one drafters.

Finish-drafted stock goes into 15-by-48-inch cans. Hand trucks move the cans to ring spinning frames; six of the frames are on the first floor, and sixteen are on the second. The frames cost around $110,000 each; twenty of the frames have 152 spindles each, and the other two frames each have 184 spindles. Spinning frames are set up to run a particular yarn count—ranging from 840 to 4,200 yards per pound. Setups require two hours.

---

*Question 2.* Why do you think Fred wants approval of the new pin drafting machines? What do you think of the proposal to acquire the machines?

---

Processing a 10,000-pound production lot through spinning *on one spinning frame* would take about five weeks, or twenty-five work shifts. Actual spinning time for a lot (on the twenty-five spinning frames) is more like twenty shifts, which includes nonproduction time such as handling, queue time, setup, and downtime. The spun yarn goes onto 12-inch flanged wooden bobbins, and trucks holding eighty bobbins each convey the yarn to the weighing and shipping area.

---

*Question 3.* About how many shifts would it take to process a 1,000-lb. production lot?

---

The last steps are testing samples for correct twist, weight, and break strength, then weighing and loading the bobbin trucks into a trailer at one of the two shipping docks on the first floor. Most of Edgeley's product goes to the Oakes plant, which is 2 miles away.

*Question 4.* How should JIT be implemented at the Edgeley plant?

## Oakes

Oakes prepares the yarn into "package form" to supply both warp and filling yarn for the weaving plants. The plant runs three shifts per day and processes about four truckloads of raw material from Edgeley and other yarn plants. The production stages at Oakes are bobbin winding, twisting, spring winding, dyeing, drying, cone-winding, warping, and slashing.

### Bobbins to Dye Springs

The initial operation at the 270,000-square-foot Oakes plant is winding yarn from bobbins onto cones; five bobbin winders are available, and they process thirty-five different yarn counts. It takes half an hour for setup to run a batch of 1,800 pounds, which takes 4.2 hours. While the machines are not prone to jam or break down, they do need a lot of cleaning (lint, fuzz, and so on), as is the case in quite a few stages of textile manufacture.

Cones on wheeled dollies are rolled to the next operation, twisting. Eighteen twisting machines with 128 spindles each twist yarn in four different patterns: Ring twisting is done for sixteen different finish yarn counts, two-for-one twisting for five yarn counts, and fancy twisting for three yarn counts. The machines require a good deal of cleaning but not much repair work. They take about six hours to set up, and batch sizes are 5,200 pounds.

Next, bobbins and tubes of twisted yarn are wheeled to spring winding, where the yarn is wound onto stainless steel dye springs. There are seventeen spring winders, with one operator for each 1.5 machines. An "autotron," linked to a computer, records completions. When one truck (500 packages) has been recorded, material handling gets a signal; it brings a new truck by forklift and takes the full truck away. The machines require a lot of cleaning but not much unscheduled maintenance. Setup time is about a half-hour, and the run time per batch is 5.9 hours.

---

*Question 5.* Is there any evidence that Oakes is using a consistent policy on batch sizes? Explain, and suggest an improvement.

---

## Dyeing to Cone-Winding

Spring-wound packages go to dyeing, and after dyeing the packages are wound back onto plastic cones. Oakes is currently dyeing and cone-winding thirty-three different yarn counts and 538 colors.

Dyeing takes place under pressure in kettles holding from 110 to 540 dye springs; the springs are placed on a dye stand, and a crane lifts the dye stand into the kettle. There are nineteen kettles, and the lot size determines choice of kettle size. Dye time ranges from two to six hours.

The dye stand goes into a pressure extractor for one hour, taking the moisture down to 65 percent, then into drying. Rayon yarns go into a drying oven for twenty to twenty-four hours, cutting the moisture to 30 percent; drying is completed in one more hour in a dielectric dryer. Yarns other than rayon go through a heat/pressure dryer.

After drying, yarn is wound from dye springs to cones in cone-winding. Oakes has fifteen automatic and twelve manual cone-winders. Dye stands are moved by forklift to cone-winding, where the dye springs are creeled (mounted on spindles and threaded through the winders). There are two different spring package sizes, 538 different yarn colors, and thirty-three yarn counts. Changeovers take half an hour, run times are 2.7 hours, and the batch size is 1,500 pounds.

Burlington pays its operators in cone-winding an individual incentive based on number of full packages wound (onto plastic cones) per shift. Each operator tends fifty to seventy-five spindles.

---

*Question 6.* Individual incentives tend to be in conflict with JIT. What is a *practical* alternative plan for implementing JIT in the case of cone-winding?

---

All of the machines at Oakes that have been described so far are of moderate size; they could be moved by a forklift truck. The final two processes, warping and slashing, are on huge machines that do *not* move easily.

---

*Question 7.* What JIT alternative is suggested by the moderate size and movability of the equipment at Oakes? In your answer, comment on the practicality and implementation approach for the JIT alternative.

---

## Cones to Beams

Warping is done on seven filament warpers, costing about $225,000 each. In warping, 500–800 yarn ends are creeled in from cone-mounted packages and rewound onto 72 1/2-inch-wide cylindrical section beams. There is one operator for two machines, and warping runs three shifts, five days a week. It takes about four to six hours to fill a section beam, and three minutes to change over to a fresh beam. About once every two weeks the product is changed on one of the warpers, which takes about sixteen hours. Startup problems are minimal after a product change. Down time is not a serious problem.

Forklifts move section beams—in thirty to forty different "constructions" of yarn—to slashing. Ten different yarns and 260 different colors are processed in slashing.

Oakes has eight large slashers for regular slashing, plus ten large dye slashers, which are partly in pits in the floor. Slashing builds the number of ends and applies a PVC sizing to protect the yarn for weaving; dye slashing accounts for 95 percent of production. Up to four colors of dye can be used in one warp.

The slashers are fed by ten to twenty section beams, each with 500 to 800 ends creeled in. It takes a two-person team eight to twenty-four hours to set up for a new dye slasher creel—with as many as 13,000 ends. The end product is would onto large loom beams ready for weaving. Production per slasher has been averaging 70,000 yards each; 90,000 is preferred. Mary Cherney, plant manager, stated that the biggest problem was a low utilization rate, about 40 percent, on the slashers; she attributed it to change times, down time, and a variety of other delays. Setup time on the slashers averages four and a half hours.

> *Question 8.* Obstacles to JIT loom large (pun perhaps intended) in warping and slashing. Comment on the obstacles and on short- and long-term solutions.

## JIT Projects

By mid-1985 Fred Doyle and Mary Cherney and their key people had developed long lists of agendas for JIT implementation in the Edgeley and Oakes plants. The lists included cutting lot sizes, cutting changeover times, transporting smaller lots, chaining up some of the material handling devices, taking operators off incentives, more cross-training, moving equipment, preventive maintenance, statistical process control, regularizing schedules, synchronizing schedules, kanban, and many more.

> *Question 9.* Developing agendas is the easy part. Doing it is sometimes not so easy. How might Doyle, Cherney, and the others on the JIT team capitalize on the competitive pressures faced by the textile industry to generate a sense of urgency? In other words, what is there about JIT that would be likely to help the plant gain a competitive advantage?

# 8

# Toyondu Company: Developing a Small Average Supplier into a Top-Notch Supplier

*Case topics:*

Effects on marketing for JIT supplier

Helping supplier to improve

Buy or backward integrate?

Growth prospects for dedicated supplier

Toyondu Company started business in 1943. Its first product was a round panel or bracket to support pipes. Forty years later Toyondu had grown to only sixty employees and annual sales of about $4 million. So little growth over so many years conjures up an impression of a precarious existence, one crisis after another. And so it was with Toyondu—until 1978. In that year Nihon Motors took Toyondu under its wing and began to develop Toyondu into a top-notch supplier

---

Company names are disguised.

of metal parts for Nihon trucks. Nihon did not invest capital but did invest a good deal of time and attention. The results, as will be explained, are probably more impressive than they would have been had Nihon merely provided money to modernize Toyondu's still ancient physical plant.

## Toyondu Five Years Later

By 1983 Toyondu had developed into a valued supplier for three Nihon truck plants. (About 90 percent of Toyondu's output went to Nihon and the rest to three other customers.) Toyondu had achieved the cherished "supplier-for-life" status that supplier companies aspire to in Japan and, increasingly, elsewhere.

Nihon contracts with Toyondu—and other "certified" suppliers—on a three-year basis. The contract cannot, of course, specify the quantities of parts to be delivered. No one can predict needs so far into the future. The contract does guarantee that, whatever the need is, Toyondu is the supplier. From Toyondu's viewpoint, that is a high degree of certainty as compared with the alternative: salesmen pounding the pavement hoping to flush out an order here and there.

At the end of each three-year period, Nihon people visit Toyondu and conduct a thorough audit of Toyondu's "quality," which means quality of management, design, waste elimination, discipline, morale, process capability, relationships with its own suppliers, operator involvement in process improvement, gauge calibration and use, orderliness, and other matters. Nihon people also do mini-audits at Toyondu fairly often within each three-year period.

What could be better for a supplier than this kind of secure arrangement with a stable internationally known customer? Toyondu can get by with little concern for marketing, since Nihon has committed to buying nearly all of Toyondu's capacity for the foreseeable future. Of course, there is no legal obligation for Nihon to keep renewing the three-year contracts. If Nihon became dissatisfied with Toyondu, if other suppliers of the same parts could show Nihon that Toyondu's costs were high and its design and quality were low, self-interest would surely compel Nihon to cut Toyondu off. Everyone understands this. Therefore, it is in Toyondu's interest to be a model supplier, to do whatever Nihon asks, so as to avoid any risk of losing this valuable perpetual customer.

---

*Question 1.* Does Toyondu's relationship with Nihon truly mean that Toyondu does not have to practice industrial marketing as it is usually practiced in industry? What *is* the proper role of marketing for such a supplier?

---

Nihon, the customer, is as happy about the arrangement as is Toyondu, the supplier. What could be better than having a model supplier who feels that "your wish is my command"? What's more, Nihon knows that Toyondu has become a model supplier through self-interest and not for some fuzzy reason like duty or loyalty.

So much for mutual admiration and self-interest. Now let's look at some potentially troublesome realities. Toyondu has a small, ugly factory crammed between some apartment houses and other buildings in south Tokyo. Its equipment is old, and its managers, staff, and operators are by no means the pick of the crop in Japan—the top people are snapped up by the top companies. As in tiny companies anywhere in the world, Toyondu does not have the managerial, engineering, and other talents to keep up with the world's latest innovations and to train its people in what is new and important. Toyondu also has hardly any clout in the financial markets and so cannot finance significant capital improvements.

In the face of those negatives, can mere self-interest and good intentions make Toyondu the kind of supplier that a manufacturer of Nihon's stature surely requires? Not likely. Nihon has much to do to assure that Toyondu's self-interest is channeled toward constant and rapid improvement and not allow Toyondu to stand still.

## Helping Suppliers to Help Themselves

Nihon's relationship with Toyondu is anything but casual. For one thing, the three-year contract that was in force in 1983 called for the price to go down by 1.5 percent every six months—automatically. Even if the amount of business—number of parts Nihon requires—goes way down, the price agreement sticks. (We may speculate that if inflation drove the price of steel up sharply and threatened to put Toyondu out of business, Nihon would negotiate a higher price or a loan.)

Even though the price is going down, Toyondu has an excellent chance to be profitable. The reason has to do with the management tools provided by Nihon. Nihon has learned simple management techniques for continually cutting its costs. Those tools are discussed below, beginning with those pertaining to design.

## Product and Process Design

With their customer's help and advice, Toyondu set up what it calls the "tear down" lab. The lab is a room about 10 feet wide and 12 feet long. A table is in the center, and a counter extends around the walls. The counter and table surfaces are loaded with samples of competitors' products—exhaust pipes, intake pipes, brackets, and so forth. Toyondu's tiny staff of designers maximize their effectiveness by spending time tearing down competitors' parts. This assures that Toyondu finds out fast whenever a competitor comes up with a simpler design, a cheaper material that will do the job, a better-bonding paint, or a way to achieve tighter tolerances.

The analyst in the lab has a full set of analytical tools. Value analysis helps find out what it probably cost the competitor to make the part. Fishbone charts tie effects, good or bad, to causes. The main causes (shown as primary bones off the spine) might be the material, the labor, the equipment, the procedures. Secondary and tertiary bones get more specific.

The competitive analysis techniques yield ideas for improving both product design and process design. In fact, since both process and product design information is found in analyzing competitors' parts, Toyondu is naturally drawn into considering questions of produceability at the same time as it considers the product design.

## Plant Management

Good plant management is not an attribute commonly found in small factories. Nihon gets high performance from the Toyondu plant manager by providing him with simple, effective management tools. The most important tool is the six-axis process check diagram.

Every Friday afternoon the plant manager tours the plant. He rates each work center on thirty-five subfactors that reduce to six main factors. He plots the ratings, from 5 (bad) to 1 (good), on a target-like card. The example in Exhibit 8-1 shows six ratings connected by lines, which makes the chart look like a spider web. The goal is for the web to shrink a little every week, for the ratings to converge on the target of perfection.

Some of the thirty-five subfactors seem not very significant. For example, one is, "whether or not work places for putting uncompleted goods are properly set." This subfactor falls under the main factor "Putting things in order. . . . "

Others seem of greater importance. Here, for example, are the five subfactors under "Equipment and tools" (not edited):

1. Whether or not daily inspection of equipment and tools is done properly.
2. Whether or not equipments are cleaned regularly.
3. Tools and metal patterns are properly put in order when they are not used?
4. Tools and metal patterns have proper numbers put on?
5. Tools and metal patterns should be cleaned regularly.

Whether of minor or large importance, the factors add up to a system in which human errors are rare. Are the operators apt to feel

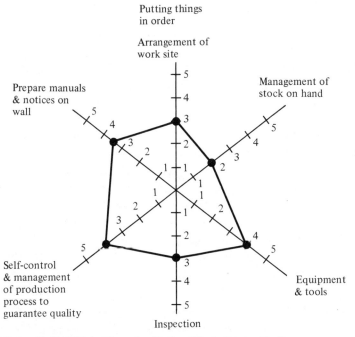

**Exhibit 8-1.** Spider-Web Chart for Rating Work Center Performance

that the boss is too snoopy, too much like a policeman? Probably not. None of the subfactors seems unreasonable. Any operator would surely agree that these are simple little things that all operators should do. Like a gung-ho army battalion, the operators at Toyondu Company may feel pride in working for a boss who has made them a sharp outfit.

Nihon provided the tool for the boss to use. What if he gets lax and fails to use the check sheets? Nihon's people would know before long, since they visit and check up on everything rather often. With the Nihon brand of attention to its suppliers, no one at Toyondu— engineer, plant manager, operator—can get away with laxity.

---

*Question 2. How* can Nihon possibly devote so much attention to a small supplier like Toyondu? In your answer think about the obstacles to such behavior on the part of buying companies in Western industry.

---

## The Operators

We have already had a peek at activities that Toyondu's operators are expected to do. There is more.

Every operator is at once a data collector, diagnostician, industrial engineering technician, quality technician, and trainer. Evidence of those operator duties is taped to walls and mounted on posts and signboards throughout the plant.

For one thing, each operator must prepare a flow diagram or written description of exactly how to make certain key parts. The operator documents every change, every improvement. The documents do not go into a file cabinet but are kept on display, and any supervisor, engineer, fellow worker, or customer is free to check the workmanship against the posted documents to see that no shortcuts are taken, no steps left out. (Some customers in Japanese industry insist that such documentation be on display everywhere in the plants where they buy products.) The operator also uses the documents to train any new people who might be assigned to the job. No one moves to another job without training a replacement.

The plant manager may use the documents as a straw man to stimulate improvements. Say, for example, that the manager is walking around checking process sheets and notices that the one for the tappet cover is faded and grease-stained. The manager could say to the welder, "Why is that the same process sheet I saw there two months ago? Aren't you involved in process improvement?"

That kind of prodding is not the whole strategy. Toyondu also has a high level of activity in formal quality control circles, and QC circle projects are recognized on charts.

## Conformance

There also are charts around the walls that deal with conformance to specifications: run diagrams and defect rates in particular. Statistical process control charts ($x$-bar and $R$, $p$-bar, etc.) are rare. Toyondu is very small and does not have the long runs of one part to yield enough data to set upper and lower and control limits statistically. With small volumes and a high variety of parts to make, conformance to specifications depends on every operator's knowing how to calibrate and use gauges, measure everything, keep the place neat and clean, keep the equipment in top condition, and do all the little things on the six-axis process check diagram.

Toyondu keeps a chart of its overall quality performance in the conference room. One representative month showed just two nonconforming parts discovered by Nihon and about thirty discovered by Toyondu itself and not sent out to the customer.

## Deliveries

Nihon gives Toyondu a thirty-day notice of requirements with two weeks of advance notice. Every two weeks Nihon sends an updated notice. Toyondu makes about 570 end items, and an average end item goes through three operations. About 65 percent of the orders from Nihon are for between one and fifty pieces.

The Toyondu employee in the shipping area prepares all delivery tags or kanban. Another employee checks them all, and any errors are charted like any other nonconformity. An error would hurt, because Nihon keeps hardly any buffer stock of materials supplied by Toyondu. Nihon requires a delivery at one of its truck plants at 1 P.M. (typically), plus or minus thirty minutes. Those parts go into a Nihon truck at 3 P.M. the same day. The truck plants are generally at least an hour's trip away through heavy Tokyo traffic. Toyondu shares trucks with other small suppliers going to the same customer plants.

## Plant Layout

Is Toyondu's plant laid out in flow lines or group technology cells? No, not at all. The plant is so small that distances from presses to drills to welding to paint are short. With short distances, inventory in transit is slight, and so are coordination problems and attendant queuing delays. If Nihon were to order a single part in a large quantity and with regular daily deliveries, Toyondu could easily move a welder and a drill press near a punch press or press brake to create a cell.

---

*Question 3.* Although Nihon seems to have developed Toyondu into a fine supplier, Nihon could have spent its time setting up its own facility to make the parts internally. Was Nihon wise in developing Toyondu instead? Discuss.

*Question 4.* What prospects does Toyondu have for growth? More products? More plants? Dim prospects? Discuss.

---

# 9

# JIT at Intel—
# Penang, Malaysia

*Case topics:*

Kanban
Number of stock points
Daily deliveries from supplier

Containerization
Multiple pieces of equipment
  per process

Intel Corporation is one among some forty electronics companies that have set up semiconductor assembly and test plants in Penang, Malaysia. Intel plants in the United States fabricate the semiconductor wafers—very much a high-technology process. Assembly and test is "medium tech"—exacting manual work at a number of kinds of sophisticated pieces of equipment. The Intel plant in Penang was established in 1972 and in 1984 had a work force of about 3,000. In each process area there are multiple pieces of identical worktable-sized pieces of equipment, each usually staffed by one employee.

## JIT Beginnings

In October 1983, Intel headquarters sent copies of Schonberger's, *Japanese Manufacturing Techniques* to Penang. Mr. P. Y. Lai, managing director at the Penang plant, states that "we were very excited by what we read.'' In March 1984, a JIT campaign was launched with the appointment of a Mr. Kumarasingam as JIT Manager. Three JIT engineers were added as Mr. Kumarasingam's staff.

## Initial Actions and Results

By May, the JIT group had removed all of the work-in-process (WIP) cabinets in the integrated circuit (IC) test building (the cabinets held boxes of ICs in tubes). The number of WIP staging points on the shop floor was reduced from six to three and a half, WIP was cut in half, and machines were moved closer together. The cabinets were replaced by locally designed trolleys (shelved carts on wheels). Each trolley holds six "pizza" containers, oblong metal boxes that hold tubes of ICs. Altogether a trolley holds 3,500 ICs, which is about seven hours of WIP. The trolleys are all placed in kanban rectangles outlined on the floor by yellow tape.

---

*Question 1.* Discuss the merits of *number of staging points* (or stock points) as a measure of JIT performance.

---

JIT status boards, about 2 feet square, are in each work center. Each board identifies the work center and the current allowable inventory. For example, one JIT board looks like this:

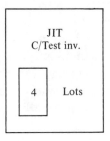

This is cold test, and the inventory is four lots (trolleys). The number "4" is on a plastic tag that fastens to the board. When a JIT improvement is made—higher rate of equipment up time, better quality, simpler handling, etc.—the *four*-tag would be replaced by a *three*-tag, and the number of lots (trolleys) would be cut to three.

The floor would be retaped so that the kanban rectangle is sized to hold three trolleys.

*Question 2.* When the number of trolleys is down to one (a *one*-tag on the status board), what comes next?

## JIT Suppliers

Most of the raw inventory comes from overseas, but there is a local supplier for the plastic tubes that hold ICs and another local supplier for packaging materials. Intel, Penang, has recently placed these two suppliers on alternate-day deliveries. Relationships with those two suppliers have improved enough so that when there is a problem, Intel staffers visit the supplier's plant and go right out to talk to the supervisors or engineers in charge.

## Multifunctional Operators

In the cold test area there had been two operators per machine. Now there is one per machine, and automatic loaders will be added to the machines so that one operator can run two machines. Intel, Penang, has established a special position called "super operator." This is the term for an experienced operator who knows how to perform some machine maintenance and also has mastered the operation of more than one machine.

## Measures of JIT Performance

The general manager, Mr. Lai, uses five new measures to trace JIT improvements:

- Space ratio: present space compared with "original" space
- Work-in-process management: percent of product on pull system and color code
- Flow distance
- Throughput time reduction
- Number of WIP staging points

With a good start in applying JIT in the IC test building—and a system of inducing further improvements there—the next logical step, as of August 1984, was to extend the JIT campaign into the assembly building and perhaps into the tin plating building as well.

---

*Question 3.* Some aspects of semiconductor assembly and test favor JIT implementation. What are some of those aspects? Discuss.

---

# 10

# JIT at Intel— Manila, Philippines

*Case topics:*

Quality assurance

Flow lines

Utilization

Employee appraisal

Under-capacity scheduling
  of labor

Length of assembly conveyor

Intel Corporation is one of some twenty electronics companies that have set up semiconductor assembly and test plants in Manila. Intel in Manila has a relation to the corporation's U.S. operations similar to that of Intel, Penang (see Minicase Study 9). The Intel plant in Manila was established in 1974 and currently has a work force of about 2,000. In 1984 it specialized in EPROMs, a type of memory chip, and secondarily produced some microcomputer component devices (MCCDs).

At Intel, Manila, integrated circuit (IC) assembly is located in a large assembly plant, Bldg. A2; IC test is in another, much smaller plant, Bldg. T9, about half a mile away. About 350 operators work in T9—about 1,200 work in A2. Assembly time averages one week, and assembly work-in-process inventory averages about two weeks' worth. Test time and WIP are greater. The number of ICs produced per month is in the millions.

## JIT Beginnings

Mr. Hermogenes ("Herb") Fernando, plant manager for assembly, has been the "prime mover" for implementing just-in-time production. In the summer of 1984 a JIT pilot test project was formulated by Fernando and his staff: Organize a dedicated production line to include the first five major steps in IC assembly:

1. Saw wafer into dies (the die is the chip itself)
2. Inspect die
3. Attach die to frame (the frame contains the leads that connect electronically to whatever the IC is used in)
4. Bond die to frame
5. Inspect

Remaining assembly steps—encapsule the die in a plastic mold or ceramic package and lid, solder coat, and inspect package—were not included in this phase of the JIT pilot project.

Herb Fernando wanted die attach and bonding included in the pilot test, because they are the two assembly steps that have the longest setup times: about thirty minutes in die attach and thirty to forty-five minutes in bonding. The setups consist mainly of changes related to "lead count" (number of leads in the frame). Most of the ICs assembled at the Manila plant have either twenty-four or twenty-eight pins or leads. The number of each type of equipment is fairly large—for example, forty-eight die attach machines. The pilot test line will be dedicated to die/frame units with a certain lead count, which avoids setup time entirely.

The dedicated-line concept contrasts sharply with the current factory arrangement. Now each stage of production, throughout IC assembly and test, is laid out and supervised by process. For example, all saws and saw operators are in one area, and all die attach machines and operators are in another area. In the pilot dedicated line, one or two of each type of equipment, plus operators, will be moved into a flow line. The work content at each station on the line will be balanced as much as possible. Small quantities of ICs will be passed from station to station. Current thinking is that a transporter channel (conveyor) will be set up to move the units from one operator to the next.

---

*Question 1.* How long should the average length of conveyor be between work stations on the line? Explain.

---

The pilot line will process plastic-coated dies. The plastic-coat processes are all on the second floor of Bldg. A2, while the hermetically sealed dies are produced on the third floor. Producing the two kinds of ICs—plastic and hermetic—involves more steps that are the same than are different. Therefore, most results obtained in the pilot test line should be transferable to the hermetic floor.

Good results on the pilot project would probably lead to organizing more flow lines, each dedicated to ICs with a particular lead count. The flow lines may be lengthened, potentially including even some of the test operations now housed in Bldg. T9. There are, of course, some stages of assembly and test that do not fit in easily with the flow-line concept, for example, a ten-hour burn-in step in assembly and a seventy-two-hour retention bake for EPROMs as one of the test steps.

## Performance

Quality assurance follows the Western approach: large inspection staff, numbering in the hundreds, who conduct 100 percent inspections and also sample-inspect from large lots. Besides weeding out bad product, the inspectors provide data for rating operator performance. Each operator (all women) is rated on quality error rate and on output. Error and output rates are plotted on charts located in the work areas, and supervisors use the data in counseling individual operators. Every three months, high-performing operators are eligible for a small gift.

---

*Question 2.* What changes in the quality assurance and employee appraisal practices would be necessary or advisable in order to blend well with the flow-line concept that Mr. Fernando was organizing on a pilot basis?

---

The supervisors, maintenance people, and quality assurance staff are physically located on the shop floor. Furthermore, in each process area (stage of production) there is a team consisting of the supervisor and the maintenance and quality staff assigned to the process. This arrangement helps get fast attention to problems.

Some of the machines—for example, die attach equipment—have multicolored pyramids on top of them. Someone turns the pyramid to indicate when the status of the machine has changed. When the white color is up, the machine is operating all right; when blue is up it is undergoing engineering; when red is up it is in need of maintenance; and so forth.

Under the dedicated-line concept, the output of one operator is the output of all, and when the line shuts down for a problem all stations are soon shut down ("soon" depends on how many minutes of ICs are between stations). The focus will be on prevention, not detection—in regard to both quality and machine operability. This tends to call for operator involvement, in-line inspection, stopping to avoid problems, under-capacity scheduling of labor, extra pieces of equipment in case one goes down, and so forth. Herb Fernando is conversant with those JIT and TQC concepts, but he wonders how they will mesh with the company's traditional emphasis on high labor and machine utilization. If the machines and operators on the pilot line are utilized less than normal—to suit JIT/TQC requirements—it is of small consequence. But what if the JIT/TQC concepts are applied plantwide?

## Timetable

Ms. Elvie, who is to be the supervisor of the dedicated line, expects to have it up and running by September 1984. In the meantime, many details need to be worked out and plans need to be formulated for the IC test operations.

---

*Question 3.* Under the flow-line concept, what changes would there be in the role of the present troubleshooting team (supervisor, plus maintenance and quality staff)? In the use of the multicolored pyramids?

*Question 4.* If the corporate concern for utilization remains in force, will Fernando have no reasonable alternative but to halt the plant reorganization? Discuss (assume that Fernando has tried but failed to get special "dispensation" from corporate).

---

# 11

# Just-in-Time Production at Hewlett-Packard, Personal Office Computer Division

*Case topics:*

Parts standardization
Supplier reduction
Forecasting and volatile demand
Commitments to suppliers
Keeping problems visible
Kanban quantities and signals
Flow-line layout
Monthly work order

Weekly count
Equipment mobility
Intermingled desks and
  machines
Simple information processing
Supervisory resistance
Robotics and automation
Role of product designer

Hewlett-Packard's personal office computer division (POD) is in Sunnyvale, California. The division's JIT campaign dates back to about summer of 1983. The JIT success story may be told by comparing manufacturing data for three generations of products.

## Pre-JIT

Before JIT (i.e., before the fall of 1983) the plant manufactured twenty different computer products, including the HP-120 desktop series. There were an average of six options per product, 20,000 active part numbers, and about 2,000 suppliers. Plant size was 30,000 square feet, and plant output was about 4,000 units per month. End-item lot sizes were 500 units, and printed circuit (PC) board lot sizes were 100–500 boards. Purchase orders, work orders, and tracking of work-in-process inventories were under the control of a material requirements planning (MRP) system.

## The HP–150

The Sunnyvale plant began manufacturing the HP-150 personal office computer in October 1983. The computer has become a $150 million business. R&D designed the 150 to be built from 450 part numbers in 7,500 square feet of plant space (a building was vacated). There were about 200 suppliers when the 150 was announced. About one-third of the direct labor time is spent on test, evaluation, rework, and repair. (Other costs associated with quality assurance—such as prevention, appraisal, external failure, and internal failure—have not been determined.)

---

*Question 1.* Should it be easier to run JIT effectively on the 150 than on the 120? Explain.

---

The 150 is sold worldwide, which amounts to seventeen different languages. That variety of languages means making a variety of keyboards but just one CPU. H-P Singapore makes the keyboards, H-P Greeley the disc units, and H-P Japan the power supplies and some PC boards. Sunnyvale ships the components to a distribution center where they may be integrated into a complete system. The distribution center keeps one or two weeks of stock on hand.

Production volume averages about 5,000 units per month. The 150 is built to a monthly schedule provided by marketing; the schedule may be changed by 5–10 percent within the month, 20 percent in the second month, 30 percent in the third month, and so forth. According to one manager, manufacturing does a lot of "second guessing," because the forecasts are "terrible." POD has committed itself to supplying service parts for up to five years. (It's considering a "lifetime buy" based on forecast demand for service parts.)

---

*Question 2.* How serious is the forecasting problem? In other words, does success with JIT depend on good forecasts?

---

In the first two months sales were 7,000 units per month. That was considerably above expectations. Sunnyvale doubled its capacity. Then in the third month sales dropped way off. For much of the rest of the year sales were only enough to run the plant at half capacity.

---

*Question 3.* What is a natural explanation for the plunge in sales in the third month?

---

## JIT Introduction

It took about two months to implement JIT in final assembly, and it took six to eight months to implement in PC board assembly. The WIP inventory reductions have been dramatic: from three weeks' down to three days' worth. According to Lee Rhodes, production manager, the WIP reductions are "entirely due to JIT."

Purchased stocks are much higher: one to two months' supply. One reason is the problem of a dropoff in demand for the 150. Orders were placed for more materials than were needed, and POD permitted some material buildup in order to honor commitments to certain suppliers.

---

*Question 4.* What is another, probably more significant, reason for purchased stocks to stay high despite the JIT efforts?

*Question 5.* "Honoring commitments" sounds like buying materials that you don't need or before you need them—which is contrary to the idcal of just-in-time receipt of materials. Is this a flaw in the POD approach?

---

When JIT is applied to a product made repetitively, the monthly scheduled quantity is divided by the working days in the month to yield the daily production rate. For the 150, the *actual* daily schedule varies a bit. If there is a lot of down time one day, the schedule for the next day calls for more than the daily rate—in order to catch up.

As in any manufacturing plant, down time at the POD plant may be caused by running out of parts, machine breakdown, and a wide variety of other problems. On the POD production floor, everyone finds out right away when one of the stations on the production line is down: The event is announced by the playing of a tune over the plant sound system. A 150 computer produces the electronic tones for the tune, and there are different songs for different causes of down time. For example, when the cause is a shortage of parts, the computer plays the "Mickey Mouse" song: "M-I-C . . . K-E-Y . . . M-O-U-S-E."

---

*Question 6.* Does it make sense to inform everybody about down time at somebody else's work station (a negative event)?

---

## JIT in Action

The plant layout in the 150 area is as shown in Exhibit 11-1. Two mirrow-image PC board assembly lines are on the outside and share an in-between area where assembly and test of the 150 are performed. A description of the manufacturing process follows, with processes keyed by number to locations on Exhibit 11-1.

### Component Sequencing and Auto-Insert

Receiving and raw material storage is number 1 on Exhibit 11-1. The first manufacturing operation is assembly of the PC boards for the 150. About ten different types of PC boards go into the 150.

The PC board assembly work centers are tightly packed into a serpentine flow line. Each type of axial lead component is purchased in the form of taped reels, and a reel rack (2) in the PC board assembly area holds one reel of each type. When an assembler takes a full reel from the rack, an empty with the same stock number information on it goes in its place on the reel rack. About two times per shift, a material handler passes by this and other stock points

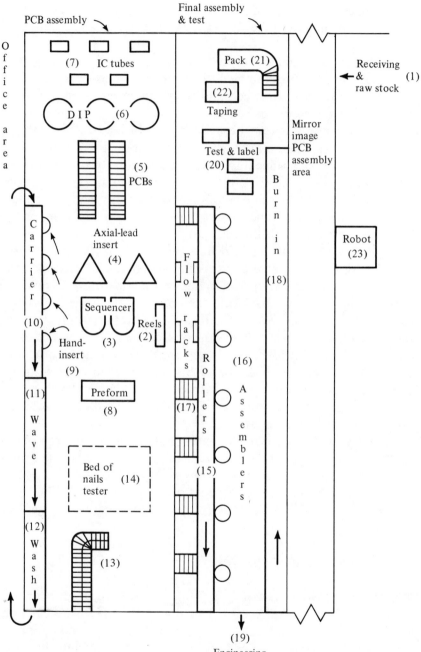

**Exhibit 11-1.** Layout of 150 Manufacturing Floor (Not to Scale)

on the assembly floor. Wherever there is an empty container (reel in this case), the handler takes it to the raw stock area and brings back a full one.

A Universal sequencer (3) is located right next to the reel rack. The sequencer is programmed to remove components (resisters, diodes, etc.) from source reels and retape them on an empty reel in proper assembly sequence.

Setup time on the sequencer is not a problem: Just put a floppy disk into the machine telling it the correct sequence. With so little setup time, it is economical to have the sequencer produce just one reel and then be set up for a different reel. The sequencer produces a reel when one of the same type is emptied on the nearby axial lead inserter machines (4), which insert the lead wires of the components into holes in raw circuit boards.

The circuit boards are held in a flow rack (5), ten boards to a box. The flow racks feed the boxes of boards to the inserter operator, who performs the insert operation one board at a time. The operator puts completed boards back into the box and, when the box is full, places it on the lower shelf of the flow rack. That shelf tilts the other way, and the tilted rack conveys the boards the short distance to the dual-inline package (DIP) auto insert machines (6) at the other end of the flow racks. When a box of boards has been emptied at the DIP machines, the empty box is turned upside down and placed back on the top shelf of the flow rack. The material handlers periodically take away the empty boxes and bring back full ones.

The DIP machines (three of them) hold about two dozen plastic tubes, each containing a different type of integrated circuit. The tubes of ICs are purchased parts held in raw storage. One set of spare tubes of each type is kept on the assembly floor in wheeled racks (7), which the material handlers take away for refilling whenever they get low.

## Hand-Insert, Solder, and Test

Near to the flow racks is the beginning of a long production line segment that completed the PC board assembly. Half the line consists of stations where assemblers hand-insert more components. These are large or odd-shaped components not easily auto-inserted. The components come from a nearby preform machine (8); the machine bends the lead wires 90 degrees into proper alignment for insert into the circuit boards.

The hand-insert stations (9) are alongside a moving carrier track (10). Boards from the DIP machines are mounted on fixtures and conveyed one at a time to the stations. There are four or five stations, where seated assemblers progressively insert components. An overhead carrier track returns the fixture to the hand-insert area after the board is removed from the fixture at the far end of the line.

After hand-insert, the boards on the fixtures are conveyed into the wave solder machine (11). A wave of molten solder passes under the PC boards, securing the leads. The last operation on this line is the washer (12), which washes foreign matter off the boards and dries them (somewhat like a home dishwasher). Setup time on the wave machine is negligible, because all of the PC boards are of the same thickness, and the few different sizes of board could all be fitted into a universal kind of fixture.

PC boards emerging from wash are placed on the upper level of an L-shaped length of dual conveyor (13); this conveys the boards to the "bed-of-nails" board testers (14). Setup time on the board testers is negligible: Just change the floppy disc holding the test program. After testing, boards go into boxes, ten per box, and the boxes are placed on the lower level of the conveyor.

## Final Assembly and Test

Occasionally a few boxes of boards are taken from the conveyor to the 150 final assembly area in exchange for empty boxes. Final assembly of the 150 is done on a line consisting of roller conveyor (15). Assembly is progressive: Each CPU is pushed from station to station, and assemblers (in standing positions) add more components and PC boards at each station (16). A maximum of two units are staged between assembly stations.

---

*Question 7.* Why have the two units between stations?

---

Flow racks (17) next to the roller assembly line hold the purchased and internally fabricated components that go into the 150. Material handlers replenish the flow racks whenever they get low. For some items plastic cards (kanban) provide identification of the part numbers needing replenishment.

**71**

---

*Question 8.* When do you need a card, and when do you not need one?

---

The computers are burned-in while resting on a length of roller conveyor (18). The procedure consists of an eight-hour ambient checkout of the 150 CPUs while they are powered up and taken through various tests. Failed test data are displayed on the screen of the 150 being tested. The screens are checked hourly. Failed units go right to engineering (19)—not far away on the same floor—where causes are immediately searched for.

Right after CPU testing comes final functional test with a keyboard; this includes attaching a label (20). There are just a few "test" keyboards, and they stay in the testing area. Next, the CPUs are packed on a low-roller pack line (21), and the boxes are taped on box taping equipment (22).

---

*Question 9.* How much does the layout in Exhibit 11–1 contribute to the JIT results?

---

Exhibit 11–1 also shows a robot (23). It is a six-axis IBM robot, which is being modified by NJB Company technicians. The modifications are to make the robot capable of automatically inserting odd-shaped ICs. It is not necessarily intended to be ready for use on the 150-generation computer.

## *Inventory Control*

Two systems are used to plan and control manufacturing: (1) the master scheduling system (MASH) and (2) the inventory control system (ICS). The ICS provides just two occasions for inventory to be tracked: when materials are moved from stock (or receiving) onto the shop floor and when finished goods inventory is put into stock.

The JIT system used in producing the 150 features one work order per month. The MRP system is still in operation but in greatly modified form. It is used for purchasing only. According to Lee Rhodes, MRP software changes have resulted in "complete decoupling of MRP from the shop floor. . . . We decapitated the MRP system."

*Question 10.* What does "one work order per month" mean? Is this a natural way to schedule a JIT plant, or is it peculiar to the POD operation?

Whereas physical inventories had been taken every six months before JIT, under JIT they are conducted weekly—since there is so little to count. Buffer stocks throughout the plant are of a fixed size—the kanban concept. Kanban squares, flow racks, cartons, boxes, tubes, and other containers of fixed sizes keep the buffer stocks constant.

*Question 11.* Is it overkill to count so often, or is there good reason for it?

## Flexible Layout and Capacity

The POD Sunnyvale plant is quite flexible physically. Lee Rhodes commented that "much of the equipment is on casters." Water hookups have also been simplified. The water pipes are in the ceiling instead of in fixed positions in the floor. Even the wave soldering machine is more movable than in many PC board facilities, because the drains for the machine are above the floor rather than in the floor.

Furthermore, according to Rhodes, major equipment could be moved over a weekend, an additional production line could be set up in two weeks, and capacity could be doubled in just six weeks. If it were necessary to double capacity, the offices next to the 150 production area (in the same large room) would be moved out to make room.

*Question 12.* Flexibility is rather opposite to stability. Is the physical flexibility at POD a liability, a "nice-to-have" asset, or a big advantage?

In the POD Sunnyvale plant, as has been traditional for years at Hewlett-Packard plants, office space and factory space are quite intermingled.

> *Question 13.* Is such intermingling a good idea in a JIT plant?

Besides the physical flexibility, there is evidence of planning flexibility. Lee Rhodes spent one day in September 1984 with a group of visitors. Their tour day ended about 5 P.M, and the plan was to meet again for dinner at 7 P.M. Meanwhile Rhodes went back to his office, where he found a note from the comptroller requesting a labor study. The comptroller wanted to know what the labor requirements would be if certain work that had been performed in the Far East were pulled back into the Sunnyvale plant. No doubt the comptroller expected a reply from Rhodes in several weeks, which was typical when planning was performed on a mainframe computer. This time it didn't take so long. Before dinner that evening Rhodes entered the data into his personal computer. A Visi-Calc spreadsheet routine that he had developed quickly converted product data to labor requirements, and he placed a computer printout on the comptroller's desk that evening.

> *Question 14.* Would the comptroller have reason to be confident in the validity of the printout? In answering, think about the ways that JIT affects labor (capacity) planning.

## Implementation Issues

It isn't easy to implement so drastic a change as JIT is without certain human problems. At POD there have been several supervisors who simply could not adapt; they have been replaced, i.e., sent elsewhere in H-P. (The supervisors who are able to adapt generally are not complete converts, however.)

> *Question 15.* Adapt to what? Why should there be a difficulty?

74

A dominant objective of the manufacturing staff was to get everyone—line and staff—to *"own* a process." That, too, is a drastic cultural change, and the objective has by no means been fully achieved. Part of the difficulty lies in changing the way managers react when problems crop up in other people's processes. Rhodes explained the way it is supposed to work: When there is a parts shortage on the line, my job is to go to the buyer and say, "Let's write down the process and see what went wrong," instead of "beating the buyer on the head."

## Successor to the 150

The half-life of a personal office computer can be as short as a year. In the case of the HP-150, the successor model has been designed and is to begin production in late 1984—little more than one year after marketing began on the 150.

The successor has been designed for manufacturability. It will have just 150 different part numbers. Purchases will come from only thirty suppliers, and WIP inventory is planned to be just one day's worth.

A six-axis IBM robot was purchased, and the design engineers studied it to learn its capabilities: what weights it can lift, what distances, heights, and angles it is capable of reaching, what grippers it can be outfitted with, and so forth. The new computer was then designed for ease of manufacture by the robot.

Actually, the intent is to start up the production line for the new computer *without* any robots—except, perhaps, for the one that was acquired for the designers to study. One visitor to the plant suggested that maybe a better strategy would be to design the product for manufacture by a simple three-axis "pick-and-place" robot instead of the large six-axis kind.

---

*Question 16.* Having prepared for robots, why not implement them? Can you think of any advantage in designing for three-axis instead of six-axis robots?

*Question 17.* In the fall of 1984, another division of H-P entered into a joint venture with a company in Taiwan. The venture called for development of what was to be the world's most highly automated plant making PC boards (the raw boards, sans components). This is in contrast to POD's not-very-automated plant making the 150. Should the POD be directing more effort into automation, more like the venture in Taiwan?

---

Details on the design and manufacturing features of the successor computer were not made public while the 150 was still in production. Some outsiders speculated that the successor might incorporate, among other things, advanced PAL (programmable array logic). The PAL approach simplifies the manufacture of a CPU by eliminating large groups of standard logic chips. (The PAL approach had enabled Apple to reduce greatly the part count in the Macintosh computer.)

---

*Question 18.* Product designers can make a contribution to JIT manufacturing by employing approaches like PAL. How important is the designer's role in JIT? Discuss.

*Question 19.* What are your recommendations for getting people involved? In your answer, assess the present situation at POD.

---

# 12

# In-Line Manufacturing (Alias JIT) at Heatilator

*Case topics*

Production speed and efficiency
In-line manufacturing
Task forces
Corporate review
Recognition
Work simplification
Carrying cost rate
Material handling "spine"
 concept
Postponing MRP development
Relayout of shears, presses,
 brakes, paint conveyor
Backward integration
Work shift policies for NC
 machines
Parts made from scrap
Hand-push vs. lift truck
Employees as "members"
Coping with seasonal demand
Incentive pay
Reduction of indirect labor
Speeding up the improvement
 rate

HON Industries is the parent company for six operating companies. HON's annual sales are about $400 million, and total employment is about 5,000. Four of the operating companies are in the office

---

Case material is derived from a paper by Stanley M. Howe, "Improving Manufacturing Effectiveness in Partnership with the Employees," *Proceedings of the Third Annual Winter Conference of the Operations Management Association,* Toronto, November 8, 1984. Numerical data are for the year 1983.

furniture business, manufacturing metal and wood furniture of many types. The fifth company is a manufacturer of material handling equipment.

The sixth company is the subject of this case. It is the Heatilator Company, an old, traditional manufacturer of fireplaces. Stanley M. Howe, HON's president and CEO, observes: "In this high-tech world one may wonder about this product, but apparently man sat in front of a fire at the mouth of his cave so long that he still has this in his system. Fireplaces are still in high demand."

Heatilator's products are called zero-clearance fireplaces. They are made of metal and are insulated so they can be installed in a home on a combustible floor and against combustible walls. They can be faced with whatever kind of brick, stone, or other material the homeowner desires. The product line includes flue systems (which replace masonry chimneys), along with glass doors and other such accessories.

HON acquired Heatilator, an employer of about 400 people, in May 1981, in what Howe refers to as "a turnaround situation." This case describes the restructuring approach taken by Howe and the corporate and Heatilator people to effect the turnaround.

## Reorganization

HON's management felt that the parent company's manufacturing know-how in metal office furniture would be valuable in upgrading the manufacturing of metal fireplaces, because both products are basically boxlike metal structures using similar materials, equipment, tooling, and processes. One of HON's office furniture companies is particularly efficient: One production line makes a file cabinet every forty seconds. A desk line makes a desk every minute. The first of those efficient lines was in place in the mid-1950s.

---

*Question 1.* Occasionally we read in the business press about some company's highly efficient production line, which, the story may say, produces a file cabinet every forty seconds or a personal computer every ten seconds, or has a line speed of 600 cases per hour. To what extent are these valid ways of judging production efficiency or excellence?

---

Howe stated that HON calls its manufacturing concept "in-line manufacturing," which it has practiced for some twenty years. "It's merely a process of bringing materials into a plant from many sources, changing their size or shape or color or combination, and then shipping them out as a salable product. Quite a simple concept. Combining or eliminating operations to speed up all these processes—the time that the materials are inside the plant, the distance they travel, the material handling devices used to move them—is vital to efficient manufacturing."

---

*Question 2.* Is Howe's description of "efficient manufacturing" reasonably complete and valid?

---

In attempting to transfer the furniture manufacturing know-how, management first set out to consolidate Heatilator operations: Heatilator had two separate factories about three hours apart in small Iowa towns; main offices in Des Moines; and more total space than it needed. One plant made fireplaces and one made flues. To ship an order to a customer required moving product between the two plants.

With a few changes, the floor space in the main plant in Mount Pleasant, Iowa, could accommodate all operations. As it has turned out, the consolidated plant, incorporating streamlined methods, now has more production capacity, in units or dollars, than the two plants had previously; the plant even has some empty floor space available for new production. While assembly runs one shift per day, the more expensive fabrication equipment generally runs three shifts.

One year after acquisition, the consolidation was on schedule and some manufacturing improvement was occurring, but management wasn't satisfied with the rate of change. The transfer of know-how just wasn't going fast enough. In a memo, Howe outlined a proposal to set up task forces to attack all phases of manufacturing. The task forces were to include, where appropriate, people from other HON divisions who had special knowledge. Ten task forces were established.

## Organization of Task Forces

Each task force had three to five people with a staff person or a supervisor as head.

Task force 1 was for workplace methods. Its charge was a plant-wide review of operators' methods at individual work stations. The review was expected to improve the actual work methods, the work station layout, and the methods of material handling. Improvements would include adding jigs, fixtures, or small tools, or combining work activities.

Task force 2 studied overall plant layout as well as individual departments in detail. The object was higher efficiency of operation and better flow.

Task force 3 looked at vertical integration. It reviewed all purchased materials to find items that could be manufactured in-house at an economic advantage. It also reviewed all outside processing of materials to determine opportunities to do those in-house at an economic advantage.

A fourth task force on material costs, primarily purchased materials, was formed. It reviewed sourcing for all significant purchased items, reviewed purchasing practices, and looked for more favorable costs through use of blanket orders, stocking programs, or other improved buying methods. It also reviewed specifications on purchased items to see if significant savings could be obtained by changing the specs or adding new approved sources.

A fifth task force focused on control of waste—namely scrap. One of the plant supervisors suggested to the task force a way he could use the computer to utilize scrap better. If he finds a piece of scrap or material that would otherwise be wasted, he can get a printout of all parts using that material that don't weigh more than the piece of scrap. Through November 1984, following the procedure, he utilized $120,000 worth of material that would otherwise have been wasted.

The sixth task force was set up to analyze all overhead costs; to determine fixed, variable, and semivariable costs; and to try to do something about them. One goal was lowering the plant's break-even point. The task force attacked all costs, including heating the plant. One action was to install ceiling fans to destratify the hot air at the ceiling.

Task force 7 had the job of reviewing all packaging methods and designs to find the lowest total costs. Packaging cost includes labor and inventory carrying costs as well as the packaging material. Packaging is a significant cost in bulky sheet metal products, because there is a lot to put a package around.

The eighth task force dealt with product finishing, which is primarily, but not exclusively, painting. It reviewed the entire process of metal preparation and finishing methods, equipment, and materials.

Task force 9 was assigned to material handling. It reviewed all material handling throughout the plant and focused on the methods, containers, and material handling equipment.

The tenth and last of the initial task forces (Howe considered task forces to be limited-life entities, so the task force list has since been modified) was product design. The group reviewed parts designs for cost reduction in fabrication and economies through commonality of parts. They reviewed product design for cost reduction and quality improvement in the assembly process and for improvements in features, quality, and performance.

---

*Question 3.* Would it make any sense to organize the task forces horizontally instead of vertically (where vertical means *by function*)?

---

## Task Force Activities

Each task force maintained a log of every idea that was generated, who generated it, the date, and the person or persons assigned to investigate it. Additional columns in the log were provided for potential advantages or savings; the cost of implementation; the date a suggestion was reported back, accepted, or rejected; and the date of implementation. Each idea remained in the log until finally rejected or accepted and implemented; ideas did not fall by the wayside.

To encourage and administer this program, management set up quarterly review meetings attended by Robert Day, Heatilator's president; Philip Hecht, vice president of manufacturing; and Ernie Sulaski, vice president of engineering. They were joined by Howe, the president of the parent company, and by Claire Patterson, the head of a small department called manufacturing research in the parent company. Manufacturing research consisted of three or four people who were devoted to searching for new equipment, processes, materials—anything that might improve operations in any of HON's companies.

The review board met with each task force individually, usually in a meeting of up to an hour, reviewing ideas and progress being made. It was important to have up-to-date task force logs. Occasionally the review board pointed out new directions and brainstormed with task force members trying to create a much-needed atmosphere of creativity and initiative. There was almost always something for which the task force could be commended.

In order to stimulate the program among the work force, a work simplification course was offered. A staff member from the manufacturing research department taught the standard course that he had developed, refined, and taught over a twenty-year period. Approximately one out of every four people at Heatilator took the course.

## Rewards

Management wanted to give recognition for the many ideas and suggestions generated by individuals—especially factory workers on the task forces—but it wanted to avoid the problems of monetary awards. The first awards were T-shirts with the Heatilator slogan on them. Many employees earned T-shirts not just for themselves but for their entire families and wore them proudly. Later the company added Heatilator coffee mugs. Again some employees accumulated whole sets of mugs. Management was considering windbreakers for the next awards. Recognition also came from posting the logs on bulletin boards in the factory so that people could see their names on them, and could see also if there was followup.

Participation was excellent. The task force on workplace methods, heavily represented by factory workers, garnered a good share of the awards. Phil Hecht, the vice president of manufacturing, requested that the work simplification course be taught a second time to include additional people. For example, one woman had always been negative and therefore was not invited to attend the first class. After she had won several T-shirts, Hecht wanted her to benefit from the course. Another example was a reclusive man who lived alone and seldom spoke to anyone. After that man, too, made some suggestions, Hecht thought he ought to be included in the second offering of the course.

*Question 4.* Is work simplification likely to support or get in the way of Heatilator's effort to cut flow times and handling?

## Restructuring the Information System

Meanwhile, drastic changes were made in the management information system (MIS): new hardware, new software, and, more importantly, a new philosophy. It happened that the lease on the firm's old IBM 4331 equipment in Des Moines was expiring just as offices there were being closed down. After much study Heatilator leased a new Prime 750 computer, then acquired totally integrated software packages. The software employs the PICK operating system, relational data base, and query/report writer with a simple English syntax. The users (key managers) selected the software. User control of the management information systems was the goal and seemed to be the reality. Only minor modifications to the purchased software were made—those essential to get the system in operation.

The new system was delivered, hardware and software, in August 1982. Conversion was completed in nine months. After the changeover, annual MIS cost was reduced about 48 percent, including costs of data-entry people and staff, as well as the hardware and software costs. As a percentage of sales, MIS costs were reduced from over 2 percent to less than 1 percent. Yet the new system had far more functions than the old. Users are pleased and like to take visitors through and demonstrate the use of the system.

The MIS program facilitated and accompanied the many changes made in the manufacturing operation, but it did not trigger those changes. The prime emphasis and direction in the restructuring of Heatilator were to improve, speed up, and shorten the flow of materials through the plant.

## Managing Materials

Stanley Howe says that, "in general, American manufaucturers have concentrated on reducing direct labor while often ignoring the important field of material flow." The company has its own way of assuring that HON is not guilty of underestimating costs of inventory: 25 percent return on assets (pretax) is the threshold for evaluating a savings. This 25 percent is added "to all costs of owning inventory to get a measure of what should be saved if the company were to invest one dollar more in inventory than it needs just to operate."

---

*Question 5.* Assess HON's way of putting emphasis on inventory costs.

---

Howe further notes that "it's surprising how much of the floor space in a plant is taken up by inventories. In a plant that has turnover of three or four or five times a year, materials sit for two or three or four months or longer." Also, "there's a general impression that when people speed up quality gets worse, but [with] excellent flow . . . much greater emphasis is put on the solution of problems, because there isn't a bank of material or parts to hide a quality problem. One has to get at the cause and correct it, because if the process is closely coupled there may be only one or two pieces there for buffer. Quality problems are discovered much sooner, and there is a completely different emphasis on the urgency of correcting the problems when you have the fast flow or 'manufacture at point of use' concept actually working.

"Another benefit . . . is improved customer service. The response time is so much shorter. You don't have to enter customer orders into the shop floor days, weeks, or in some cases months ahead of delivery. With fast flow through the shop, orders are rapidly processed. The benefits of less inventory—smaller factories, improved quality, better customer service—are so important to a manufacturer that great effort should be put into improving the material flow, which is too often neglected."

## Material Flow

One of HON's manufacturing concepts is that good material flow through a shop requires a basic material handling "spine." The spine is a series of conveyors and other material handling devices, such as automatic guided vehicles, which move the material through the entire plant.

The work of the task forces led to a much more efficient and complete material handling spine than the assembly line that was in place on acquisition. The spine at the Heatilator plant—see Exhibit 12-1—now comprises, first, a roller conveyor, shown as a vertical line at the top of the exhibit. It moves the heavy refractory material toward its point of use. Then a chain conveyor, the rectangular-shaped loop, moves parts from fabrication through finishing and to

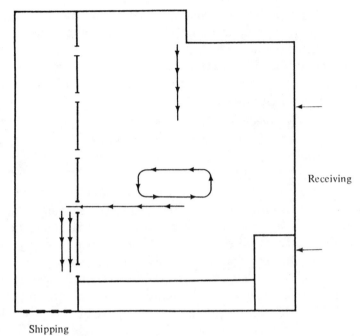

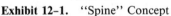

Shipping

**Exhibit 12–1.** "Spine" Concept

the final assembly line. The short horizontal line in the middle is the assembly line itself, which ends up taking the product to the conveyors in the finished goods warehouse. The vertical lines in the lower left corner are conveyors in the warehouse, which take the product close to the truck docks, where they can be shipped. Many components and subassemblies in the plant are fed to the main spine from the production cells, where they are manufactured along supplemental conveyor systems.

---

*Question 6.* Does the description of the material handling spine fit fully with JIT concepts? Discuss.

---

Management firmly believes that such a spine must be conceived, together with the methods by which it is scheduled and operated, before a computerized manufacturing system can be devised and installed. Howe states: "It's putting the cart before the horse to adopt a manufacturing system, such as MRP, first and then have it dictate the method of running the manufacturing operation and the flow of materials. A properly conceived spine and manufacturing system greatly simplify the software and the programming required from MIS." Howe notes that with in-line manufacturing, "by the time an operation would have been reported [to the MRP system], the part [could have] moved on to two or three or more operations. It might even be in the warehouse."

---

*Question 7.* Do you agree with Howe? If not, explain.

---

Much of the work of the task forces resulted in improvements in the flow of materials through the plant. For instance, the task force on improving workplace methods eliminated many unnecessary operations, combined operations, and reduced setup and operating times. One example was a part that was spot welded, then put into storage, and later brought out for riveting. The operator noted that the two machines were close to each other, and if they were pulled a little closer together, the operator could spot weld and rivet the part and cut out the handling.

The task force on packaging also made improvements. For example, a simple machine called a "pad locker" automatically closes and seals any size carton coming down the packing conveyor. The pad locker eliminated the high-labor-content packaging steps that had been the former practice.

Attached to the pad locker is a jet ink printer, used to spray onto the side of the carton a new designation, eliminating all the former labeling.

The task force on improved finishing led to the introduction of a paint conveyor; it is a key part of the material handling spine.

In sheet metal work, as soon as the metal is formed it gets bulky and is easy to damage. Therefore, the goal was to get it to the customer fast. The sheet metal parts are formed on one of the six press brakes, and the operator immediately hangs the parts on the chain conveyor, which takes them through painting and drying and, automatically, to the assembly line, where the assembler takes them off and uses them.

## Changing the Layout

The plant was previously organized in typical machine departments: all the shears in one department, all the presses in another, all the brakes in another. Parts would have an operation performed, then be transported on skids to a storage area, and then later returned somewhere for another operation. This involved making long runs to amortize the setup costs. The plant had sufficient press brakes for an improved solution: Pull six of the brakes over beside the paint conveyor and permanently set up each one to produce one or a group of related parts. Since setup time was virtually eliminated, parts are formed only as needed and hung on the conveyor. The flow is improved; see the short lines on the right side of Exhibit 12–2.

---

*Question 8.* How could the press brake and paint sequence be streamlined further?

---

## Other Task Force Recommendations

The purchasing task force found ways to eliminate sixty-three of the many different types of coil steel that Heatilator had been buying;

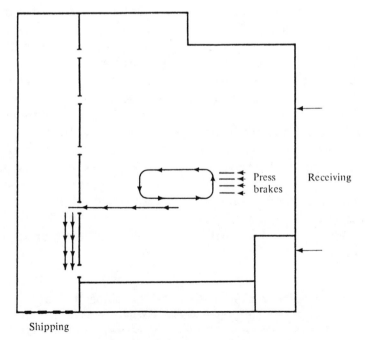

**Exhibit 12–2.** Dedicated Press Brakes at Point of Use

they found that in many cases common types of coil could be used instead of "special-spec" coils that had been bought.

The task force on vertical integration investigated an in-house operation for V-grooving the insulation blankets used for the chimney flues. Because it was a rather unusual operation, Heatilator had only one willing supplier in the United States. As a result, purchase quantities and price were high, and inventory turnover was poor. Acquisition of a $12,000 V-grooving machine for in-house production promised annual savings of $90,000 a year. More important, the right parts could be made at the right time rather than having to maintain huge inventories of every size.

---

*Question 9.* While we do not have enough details to judge that decision, we can assess the backward integration effort at Heatilator in general terms. Is it well conceived? Explain.

---

## Flexibility

The work of the task forces led to the purchase of a number of numerically controlled (NC) punch presses. Those machines are versatile, carrying as many as fifty different punches in their turrets. They eliminate the need in many instances for clanking and piercing dies. Setup or changeover time is negligible: just change a tape or a few work-holding clamps. Because the investment in the setup is so small, the operator makes the exact number of parts needed and no more. Long production runs are eliminated. The machines also eliminate many separate operations, because they can make a complete blank with any variety of notches, holes, or outline of the part, in one operation. The first machine of this type was soon up to twenty-four-hour-a-day, seven-day-a-week production. At that point a second was bought and also run twenty-four hours a day, seven days a week. Then a third was bought. At the moment three suffice.

---

*Question 10.* Should the NC machines be run that many shifts per week? Explain.

---

## Tooling Costs

An added benefit of the NC machines was reduced tooling expense. When HON purchased Heatilator, Heatilator's management had boasted about having spent a million dollars tooling up a new line of fireplaces. The new management boasts about bringing out a number of new lines with tooling in the $50,000–$100,000 range. Because there are no blanking dies to build, the time for introducing a new product is greatly reduced and the quality is improved.

If a conventional $5,000 or $10,000 blanking die produces parts that aren't quite perfect, management hesitates to rebuild or scrap the tooling. Now, with versatile NC machines, a Heatilator operator can cut another tape with a dimension altered by a few thousandths of an inch to obtain the desired quality.

## Simplification

The task force on product design found many ways to simplify parts, reduce operations, and in many cases actually eliminate certain parts. For example, one particular part—a blank—used to be designed with a big hole in the middle, and the hole punched out became scrap material. The NC machine was programmed to use the punched-out hole, to pierce it to form another part simultaneously with the blanking of the main part. So Heatilator got two parts for the price of one.

## Material Handling

The task force on plant layout shortened and straightened the assembly line for fireplaces, which greatly improved material handling. The initial line had four 90 degree turns and strangely ended up against a wall of the plant that was a rail siding. From there a fork lift truck had to take each fireplace to the warehouse door, which then was back somewhere in the long western part of the plant. The task force's single straight line ended up going through a door right into the warehouse. This greatly reduced the space occupied and facilitated fast production.

This task force also rearranged feeder operations to reduce material handling. One example is the cross-hatched area in the lower

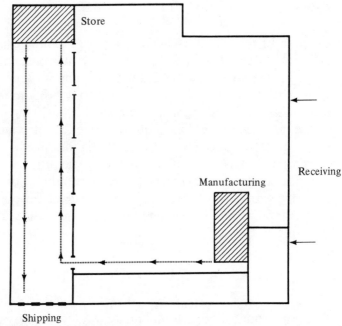

**Exhibit 12–3.**   Accessories Department—Before

right corner of Exhibit 12–3, where accessories like glass doors were manufactured. Those are the kinds of components that usually would be stored in the back of the warehouse, but that out-of-the-way location would add to forklift travel time. Travel times are long anyway in the plant, which is about two blocks square. That is almost four blocks of fork truck travel in and out of production for every one of the accessories. The shipping doors are at the southwest corner, which is two more blocks to get an accessory and two blocks to bring it back to ship. The floor space between the shipping docks and the accessory manufacturing department was empty anyway. So, to save endless transportation, the accessories would be stored between where they're made and where they're shipped. An unused rail siding that divided the building in half hadn't had a car shipped out on it for years. The pit was filled to make the building whole and provide more space for the accessories.

---

*Question 11.* We could expect usage of accessories to be irregular, thus making conveyors an illogical choice to move them. So the alternative to forklift trucks would be hand-push wheeled carts or dollies. What are the merits of wheeled carts or dollies as compared with lift trucks in this case?

---

Fireplaces are lined with a refractory-like material, which is cast in the plant. The cement product is poured in molds and stored on roller conveyors. When the material sets up it can be taken out of the molds and installed in a fireplace. The department had been laid out so that the conveyors took the material far away from the point of use, which is the start of the assembly line. By reorienting the conveyor 90 degrees to take the material closer to the assembly line, a good deal of handling was eliminated.

The material handling task force added conveyors in the finished goods warehouse. Those are critical, because not all fireplaces have to be handled by fork truck into storage and then hauled to the shipping docks. Now a simple little air cylinder with an electric eye automatically reads a piece of tape on the carton and pushes fireplaces to be shipped immediately onto roller conveyors, which roll it close to the truck docks. There the whole load can be accumulated on conveyors and loaded promptly.

## Employee Cooperation

Management conducted a number of programs to win employee cooperation and motivate employees in the restructuring. An early step was to refer to employees as *members*. If people thought of themselves as members of the organization rather than "just employees," management felt, there was a better chance of getting the people involved.

Another program began with a quarterly meeting conducted at Heatilator by Robert Day, the president. Now it is a monthly meeting with all the employees. It takes about three sessions to get them all together in the cafeteria and to go over problems and progress, for the company as a whole as well as in the work areas.

HON Industries has had profit-sharing programs since very early in its history. The company actually paid profit-sharing to people in the company before it ever paid a dividend to shareholders. The profit-sharing program was extended to Heatilator.

The fireplace business is seasonal. Shipments in the second half of the year are normally double those in the first half. The result, traditionally, was large-scale hiring, then layoffs. Management undertook a program to stabilize the work force in which it:

- Scheduled its vacation shutdown in June before the busy season rather then allow vacations during the busy season
- Shifted annual inventory taking to March during the slow season rather than in November at the height of the busy season
- Decided not to use overtime in the slow season, which made people more receptive to working overtime to increase production during the busy season
- Sought out more Sunbelt business, because it is less seasonal
- Ran special promotions during the dull season of the year to bring in orders and help stock distributors
- Built inventory during the slow season and drew it down during the busy season, a practice not formerly followed

The result of those actions is elimination of the seasonal layoff-and-hiring cycle, which management expected would improve members' attitudes and morale and the quality of people who could be attracted into employment.

Heatilator also developed an incentive plan for the busy season only. Management asked people for extra help and extra effort during that period and thought it only right that people be rewarded for this extra effort. The plan was quite simple. It was based on the sales value of goods produced per labor-hour in the plant. A basic standard was established. Management put into a bonus kitty a certain number of dollars for each thousand dollars of production in excess of the standard. Everyone in the plant shared the kitty, based on number of hours they worked during that period. Under this plan the output per hour increased significantly. When the plan was discontinued at the end of the busy season, there was virtually no change in productivity.

The net result of the various programs to elicit cooperation was positive: no overt resistance from members.

---

*Question 12.* Is the employee cooperation effort well conceived? Explain.

---

# Results

One of the benefits of the improvement efforts is improved customer service. Now over 96 percent of shipments are completed on time due. Orders can be processed promptly, and customer complaints are few. The president of the company used to dread the busy season because of all the calls he would get from unhappy distributors. He claims to have had none last year during the busy season.

The product line has been expanded greatly. The NC machines have made it easier, quicker, and less expensive to tool new products. Two or three fireplace product lines are being added each year, and with less trouble than there was in introducing one line per year in the past.

Manufacturing efficiency has improved, and costs have been reduced dramatically. The initial task forces were formed during the third quarter of 1982 and had not really affected the fourth quarter, which was the base measuring period. Comparing the base period against the fourth quarter of 1983, the number of fireplace units produced increased 49.2 percent. The total direct labor hours declined by 27.3 percent per unit.

The reduction in indirect labor, because of the flow improvement, is more dramatic. During this same period when units produced increased 49.2 percent, the total hours of indirect labor in the plant declined by 12.5 percent. Thus the indirect labor per unit produced declined by 41.5 percent in a one-year period. There was a change in product mix during the same period. Because some of the new products introduced were lower-priced and better designed, the sales value of units produced per direct labor hour increased from $58.61 to $66.83, which is a 14 percent increase. Current estimates are that in the fourth quarter of 1984 it will be about $80 per direct labor hour, or approximately a 35 percent increase for the two-year period.

Cost savings generated by the task forces now come to approximately $1 million a year. Those are the measurable savings of major projects. Many small improvements haven't been valued. Inventory turnover improved about 50 percent. Steel, the principal raw material, has increased from 4.4 to 8.1 turns a year. That is a lagging indicator, because it takes a while to use up raw material, so it will continue to improve for some time. Morale in the company seems improved. People seem proud of what they're accomplishing, and management is quite pleased with the results. The rate of change has slowed some since the beginning, but people continue to find ways to improve the operation.

---

*Question 13.* How can the rate of improvement be speeded up again?

---

# 13

# H-P—Computer Systems Division

*Case topics:*

Statistical process control  
JIT supplier  
Kanban  
Performance data on display  
Kitting  

Oversight of improvement effort  
Clustered engineering changes  
JIT software  
Disappearance of maintenance as a function  

The Hewlett Packard Computer Systems Division is headquartered in Cupertino, California, but the division's popular HP-3000 Series 68 minicomputer is made in nearby Santa Clara. Another H-P division provides the manufacturing space, which is in part of the top floor of one building. The space loan was supposed to be temporary, but it has gone on for seven years. Through just-in-time production and total quality control, space needs for production stock and for rework have gone way down, and the Computer Systems Division has given back unneeded space to their hosts. The manufacturing space for the HP-3000 is not at all crowded, and it appears that more space could easily be given up. The HP-3000 Series 68 will finally move to a permanent home in Cupertino later in 1985.

The Series 68 was released in March 1982 and has been a steady seller for H-P over the years. Recent production volume has been "several" systems per day.

Each unit has twenty-five to thirty printed circuit (PC) boards—about seventeen basic PC board types. This amounts to about 12,000 components per unit.

A statistical quality control (SQC) program was begun in 1980 and has become a normal part of the job for many of the operators. JIT production was implemented more recently, as is explained below.

## Just-in-Time

JIT was launched in early 1984. It took only two or three months of planning before the JIT cutover date. The cutover featured setting up kanban areas and converting to pull signals. The planning prior to cutover included a pilot JIT project run in PC board assembly (PCA).

Before the pilot project, materials were fed to the line by work orders once a week in batches. There were three stocking areas. In the pilot approach, materials from line-stock areas were fed to PCA in kits on demand. Inventories were pushed back to prior stages.

The date of cutover to full kanban was March 1984. A deck of pull cards was issued, as had always been done in the previous batch system, but decks were converted to individual unit quantities instead of weekly quantities. The computer no longer generates new decks; instead the deck is just photocopied over and over.

After cutover, some boards did not need to be built for three weeks. The material control people kept going over to PCA and asking, "Don't you need any more material yet?" "Are you making anything?" After the three weeks of lot-size stock had been worked off, safety stocks and safety days of stock were gradually pulled out.

On a main interior wall are three large display panels with the overall title, "SQC and JIT in Synergy." The panels are prominent and visible to all workers either from where they work or when they pass by during the day. Visitors to the plant always spend time hearing about the content of the panels, which includes the following:

1. One panel displays the JIT material flow (see Exhibit 13-1). For comparison purposes, see Exhibits 13-2 and 13-3, which show the material flow as the JIT team *thought* it was and how they found it actually was before JIT.

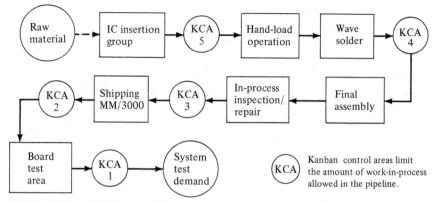

**Exhibit 13–1.** JIT Material Flow

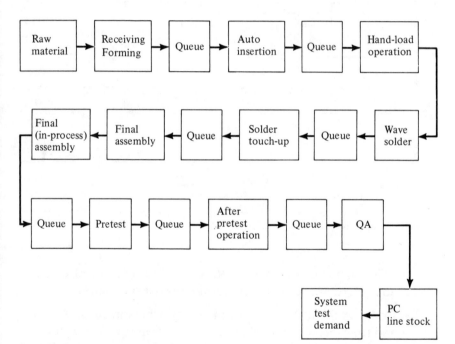

**Exhibit 13–2.** Assumed "Batch" Material Flow

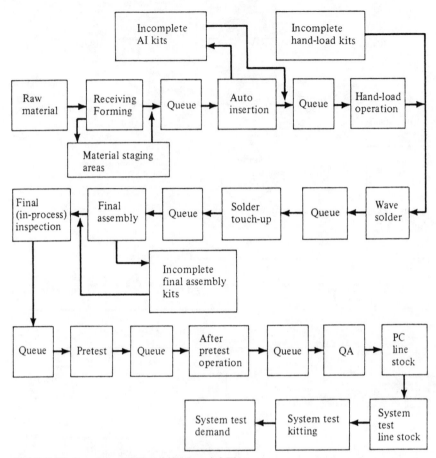

**Exhibit 13–3.** Actual "Batch" Material Flow

2. The next panel displays data on several categories of waste reduction. Here are some of the results posted on charts:

- PCA "cycle time" (see Exhibit 13-4), which includes all queue and run time, dropped from fifteen days in fourth quarter 1982 to about seven in most of 1983, and to 1.5 days since March 1984.
- PCA inventory in line fabrication is down from $670,000 in May 1983 to below $200,000 in October 1984, and to about $20,000 in January 1985. There was a gradual decline (stemming, perhaps from quality and other improvements) through February 1984, then a sharp drop when the cutover to JIT took place in March 1984. The drop to $20,000 in late 1984 and

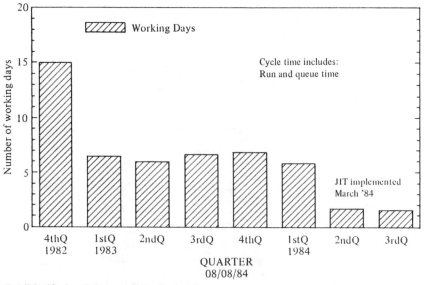

**Exhibit 13-4.** PC Assembly Cycle Time

early 1985 resulted mostly from elimination of stock on old products; these unneeded stocks became visible when overall inventories were cut.

- PCA scrap used to be high one month and low the next, and sometimes was above $100,000 worth in a quarter. In the last year and a half it has stayed below $50,000 in every quarter.
- PCA floor space is down from 8,500 to 5,000 square feet.
- Wave solder defects dropped from more than 5,000 parts per million in 1982 to less than one part per million in 1984. Data on defects in wave soldering, and in other processes as well, are posted daily and also plotted on weekly and monthly summary charts. The daily charts give some details on such things as numbers of bent leads, missing parts, reversed parts, wrong locations/values, missing solder, and raised parts.
- Labor hours to produce a complete PCA kit for the S68 model are down from 85-90 hours to about 40 hours.

3. The third chart displays the total quality control process. See Exhibit 13-5.

---

*Question 1.* How important are the wall panel displays? Are they well conceived? Are they the *right* displays?

---

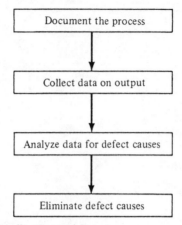

**Exhibit 13–5.** Total Quality Control Process

## Kanban/Pull System

There are five KCAs (kanban control areas). Three are in PCA, and two are in board test. The kanban, or signals, at the KCAs are large cards, red on one side and green on the other. Work does not move from one PCA process to another until a complete set of PC boards (a kit) for one HP-3000 is ready to go.

Operators go to a KCA to get more work. When all cards are green in a KCA rack, operators stop and don't make more until the next process takes some away. When operators from the next process take work away, they turn the card to its red side, which is the pull signal authorizing more work. The red also tells the next process not to take the kit yet, because it is not complete.

Example of the KCA procedure: KCA-5, located after auto-insert, is an old wheeled cart modified with slotted shelves to hold circuit boards. One set of twenty to twenty-five slots holds a full kit of boards for one unit. An operator completes a board and puts it in one slot, completes another and puts it in a slot, and so forth. When all are completed for a kit, the operator shows completion by putting up an 18-inch-long green card. The card is fastened by a couple of pieces of velcro and has a model number on it ("142-A", "143-A", etc.). At this early stage of manufacture, there are only five or six model numbers. When someone from the next process, hand-load, takes the kit away, that person turns the card over to its red side, which tells auto-insert to produce another kit.

---

*Question 2.* Discuss the merits of treating a kit of PC boards as the move quantity.

---

## Under-Capacity Scheduling

Under-capacity scheduling is used to plan labor. The average is one hour under capacity each day (or shift). The one hour is cumulative throughout the day (not just the time available at the end of the shift after making rate).

Operators go off direct labor when they run out of work (all kanban cards green), and also when problems cause stoppages. When they are off direct labor, operators do things like simplify procedures, modify assembly drawings, hold a meeting, SQC, etc. A visitor asked what keeps people from running off to drink coffee or just disappearing instead of taking on an improvement task. Answer: "We have great people," dedicated enough not to goof off. Also, "our supervisors do a good job in keeping people busy."

Six-pen computer graphics equipment is available in the office cubicles right next to the production areas. Steve Balsbaugh, PCA supervisor, says, "We let our operators go enter data and produce their own progress charts and so forth."

A visitor to the plant will see a good deal of evidence that operators, supervisors, and others are active in measuring, recording, posting results, and so forth. In fact, few factories in the country have as much visual evidence posted on shop walls as there is in the HP-3000 facility.

---

*Question 3.* Good people, good supervisors, and graphics equipment help keep problem-solving going on when direct production stops. What else should be done? (Consider, for example, the role of the supervisor's bosses, and consider systematic procedures and controls.)

---

## PC Assembly

JIT has altered PC assembly procedures considerably, as the following indicates.

## Auto-Insert

Change time in auto-insert, which used to be long, now is about ten seconds. Fast changeover is possible because of (1) an adaptable tooling plate, (2) easy-to-change programs stored on floppy discs, (3) dedicated auto-insert machines—just keep the tube feeders full.

There are two AMISTAR DIP auto-insert machines: a CI-1000 that cost about $80,000 several years ago and a fairly new $125,000 CI-3000 that "does everything" (when it works).

Each machine is dedicated to inserting certain integrated circuits (ICs). Most boards have part of their ICs inserted on the 1000 and part inserted on the 3000. Some of the simpler boards require insertion on only one of the two machines.

## Hand-Load

Hand-loading of odd-size and low-use ICs is the process following auto-insert. One operator completes an entire board—no progressive slide line—and the board goes into the KCA rack. Formerly an operator loaded four boards at a time—for "efficiency." Now it is one at a time, and the drop in inventory is sizable.

---

*Question 4.* What "efficiencies," if any, are lost in going to one board at a time? Can the efficiencies be gained back? If so, how?

---

## Wave-Solder, Wash, and Touchup

The next KCA location includes wave-solder, wash, and touchup. Touchup consists of just one part-time station, which is also used for record-keeping, and so on. There used to be *many* touchup stations, but now there is little to do. In fact, the touchup person is not allowed to turn the boards over.

Each time a board comes out of the washer, the operator rolls a twenty-sided die—the kind used in Dungeons and Dragons games. If it comes up "7," the board is thoroughly tested. (The same random sampling approach is used elsewhere, including in hand-load.)

## Equipment Maintenance

There is scheduled maintenance every day on auto-insert equipment, wave-solderer, washer, and so forth, and operators are "very involved in PM."

There are four levels of maintenance:

1. Operator level: lubrication, etc.
2. Supervisor level: Supervisors sent to AMISTAR in Torrance for two weeks of training
3. Factory maintenance department
4. Manufacturer's representative

The results have been good:

The CI-1000 used to have 35 percent availability and now is available 99 percent. The CI-3000 is much more complex. Though up time has improved by a factor of two recently and defects are down by a factor of two, the CI-3000 is still down quite a bit. Bob Tellez, manufacturing engineer, notes that "we would not buy that complex a machine today." H-P does not need all the features and could get along fine with a mid-range machine like AMISTAR 1800.

The wave solderer, an Electrovert Sys/10 with several times more capacity than is required, was installed in August 1983. It is kept spic and span. The metal plates inside look clean enough to cook pizza on, and the glass sides are crystal clear.

The wave is cooled down periodically so that someone can crawl through it and wipe everything. Operators check the specific gravity of flux fifteen times a day and plot results on $x$-bar and $R$ charts. Operators also plot surface temperature many times a day. Wave defects were just 2.2 per million in January 1985. (Defects are so low here and in the other PCA processes that it has become reasonable to measure number of boards that go through with no defects.)

The washer, a large model (a small degreaser cannot be used, since water-soluble flux is used in the wave) is similarly cleaned and maintained.

---

*Question 5.* Equipment maintenance is still identified as a *function,* although operators are taking over some of it and making it part of their job. As this trend continues, where will it lead? That is, what will become of the maintenance function? (In your answer, consider also what is happening to process engineering, industrial engineering, production control, and quality assurance.)

## PC Test

KCA-1 and KCA-2, in PC test, are about 80 feet away, separated by a cable subassembly area and a wall. A KCA red/green signboard is high on the wall, so that wave-soldering people can see it easily.

PC test takes one hour, and bay-test takes two hours. At bay-test, KCA-1, the lot size used to be two kits. Now it is just one kit, and cycle time in testing has been cut in half accordingly.

## Cable Subassembly

There are three rows of three people, each assembling cables. Also, there are stations where cables are strung on large template-tables and a station where wire ends are lugged and attached. Some of the cables are rather complicated, requiring many colors of wires. It takes nine people six hours to build three typical cable sets.

Cable subassembly is not yet on the pull system. The material requirements planning (MRP) system still is issuing work orders, although several steps (e.g., producing to a daily rate) were taken to cut the amount of work on the floor. The shelves holding tubs full of cable components will be considerably shrunk when this work center converts to the pull system sometime in early 1985.

## Final Assembly and System Test

The HP-3000 is assembled to stock through most of the manufacturing process. Units that are nearly finished (typically a dozen or so) wait for receipt of the sales order to find out the final details of the customer configuration before they are completed. Shipments are made every day.

Taped squares on the assembly floor are kanban squares. There are four assembly locations on the floor, each with a limited number of taped squares, so as to hold down the maximum amount of units on the assembly floor.

Frames and skins are purchased from a local supplier ten minutes away, Touche Manufacturing Company, a minority supplier. H-P has worked very closely with Touche, and "Touche is excellent—like family."

Touche used to deliver in large lots, but now it delivers frames daily. Touche receives its scheduled quantity from H-P's MRP system, but H-P requested that Touche deliver just what H-P uses and asks for—just in time—rather than the MRP quantity.

Touche does the quality checks so that H-P does not need to inspect frames or skins. Touche gives six-hour turnaround on any defective part, and Touche's people come right to H-P's assembly floor to make corrections. Touche became a believer in the idea of JIT deliveries on one occasion when it had to send people to H-P's assembly floor to correct a problem. The number on the floor was large and took a long time to fix, which gave Touche's people cause to conclude that keeping H-P's floor stock low was a good idea after all.

The floor stock of raw frame materials is no more than one day's worth. There is hardly ever a quality problem, and Touche now does certain things to the frames (e.g., install metal tabs) that H-P used to have to do.

Final test takes 5.5 days, and there are two dozen or more units in test at any given time. It takes only about four hours to run through a test cycle. The rest of the time is burn-in time, which is considerable, since there are 12,000 components that could experience infant-mortality failure.

## Planning and Control Support

Plans were under way to convert to the new H-P JIT software package in place of MM-3000, which is H-P's several-year-old MRP package. But conversions to new systems are not easy. Kate Jarvis, production control manager, indicated that there are thoughts about just making a few simple modifications to MM-3000 instead. (Visitors from a Lever Brothers plant in South Africa had explained how they had made such a conversion.)

## Engineering Changes

There were also tentative plans to adopt a fixed-interval approach to engineering change releases: Once a month was discussed—with ECs during the month only for emergencies.

## Organization

The TQC effort began several years ago at the managerial level. Supervisors were involved in the learning phase and then started up projects. Operators got involved in measuring and plotting results, and eventually learned most of the basics of TQC.

Just-in-time progress was much faster. After managers had been exposed to JIT, a "Stockless Production" skit on videotape (developed in another H-P division) was used to teach JIT to floor operators. A steering committee of managers, engineers, and a scheduler was formed to get JIT launched, but all the details were worked out by line supervisors and operators.

Rick Walleigh, production manager, has worked in the HP-3000 product line almost since its release, and he has been in the thick of the improvement process as it has gathered steam. As Walleigh puts it, "It is an exciting time to be in manufacturing."

---

*Question 6.* Would the clustering of EC releases have an impact on computer software needs? Explain.

---

# 14

# Toyota Auto Body, Inc., of California

*Case topics:*

The five whys
Bypassing stockrooms
Cordoning-off space
Effect of mixed-model
   production on finished goods
One-way kanban and
   bar-coding for financial
   reporting

Standard containers
Kanban removal
Batching models within a daily
   make schedule
Effects of JIT/TQC on
   personnel retention
Visible measures

Toyota Auto Body, Inc., of California (TABC), began operations in Long Beach, California, in 1972. The product, truck beds, is made in three models and ten colors. The beds go to eight U.S. ports of entry for trucks arriving from Japan, and the beds are installed at those locations. More than a million beds have been produced since 1972, and sales have risen a good deal in recent years: 140,000 in 1980, 240,000 in 1984, and 300,000 in 1985. The Long Beach facility comprises 300,000 square feet in fourteen buildings on a 20-acre site. The annual payroll is $10 million, and 350 people are employed.

The manufacturing process is stamping (the sheet metal comes from Japan), assembly, paint, and ship. There are approximately 120 stamped components in each truck bed; but since many of the components are common to the different models, they are stamped in lot quantities of about four to six shifts.

Thanks go to Dr. Mehran Sepehri, Long Beach State University, for sharing data he had collected on Toyota Auto Body, Inc., of California.

Welding is a key step in bed assembly. A new framing fixture, designed by Toyota and produced by a U.S. company, provides for automatic welding of some of the more difficult welds. The fixture also includes a computer-monitored weld-fault detector that checks for poor welds. The equipment shuts down production when there is a problem, so that no bad product is passed on.

## Just-in-Time Beginnings

The just-in-time commitment was made in 1979 by TABC and not mandated by Toyota, Japan. The managers in Long Beach, Americans who came mostly from other U.S. auto companies, decided to implement, and it took several months of training for the management group to be convinced. Then, in 1980, JIT projects were started in final assembly and with a few selected suppliers. The raising of the U.S. truck import tax from 4 to 25 percent meant losses, which added urgency and reason for rapidly implementing JIT.

Progress was being made on a few JIT projects when, in April 1981, a new general manager came on board. The new man, Don Haller, came from Ford. He was dubious enough about JIT to put it on hold. In the next few months Haller reviewed the plans and participated in JIT walk-throughs. He heard the arguments of strong advocates and of others who were not advocates. Haller agreed to proceed but with larger safety stocks and lot sizes than had been planned initially. Haller is still general manager, and JIT has progressed from mere projects to "a way of life."

Much of the planning for JIT has come out of a task force headed by Edgar Manrique, the production control manager. (Manrique, who was once employed at GM, came to TABC in 1976.) The task force set up training and retraining programs that touched the whole work force. Everyone in the managerial ranks has been to Japan, and first-line supervisors are going to Japan as well. Associates (as TABC employees are called) have learned the Toyota "five whys":

1. Manufacturing overhead cost is too high. Why?
2. It can be traced to high investment, space, and handling costs. Why?
3. To handle the required amounts of material, two miles of conveyors were installed. Why?

4. Because the routing was long—through many departments. Why?
5. Because when we laid out the plant, the processes were separated into departments. Why?

---

*Question 1.* What kinds of questions and issues warrant the five-whys treatment at TABC? Should they ever stop with less than five?

---

## JIT Actions

The fifth why reveals the culprit: bad plant layout. It has taken time for TABC to correct the problem, but recently two presses were moved from the press building to assembly, and more may be moved in the future. That greatly shortens the flow path and cuts conveyor needs.

While the press relocations are recent, another important action to short-circuit the long flow path was taken in 1981 as one of the initial JIT projects. The assembly warehouse, a separate building, was bypassed; instead stampings went direct to assembly. Large amounts of lead time and inventory were shed, as well as handling costs.

---

*Question 2.* What are the pros and cons of bypassing a stockroom? Is it good as an early JIT action, or are there serious risks?

---

### Storage Areas, Suppliers, and Freight In

Another early step taken by Haller was to put everyone to work cleaning up the warehouses and shipping yard. Also, obsolete and unnecessary items were purged from buildings bulging at the seams. The idea was to clear away the confusion so that reviewing lot sizes and buffer stocks could proceed in an orderly way.

Storage areas have been progressively compressed. TABC's technique is to cordon off the target racks and material—not allow any use of it—for a time. Get comfortable without it; then eliminate it. Vacated storage areas and warehouses have been converted to other productive uses.

> *Question 3.* How strict should TABC's JIT rules
> be on not using cordoned-off space, keeping un-
> necessary items out of the way, and so forth?
> Who should enforce the rules, and how?

Materials that used to go into warehouses and later out to the
shops now are delivered from several suppliers right to the user
building. Double handling is thus eliminated.

Mr. Manrique has made some progress in negotiating JIT deliveries from U.S. suppliers. For example, one supplier of steel had
previously insisted on a minimum of 40,000 pounds per delivery;
now it is down to 20,000, and TABC is pressing to have the delivery
amount cut further to a target of a delivery every other day.

The average inventory of steel from all sources, including sheet
steel from Japan, is currently less than one month's supply. It was
cut by 55 percent in the last year as delivery quantities have been cut
and frequencies increased. Steel prices have gone up very slightly as
a result of more deliveries, but Manrique sees reason to believe that
prices should fall rather than rise: TABC does not buy a whole ship-
load of steel, which means delivery costs by ship are not related to
quantity. But when larger quantities are delivered per ship, the steel
has to accumulate somewhere; the accumulation has its carrying
costs, which someone has to pay and pass on in the price.

## Lot Quantities and Changeovers

Lot sizes and change times have been steadily cut. In 1979 model
changeovers in assembly were monthly, and it took ten hours to make
the change. Since 1982 all models have been made nearly every day.
Changeover time is negligible, and currently forty truck beds of a
model are made in each repeating cycle of models. A dominant mo-
tivation for cutting assembly lots was to cut finished goods; in fact
it appeared that assembly lot sizes and finished goods relate one to
one: Halve the lot size, halve the FGI.

> *Question 4.* What is the impact on marketing of
> the one-to-one ratio between the mixed-model
> schedule and FGI?

In stamping, press die change times were five hours or more in 1979. Today changing one line, consisting of six presses, takes about seventeen minutes. Stamping lot quantities are down from twelve shifts to six shifts with a 1986 target of five shifts.

## Kanban

While lot sizes relate to how quickly equipment can be set up, buffer stocks are there to absorb shocks, like late deliveries and production stoppages or slowdowns. Kanban is a JIT technique for disciplined management of the buffer stocks.

Early kanban attempts came close to utter failure. In the first week of kanban, managers stayed long hours, and some were counting kanban tickets and monitoring material movements and correct placements to make sure that kanban rules were followed. Not all the managers fully understood the approach, however, and some supervisors fell into old habits of going to the stock area to fetch material instead of letting kanban deliver "just in time." Kanban was kept alive by solving some basic problems. Finally, after more than a month, the general feeling was that kanban might work, but it took another three or four months before people believed in the approach and were making it work.

The kanban tickets in use at TABC hold more information than do kanbans at Toyota in Japan. Also, Long Beach uses circulating kanbans. Kanbans currently cover all internal operations and several suppliers.

There is a plan to bar-code all the kanbans, not so much for shop floor control but for making cycle counting simpler and providing information for tax reporting, as TABC is an active foreign trade subzone.

---

*Question 5.* Does TABC really need the extra information provided by their kanban and bar-coding? Or do they just provide comfort to TABC's American managers, who came from companies that had such information?

---

TABC uses numerous kinds of kanbans, both internally and back to suppliers. The classical Toyota dual-card kanban approach—one kanban for delivery and another for production—is not used; instead a single kanban (for a given part number) goes with the container and often authorizes production as well. The delivery containers, one for each kanban, are standardized, and they are always filled with the standard unit-load quantity.

Kanbans are put up on a hook board near the entrance to each area. For example, the receiving warehouse has a kanban board for material from suppliers; the press department has kanbans for material from the warehouse. Typically hook boards have seven hooks per row, each hook holding kanban tickets for a different part number. TABC circulates 4,000–5,000 kanbans a day, a feat that takes considerable sorting and placement on hooks each day. Kanbans are sorted by color. For example, green is for right-hand parts, gold is for left, and blue is for common components.

In painting and stamping, the normal rule is to accumulate enough kanbans to trigger another production run. In those areas and other areas as well, there are normally several kanbans and containers of parts for each part number. The number of kanbans drops over time, however, because TABC Long Beach employs Toyota's fabled kanban removal technique: Periodically—often monthly—remove a kanban ticket along with that much buffer stock. This stimulates the need for process improvements to solve problems that cause output to vary.

---

*Question 6.* Is TABC's kanban approach sound? Any recommendations?

---

## Scheduling

Kanbans, when generated, are controlled by computer explosion of the bill of material, along with a formula for determining the number of kanbans per part number. Kanbans are issued about seven days before the start of the next period in which lot sizes are reduced.

While kanban quantities can change monthly, the production schedule is based on a frozen quantity for a period of months, with a variable mixture of models and colors within the month. In other words, the TABC approach is to make quantity to plan, make models and colors to order. There is some flexibility for changes. A new master schedule is made up daily for the second day forward (a rolling two-day schedule). The master production schedule sets the model sequence first, then sets the color sequence within models. The final sequence repeats itself a number of times in the normal two-shift work day.

---

*Question 7.* Why repeat the sequence "a number of times in the normal two-shift work day"? Why not at least batch the colors and models so that each is run just once every day?

---

## Respect for People

TABC production employees have taken on a good deal of responsibility as JIT implementation has progressed. For example, everyone has the authority to shut down production in order to avoid making something wrong.

TABC does not evaluate employees on individual output against standards. Instead, they are evaluated based on long-term performance, including versatility to move to nondirect labor when occasions arise.

Use of kanban and cuts in material storage and handling have led to commensurate reductions in staff costs. There is little paper processing and no need to report material usage and progress at each stage. Overall production reporting is down.

Quality is similarly affected. For example, in painting, some inspection has been turned over to line operators. In this case the inspectors' jobs changed. Now they work on verification of product acceptability, check for correct placement of parts, perform some graphic analysis, prepare process control charts and go over them with the painters, look for causes of major defects, and conduct some process-improvement studies.

At TABC voluntary quality control circles meet weekly on paid overtime. The first circle was formed in 1983 in the press area, and the next were in paint and in maintenance. The number of circles and the number and complexity of suggestions have grown rapidly. TABC management feels the circles are most effective on issues in which there is initial shop floor opposition; part of the reason is the forum for discussion and dissemination of information that QC circles offer.

Increases in production volume have absorbed most of the excess labor generated by the improvements. Also, TABC has backward integrated in a small way: They are now doing their own packaging; packaging costs have dropped by 38 percent since TABC took over the function in 1984. TABC plans to continue to look for new business—not necessarily through backward integration.

---

*Question 8.* Did TABC do a brilliant job of handling the job of personnel retention? Or did they have circumstances on their side? In your explanation, compare TABC's situation with that of some of its competitors.

---

## Results

TABC's improvements since 1980 have been gratifying:

- Throughput time: down from six days to 1.5 days
- Average work-in-process: down 45 percent
- Average raw material: down 58 percent (steel down to 3.5 million pounds in the most recent year)
- More than 100 racks removed
- Forklift trucks: down from eighteen to twelve
- Number of presses reduced by 30 percent as setup time reductions yielded more time for production
- Substantial reductions in absenteeism, nonproductive time, and labor turnover
- Outgoing quality up, and warranty costs and replacement parts cost down substantially
- In-process scrap reduced almost to zero—since defectives are caught and corrected right away
- The plant received a safety award in 1984; only four safety awards were granted by the insurance company in the past five years
- Labor productivity improved by 58 percent over 1980 levels

The last item, productivity, derives from TABC's sizable increase in production volume with no increase in headcount; TABC has been able to avoid layoffs as a result of productivity improvements. Labor had been scheduled in two ten-hour shifts plus two Saturdays per month; then two nine-hour shifts, no Saturdays; and finally, today, two eight-hour shifts.

---

*Question 9.* Are these the most relevant measures of JIT performance—for Toyota Truck? To what degree should the 350-person work force be kept informed of results on these performance criteria?

---

Don Haller, the general manager, attending Toyota's annual QC circle meeting in Japan in 1984, told the audience, "We are coming back. Every measure of productivity and production savings is comparable to the one in Japanese plants."

# 15

# 3M Videocassettes—
# Hutchinson, Minnesota

*Case topics:*

Computer vs. manual planning/ simulation

Process ownership

Machine and shift imbalances

Standard containers/kanban

Smooth implementation of JIT

3M's Hutchinson, Minnesota, plant manufactures videotape cassettes. The old way was job-lot production: large stocks of material separating one work center from another, large lots moving between them, and each machine making as much as possible and pushing it onward. The new method is just-in-time (JIT) production: Pull only the amount needed from the previous work center. The way Production Superintendent Paul Behrens and his staff planned and implemented JIT is as notable as the results.

## Brown Paper and Coffee Cups

The JIT planners at Hutchinson placed a large sheet of brown paper on a big table and drew squares on it. Each square was a machine.

Adapted from G. P. Behrens, "3M," *The Just-in-Time Technical Development Newsletter,* no. 5 (Association for Manufacturing Excellence, Inc.), September 30, 1984, pp. 2–3. Reprinted with permission of Association for Manufacturing Excellence, Inc., 380 W. Palatine Rd., Wheeling, Ill. 60090.

---

**NOTE ON KANBAN**

Where containers are used as kanban signals, they must be standard containers. Any old box, tray, or pallet *won't* do. A standard container holds a standard quantity, and partitions often divide the container so that putting more or less into the container would be easily noticed at a glance. Also, the container needs a card or tag to identify the part number, the quantity, the source, and the destination. (Any of these could be omitted if obvious.) With lean JIT inventories, you can't risk any mistakes or uncertainty as to kind, quantity, or location—hence the need for rigor in container design, labeling, filling, and handling.

---

They wrote the machine's hourly capacity and its changeover time inside the square.

The machine locations and operating data were considered fixed, while other factors of production were altered—on paper—in order to find the best ways to change from push to pull. Pull signals (or kanban) are necessary in order to make a pull approach work.

In the video cassette area, the pull signal would be an empty container needing to be refilled. Coffee cups on the brown paper were used to represent containers of cassette components and assemblies.

Each coffee cup was stuffed with a card (kanban) with all the right information on it. Now the pull approach could be refined by a coffee-cup simulation.

## Brainstorming

How many coffee cups—standard containers full of cassette components and assemblies—should go beside each machine? That is an obvious question, but its answer depends on many factors: reject/defect rates, machine down time, changeover time, lot sizes, schedules, machine staffing, coffee and lunch breaks, what to do when a tool breaks or someone runs out of parts or gets sick and leaves the machine.

The planners and managers are not close enough to the work to be able to compile and expound on a full list of such factors. The people on the shop floor—operators, handlers, inspectors, maintenance people, supervisors, and so forth—have much of the required knowledge in their heads. Therefore, the simulation proceeded by bringing groups of people from all parts of the cassette operation to the simulator room and getting their questions and concerns out on the table—literally. Rather firm decisions were made in the simulation mode; for example, a decision to dedicate a certain winding machine to winding only certain products (like T-120 or T-30 tapes).

Those were brainstorming sessions: The simulations showed the amount of inventory in queue each simulated hour, and observers freely threw out their "what-ifs." The what-ifs that did not have obvious answers were posted on a blackboard. One hundred or more problems and issues went up on the board. It took nearly two months to solve them—on paper. Then the simulated plan became a reality.

---

*Question 1.* The simulation could probably have been done on a computer. Would a computer simulator have served the purpose just as well? Discuss.

---

## Implementation

Implementation went off without a hitch. The mismatch between running injection molding three shifts and assembly only one shift was a problem, but not a serious one. Each day the assemblers would see the pile of containers of molded plastic components shrink. They did not need to worry about running out (though some did anyway), because they saw it happen with coffee cups, and they knew the containers would be filled again overnight. Furthermore, the schedule had been "regularized"—a fixed daily rate—and packaging people posted progress against the rate hourly.

The Hutchinson kanban approach does *not* have tight restrictions on the possibility of a maker's producing more than a user can soon use up. As a matter of fact, makers deliver parts forward instead of users fetching parts from makers—the more classical form of kanban. Old habits of making and delivering too much have resurfaced from time to time, and people have to be reminded about the commitment to make only what is used. This problem—one of continued correct execution—has not been serious.

*Question 2.* Since in manufacturing things rarely work without exasperation, struggle, and heroic measures, we tend to shake our heads in wonder or disbelief when an implementation goes smoothly. What was the secret?

*Question 3.* What has been described is just the initial JIT/kanban planning and implementation at Hutchinson. What improvements and enhancements do you recommend? In your answer, consider the limitations and restrictions of JIT as initially installed at Hutchinson.

# 16

# Getting Ready for Mixed-Model Production at Kawasaki Motors in Lincoln, Nebraska

*Case topics:*

Pre-automation
Mixed-model assembly sequence
Benefits of mixed-model
  assembly when sales are
  falling

Benefits of setup time reduction
  on presses

## Mixed Models in Motorcycle Assembly

In September 1981, a Japanese management team replaced the American plant manager at the Kawasaki motorcycle plant in Lincoln, Nebraska. One goal of the new managers was to convert the main motorcycle assembly line to mixed-model production. The line had been running production lots of at least 200 of each model between line changeovers.

The conversion was expected to take about three months. It required two kinds of exacting preparation:

## WHAT IS MIXED-MODEL PRODUCTION?

Most goods manufacturers make several models of each end product. Most producers produce large lots of first one model and then another on the same machines or production lines. JIT manufacturers have developed ways to produce mixed models, that is, a mixture of single units of each model, one after the other, on a machine or production line. The benefits are impressive. The factory can be scheduled to produce each day about the same mix of models that are sold each day. The right models are being made, and the need to warehouse large amounts of finished goods fades. The same is true of subassemblies and component parts: The right parts are produced in the same mixture as they are used, so that inventories are small. Furthermore, since small quantities of each model are made steadily, peak capacity may be shaved. That is, smaller and simpler tools and equipment may sometimes be used—and kept busy at a steady rate.

To make it economical to fabricate component parts in mixed models, machines and production lines must be engineered so that tooling, machine settings, part numbers, and load/unload operations can be done quickly. It is called "single setup"—a single-digit number of minutes—when a machine can be set up for a new model in less than ten minutes. When the machine requires no adjustments at all—just load and unload time—it is called "one-touch setup."

1. *Identification.* All parts, tools, cartons, racks, and so forth had to be clearly labeled so that an assembler would be able instantaneously to identify and select the right one. With a different motorcycle model next on the conveyor, delay in identifying it and all of the parts and tools to go with it would be intolerable. A color-coding system was devised so that, for example, all items related to a KZ650 motorcycle would be labeled with a gummed red dot. Even the position of the colored dot on the carton, part, or tool had to be precisely designed.

2. *Placement.* Engineers, material controllers, foremen, and assemblers all pitched in to devise exact locations for all parts and tools at work stations along the assembly line. The assembler, on seeing what the next model of motorcycle is, should be able to reach for the correct parts and tools blindfolded. Better racks, containers, and holding fixtures were designed to feed parts and hold tools in the right positions.

The preparations (which today we would refer to as *preautomation*) were successful. On January 1, 1983, the main assembly line converted to fully mixed-model production.

At that time the production volume was at about 200 motorcycles per day. That 200 might consist of the following models: 100 KZ440s, 60 KZ650s, and 40 KZ1000s.

---

*Question 1.* For that mixture what is the ideal mixed-model assembly sequence?

*Question 2.* Would there be any benefits of mixed-model assembly in a period when motorcycle sales were falling and excess bike inventories were building up in the distribution system (as in 1982)?

---

## Mixed Models in Motorcycle Parts Fabrication

Perhaps the main subassembly made in the Lincoln plant is motorcycle frames. The frame parts are formed from steel tube stock, and the parts are welded together into frames.

At one time frame parts were "punched out" on punch presses in lots of thousands at a time. The large lots were economical, because it typically took half a day or so to move a heavy die into place on a large-size punch press and to get all of the die adjustments and machine controls just right. Part of the setup time was running off trial pieces, inspecting their dimensions, changing settings, running and inspecting a few more, and so forth.

In 1980–81 the presses were modified for quick die changes and adjustments. Common roller conveyor sections were welded to form a "carousel" around the punch press; all dies were shimmed up so they had standard "shut heights"; and insertion and fastening were simplified. A dozen or more dies could be lined up around the carousel conveyor in the morning, and each die could be quickly and precisely rolled into place during the day in shifting from one frame part model to another (see Exhibit 16–1). The changes cut setup time to under ten minutes (including zero inspection time)—achieving single setup. Instead of running thousands of a model between setups, it became economical to run in lots of 200, 100, or perhaps 50; while that is not the one-piece-at-a-time mixed-model ideal, it comes close.

But Kawasaki wanted to achieve the ideal: one-touch setup and one-piece-at-a-time production. That was accomplished for high-use frame parts in the summer of 1982. To achieve one-touch setup, large

**Exhibit 16–1.**  Carousel Conveyor on Punch Press

general-purpose punch presses were replaced with small special-purpose screw presses. Each screw press has a die permanently built in so that there is no die change time and therefore no setup time—a dedicated machine. The small screw presses apply pressure slowly rather than punch suddenly, but their slowness is more than offset by the zero setup time. With dies exactly positioned, defective parts are much less likely. Now the screw presses are in the welding shop, where a welder can set up several screw presses to make several different frame parts; as each part is completed, the welder may immediately weld it onto the growing frame. There are no lot-size inventories. Much of the punch press shop has been abolished, since welders now make each part as they go.

---

*Question 3.* What kinds of resource costs did Kawasaki reduce through their way of achieving, first, single setup and, then, one-touch setup?

---

# 17

# Ultrix Corporation

*Case topics:*

From autonomous to sequential assembly

From batch to rate-based scheduling

Changing mind-set of buyers

Dock-to-line delivery

Cross-trained direct and indirect labor

ABC analysis

JIT computer software

Bar-coding material receipts

Backflush

100 percent stock record accuracy

Space compression

Consignments

Containerization

Layout improvement

Ultrix began operations in 1979 and moved into a new building in 1982, where it produces the 5080 roll-top printer, the Jet-Pac Printer, and the 901 impact printer. The new building has about one-third the space of the former facilities, but production volume is about the same. Bulk inventories were cut from $6 million to $1.5 million, and printed circuit (PC) board inventories were cut from $450,000 to $150,000. Those reductions are the result of Ultrix's just-in-time campaign, aggressively led by production manager, Burton Cash, and his staff.

---

*Company name is disguised.

## Job Changes

JIT altered everyone's job at Ultrix. Assemblers used to build whole units at single work stations. Cash and his associates Hank Olson, Bill Wurtman, Dick Labich, and others were instrumental in bringing about a conversion to assembly lines. Now the assemblers build printers sequentially.

---

*Question 1.* What are the pros and cons of autonomous versus sequential assembly at Ultrix? Did Ultrix go in the right direction? Explain.

---

Scheduling of final assemblies and subassemblies has been greatly simplified. Now scheduling of final assembly and pack is to a daily rate instead of off and on in batch quantities. There is a small stockroom for finished goods inventory (FGI); it holds just one day's supply and is usually half full. That space provides a small buffer between batch shipments and one-at-a-time production. The final assembly people set the pace for the plant. Their completion of a unit prompts people at prior stages to make subassemblies.

Gary Hudson, purchasing manager, states that one of his main tasks was to try to change the mind-set of his buyers. They had always bought in large quantities to long lead-time schedules. Now the need was to synchronize deliveries from outside suppliers with assembly rates. As part of a training program, Hudson had buyers work on production lines, where they could become familiar with use rates and how much space was available for parts. ABC analysis was used as the basis for purchasing policies. "A" items, large, costly, locally sourced items like manuals, are delivered daily on a space-available basis. "B" items are deliverd every two weeks, and "C" items are deliverd every four months.

---

*Question 2.* Is Ultrix's use of the old ABC system compatible with its JIT purchasing efforts? Explain.

---

Most suppliers are on some form of total quality control; line shutdowns caused by problems with purchased parts, which initially averaged two per week, are now rare.

## Material Control

Material control has been greatly simplified. Most incoming materials bypass the stockroom and are stored on the production lines. This cuts the number of storekeepers needed, so stores people have been cross-trained to work on the line, and they also train production people in right ways to handle material.

The division handles about 5,000 part numbers. Manufacturing lead times and work-in-process (WIP) have shrunk to the point where it is easy to keep inventory records virtually 100 percent accurate. For example, WIP is only four hours' worth in the Jet-Pac printer area, and this includes burn-in test time. The short manufacturing cycle also makes it possible for engineers to spot trouble resulting from engineering changes the day after the changes are introduced.

Ultrix once had three carousel storage units on the floor and in the stockroom to hold WIP. All three were sold to another division, which uses them for finished goods storage. Also, parts that used to move around the plant in big carts now move in small carts. With the WIP reductions, production space has been cut 60 percent. WIP turnover has risen from six to twenty-nine.

Certain of the purchased materials and the WIP are controlled by kanban, or pull signals. For example, a foam molder and a maker of plastic bases (both located less than 100 miles away) ship only when Ultrix uses up the previous trailer of material. The trailers are parked at receiving docks, where they serve as storerooms as well as kanban containers. This arrangement avoids extra handling and storage steps.

Handling has been simplified in another way for a fan assembled by a local subcontractor on consignment. Ultrix provides kits of unassembled fans in boxes; the subcontractor assembles the fans and returns them in the same boxes. The boxes are of a special design: Small parts go into honeycomb dividers on a lower layer, and two larger fan castings are placed between a separator on an upper layer. The subcontractor just folds up the honeycomb and puts it in the bottom of the box to make room for the assembled fan. In an average day two pallets of the kitted fans go to the subcontractor and two come back assembled.

Another special box has been designed for small hardware items: screws, washers, grommets, and so forth. The box is oblong, and it is creased at one end. The local suppliers are required to deliver hardware in these boxes. Then they go right out to the production lines, where they serve as parts trays. The assembler merely folds the end of the box at the creases so that the box is much like the commercial plastic parts trays that are in wide use in industry. The object again is to avoid handling: taking out of one container and putting into another. The special box was designed by an Ultrix employee, and a patent has been applied for.

---

*Question 3.* Do such special container, handling, and kanban requirements sound like an undue burden upon suppliers? Explain.

---

## JIT Software

Ultrix is one of the first American companies to use a new computer software package called Pro-JIT. Bar codes are applied to boxes of incoming stock as they come off the truck, and as the boxes pass by a reader, the Pro-JIT system records the addition in an inventory item master file. Parts used in manufacture are deducted from the item master file when the bar code on the finished product is read as it goes onto the outbound truck. (This is commonly known as backflush or post-deduct.) A limited amount of bar-code-based transactions can be entered into the computer in between the raw-material and finished-goods stages.

---

*Question 4.* What is the proper role of bar-coding at Ultrix? (Where and to what extent should they plan to use bar-code readers—now and in the future?)

---

## Appearance and Arrangement

On a clear day, one can look out one of the large east windows and see spectacular Mt. Jefferson looming "in the back yard." Perhaps that kind of a view makes it easier for people at Ultrix to accept the uninspiring look of a factory.

Actually, many factories in the electronics industry are well lighted and nicely furnished with modern partitions, potted plants, and good-quality work benches. And so it was at Ultrix—until it began to respond creatively to the problems that surfaced from the JIT campaign.

## Cut, Paste, and Jury-rig

Take the work benches, for example. They were nice-looking Herman Miller modular benches. But those benches could not be adapted easily enough—length changes and so forth. JIT means flexibility and change: As stock between processes shrinks, work stations move together, and this never stops. Ultrix got rid of the Herman Miller benches and devised their own, which were made simply from tubular T-shaped steel frames and common sheet materials. They are not pretty but arc flexible.

Many of the kanban containers are not aesthetically pleasing either. For example, in several areas corrugated boxes have been cut up and pasted together into pigeon-hole kanban racks or partitioned totes. The pasted racks and boxes are, of course, quick ways to get started and may be replaced by something more durable later.

---

*Question 5.* Would it have been better to go slower and find nice-looking storage and handling devices? What is a good JIT strategy in the area of aesthetics?

---

## Layout

Manufacturing space at Ultrix is on two floors. Printed circuit board assembly (PCA) is upstairs, and that floor is arranged mostly by process: Auto-insert is in one room; hand-loading and testing are in another area; soldering is done on a single large wave-soldering machine; and so forth. Assembly, test, and packing lines are on the lower floor, one line for each of the three major products.

The sharp reductions in WIP have left the entire plant quite uncrowded. It appears that there is room to fit production lines for more products into the building. Future JIT improvements are sure to cut WIP and space needed for the existing products even more.

*Question 6.* What, if anything, ought to be done with the plant organization?

## Midlife Challenge

Ultrix is one of the first of North America's JIT success stories. Like two dozen other early JIT successes, Ultrix has entertained a steady parade of visitors from other companies looking for a model to follow. Ultrix has grown a staff of managers, technicians, and operators who have acquired a wealth of JIT know-how, and some, like the managers Hank Olson and Bill Wurtman, have gone on to work the same magic in other plants.

Is there any concern that complacency will set in among the Ultrix regulars? That is hard to say for the long run. For the next few years, however, there are worthy new challenges that seem sure to keep up the interest. Ultrix is in the vanguard in the world in developing simple computer-system support—to replace the complicated manufacturing computer systems that do not fit well with JIT. The Pro-JIT package is an early release, and there will be plenty for everyone to do at Ultrix in melding it with the JIT procedures in place.

*Question 7.* What if Burton Cash, Gary Hudson, Dick Labich, and other early JIT champions follow Hank Olson and Bill Wurtman out the door? Would Ultrix need a new champion in order to ensure continual improvement at a rapid pace in the future?

# 18

# JIT in Premanufacturing, North American Gear, Inc.: Part A— Detail Engineering

*Case topics:*

Organizing for JIT
JIT in office work
Work sampling as JIT tool
Preserving flexibility in
  engineering

Kanban in engineering
"Doing it right the first time"
  in engineering
Continual improvement

North American Gear (NAG) is a subsidiary of Western Engine Company, a manufacturer of power transmission devices of all sorts. NAG is the dominant employer in a small city located in a remote area. Compared with labor in urban areas, the local labor pool is unsophisticated, stable, and not highly paid.

---

Adapted from case originally prepared by William A. Wheeler III, Partner-in-Charge, National Just-in-Time Practices, Coopers & Lybrand, 1 P.O. Square, Boston, MA 02109. Company name is disguised.

130

NAG recently has averaged about $45 million in sales annually. It makes a specially engineered product for the steel industry. The units sell for more than $75,000 each. All the units are round and contain gears and shafts. They vary in gear-tooth pitch, number of assembly components, and size: 1 to 5 feet in diameter, 3 to 15 feet in length.

## The Market

Order volume is about equally split between OEM (original equipment manufacturing) customers and service parts. The OEM market is hard to service because of constant specification changes from NAG's own designers as well as from final customers (steel manufacturers). The other market is just as difficult, since the high unit cost induces end users to squeeze service parts inventories and to order irregularly based on dire need.

Both markets have been cost-driven. Even with all the design changes, OEM business was usually bid firm, with bids then frozen into customers' budgets.

Replacement business usually arose from "crashes" (as they were known in the steel industry) in a customer's plant. Therefore, technological advances in heat treating, quality, or design were selling points but not determining factors.

The industry lead-time standard was thirty-two weeks, and a premium cost add-on for less than normal lead time was not unusual. There were three major manufacturers in the United States, each with about equal participation. Management at NAG thought their two competitors had similar cost structures. That would explain the aggressive pricing and "at cost" bids when the market was slack and order backlogs were falling. There seemed to be no brand loyalty, even for replacement items. Assuming delivery could be assured within the thirty-two-week bogey, the choice of supplier was strictly cost-driven (except in emergencies).

## New President

A few months ago Harold Hagge assumed the presidency of NAG. Hagge's background was in marketing and sales for a large con-

sumer-goods manufacturer. He admitted to little knowledge of manufacturing, much less a job-shop environment.

Hagge was greeted with the following operating data:

- Return on net assets (RONA): 21 percent
- Inventories: nineteen weeks of raw material (2.7 turns), six
  weeks of work in process (8.7 turns)
- Delivery timeliness: 61 percent within five days, 88 percent
  within twenty days
- Backlog: seventeen weeks full, forty-one equivalent weeks
  booked
- Capacity available: 56 percent (estimated)
- Wage incentive payment: 181 percent on average standard day
  of five hours
- Profit projection: $380,000 loss for remaining eight months of
  year
- Industry projection: down 15–20 percent this fiscal year
- Ratio of direct to indirect labor: 1:2.7

Coming from consumer goods, Mr. Hagge was understandably
aghast. He was used to product differentiation, tight asset management, high productivity, and customer service approaching 95 percent. Hagge set his sights on these potential improvements in the
short term:

- Morale, especially a desire to improve
- Improved RONA via better capacity utilization and inventory
  reduction
- Higher productivity via revision of the wage incentive system
- Cost improvement via indirect labor reduction and/or pro-
  ductivity improvement

For the longer term, Hagge's prime goal was added volume to
absorb underutilized capacity. To get more volume, NAG would have
to differentiate itself from the competition. Hagge suggested to his
staff that the best way to gain the edge was to cut deeply into the
thirty-two week industry lead-time standard. He set a goal of eight
weeks, with this reasoning: It takes six weeks to manufacture something now, and with over 50 percent unused capacity, production
could be done in three weeks; that would leave five weeks for order
entry, engineering, and procurement.

## Plan of Attack

Hagge and his plant manager, Kevin Rutten, decided the best course of action was to build on strengths. Rutten made up a list of what he thought were NAG's strong suits:

- Almost every employee knows the product intimately, through years of experience. Most consider it an honor to be asked to work overtime, and there is evidence of fierce loyalty.
- Engineering and cost-development records are extensive and easily accessible.
- The purchasing group is unusually young and eager to learn. It is proud of its self-initiated cost reduction program, which cut costs 1 percent or better for three straight years.
- An aggressive quality improvement program brought scrap and rework down from 4.0 to 0.3 percent. The program's principal focus is failsafing, especially in engineering.
- The sales department is championing improvement.
- The majority of the lead time, twenty-five to twenty-nine weeks (not including shipping), is up front, in the office, as is more than half of the indirect labor. (See Exhibit 18-1.)
- The union (International Association of Machinists), which represents both the office and the factory, understands the

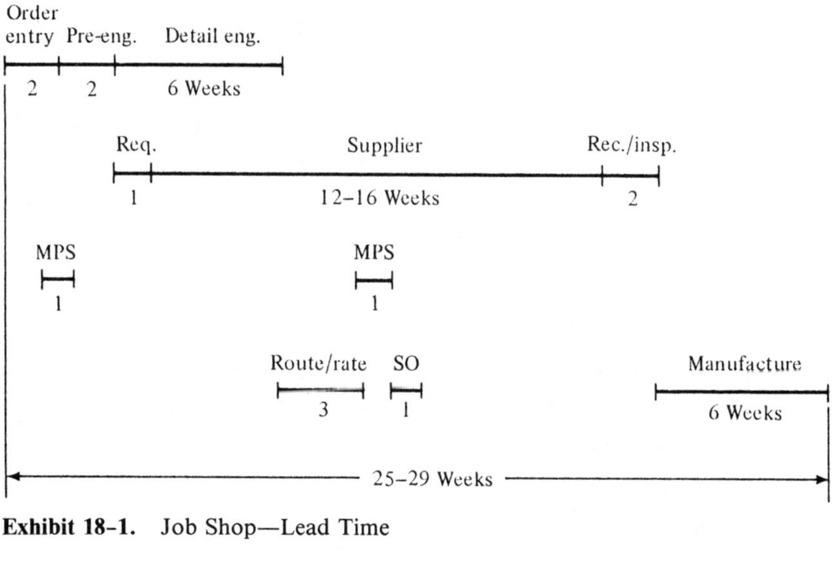

**Exhibit 18-1.** Job Shop—Lead Time

tough competition and seems to favor improvements that will keep the plant afloat. Rutten stated that the union leadership expressed this concern a number of times, but never in the presence of other members.

- Through extensive use of phantom job orders ("phanjos"), the master scheduler is efficient at rough-cut capacity planning and preliminary scheduling (prior to completion of design engineering). About fifty phanjos represent common configurations. Each phanjo has an associated shop routing and work standards.

## Lead-Time Reduction

Hagge decided to tackle the long-range strategic goal—cutting lead times and generating more volume—first, since improvements there would enhance some of the short-term indicators at the same time. The starting point would be in premanufacturing in the office, where a large potential for head-count reduction existed.

Hagge had some exposure to concepts of JIT production in his previous job. He thought JIT should apply to a job shop, and why not the office, too?

## Steering Committee and Improvement Groups

Hagge appointed an improvement task force, including himself, Rutten, and five other key managers; they were to guide the lead-time reduction campaign. The task force quickly saw that it lacked the resources or background to perform studies and suggest specific actions. Therefore, it evolved into a steering committee that tasked subgroups, called improvement groups (IGs) to do the "leg work."

Each IG was composed of office people (mostly from the bargaining unit) from different departments and one member of the steering committee. Each IG was assigned areas to study. The IG was to detail the problem and submit recommendations to the steering committee. Implementation was up to the department head.

---

*Question 1.* Is Hagge's way of organizing the improvement effort sound? Discuss.

---

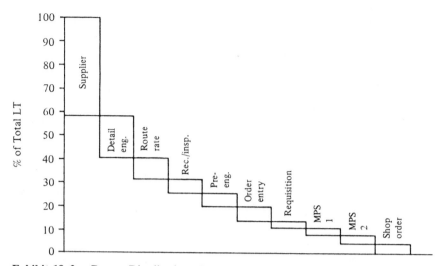

**Exhibit 18–2.** Pareto Distribution, Premanufacturing Lead Times

The steering committee adopted Mr. Hagge's goal of a five-week throughput time from order receipt to first factory operation. They prioritized options by a Pareto analysis of lead times (Exhibit 18–2). The Pareto chart shows that the supplier, detail engineering, and route/rate consumed nearly 70 percent of the lead time. One IG was established for each of those three areas. A fourth IG was assigned the full order-entry procedure: order entry through shop order. All of the improvement groups made swift progress, with the IG for detail engineering completing its studies and recommendations first.

## Detail Engineering

Throughput time in detail engineering was six weeks. Detail engineering was segmented by size of product, not type. One negative result was an ever changing imbalance of workload between design groups.

Competing with the normal design function was preparing estimates for proposals, which accounted for about one-third of each group's time. Marketing insisted that proposals take priority over finish design for booked orders; thus, proposals constantly interrupted the regular design work. Work sampling in the detail-engineering department indicated the following:

| Productive Time | |
| --- | --- |
| Prepare proposals | 32% |
| Design | 18 |
| Detail | 23 |
| Check | 5 |
| Review order | 5 |
| Reacquaint | 11 |
| Reassignment | 6 |

The engineers work-sampled themselves, which may explain why no idle time was reported. The IG still found the results useful, since they indicated relative uses of time.

## Interruptions

The IG zeroed in on the last two items: 17 percent spent going back and getting reacquainted with an interrupted job or getting up to speed (holding discussions with another engineer) when a job was reassigned from one engineer to another. Most of the "review order" time was spent with the order-entry group seeking clarification of the actual order.

> *Question 2.* Work sampling has British and American roots and dates back to the 1920s. Does it have a legitimate role in connection with JIT? Or is the IG "spinning its wheels"?

Further study revealed causes of the interruptions:

1. Stop detail engineering to prepare a proposal
2. Imbalance of work among the detail engineering sections
3. Order-entry data missing or incomplete

The last problem was easy to fix. A joint order-entry and engineering team worked up checklists for each product type, and order-entry people were trained to use them. A bonus was that customer service people spent less time clearing up questions with the customer, which fostered a professional image.

The IG felt the first two problems required reorganizing the detail engineering department. It rejected setting up a separate proposal group. Instead, it recommended design groups specialized by product subtype, with each group also generating proposals. The steering committee turned down the recommendation. The committee felt that organizing by subtypes would reduce flexibility, a no-no according to JIT principles.

---

*Question 3.* Is this overdoing it? How strong is this "no-no," and should an exception be made in this case?

---

The interruption problem had to be solved another way. A type of kanban was devised: When assembly is completed, a signal (kanban) goes back to the route/rate group to prepare another job packet; route/rate sends the signal back to detail engineering.

The production rate in assembly was fairly constant: about two units per day. Unfortunately, job completions per day in detail engineering were not constant. Therefore, detail engineering was required to stockpile two to four days of "finished goods" (completed detail engineering jobs). When the queue fell below two, detail engineering would work overtime; when it rose above four, people could be reassigned to task forces, tooling reviews, troubleshooting, quality problems, value analysis, and other useful work.

As it turned out, the queue upper limit was forever being exceeded. The steering committee elected to reassign less technical personnel to other departments, which cut the department payroll.

---

*Question 4.* Is this a true use of kanban? Is the "finished goods" inventory consistent with good JIT practices?

---

Other ways the IG found to cut engineering lead time include the following:

- Undimensioned drawings were found to be suitable for 80 percent of requirements.
- Cross-footing of dimensions on drawings offered some "fail-safing."
- Sketches were acceptable for forgings and for packing and shipping.
- Repetitive calculations, especially for gearing, were done on the computer.

- Most prints were refiled by size and by phanjo; the old way, which seldom was useful, was to file by job number, with cross-referencing by customer.
- Instead of preparing sepia or mylar drawings for everything, "same as, except" ("red-line") drawings were used in copying machines.

## Proposals

The next question for the engineering IG was what to do about the 32 percent of department time spent on proposals. The proposal success rate was about 40 percent. As Rutten put it, "Almost 100 percent of the jobs are conceptually engineered twice! You could say that 60 percent of the proposed work is for nothing."

The long-range strategy of gaining higher market participation dictated care in responding to customers' queries. Engineering review for every proposal request would have to be continued. The engineering IG recommended a do-it-right-the-first-time solution: Prepare proposals more thoroughly so that, if accepted, most of the detailing would already be done, which would cut lead time. The number of change orders would also drop, since the customer would have access to a more complete engineering package.

---

*Question 5.* This solution involves doing some work in advance of need. Is it a violation of JIT concepts?

---

Proposals would be treated like any other job. Marketing's old requirement for putting first priority on proposals could be set aside, because the engineering lead times, down to eight to ten days, would erase concerns about priorities; that would take care of the interruptions problem.

Engineering had three control clerks. They tracked progress, prepared ETC (estimated-time-to-completion) reports, accumulated cost data, and checked inventory against bills of material (BOM). The IG reasoned that when the lead time melts, so does the need for tracking and reporting. The pull system with route/rate simplified material management and cut out the need for checking materials against BOMs. The control clerks could be reassigned or, if lacking in seniority, laid off.

While the office changes were being planned, things were happening in the factory as well, and some of the factory changes opened up opportunities in engineering. For one thing, formation of work cells in the factory caused BOMs to collapse; BOM clerks had fewer levels to identify in the product structure. One of the two BOM clerks could be eliminated.

Cell formation yielded similar benefits in routing. A manufacturing cell operator or supervisor could do much of the routing from the blueprint.

The IG came up with still more staff-cutting recommendations, which are reflected in the before-and-after summary below.

| Position | Before | After |
|---|---|---|
| Manager | 1 | 1 |
| Working Supervisor | 3 | 0 |
| Control Clerk | 3 | 0 |
| Detailers | 7 | 4 |
| Designers | 10 | 10 |
| Checkers | 1 | 0 |
| BOM Clerk | 2 | 1 |
| | 27 | 16 (41%) |

The net result of the IG's efforts is a 41 percent reduction. Furthermore, a computer-aided design (CAD) system, which had been approved earlier, no longer was justified, given the simplifications and changes.

*Question 6.* What's next?

# 19

# JIT in Premanufacturing, North American Gear, Inc.: Part B—Purchasing and Order Entry

*Case topics:*

JIT/TQC procurement strategies

Sole-sourcing

Joint customer-supplier leverage with common suppliers

Supplier limits on share of their business

Penalty payments to suppliers for quantity changes

Effects on sales and employment

North American Gear (NAG), under its new president, Harold Hagge, had embarked on a campaign to slash lead times and thereby gain market share. A steering committee had tasked four improve-

Adapted from case originally prepared by William A. Wheeler III, Partner-in-Charge, National Just-in-Time Practices, Coopers & Lybrand, 1 P.O. Square, Boston, MA 02109. Company name is disguised.

ment groups (IGs) with planning for JIT implementation in the pre-manufacturing (office) areas.

Part A of this case study (case 18) provided background and a discussion of one IG's recommendations for cutting lead times in detail engineering. Part B concerns the continued efforts to introduce JIT in purchasing and in order entry.

## Purchasing

The IG for purchasing found three commodities—steel rounds, forgings, and bearings—to be consistently outside the one-week bogey set by the steering committee (see Exhibit 19-1). Purchasing usually bought steel and bearings from the manufacturer in large lot or mill quantities. They ordered forgings from the supplier that could best meet due dates, that is, had capacity available. For that reason, price was secondary most of the time.

The IG developed a common set of procurement strategies for the three commodities:

- Eliminate purchase orders and requisitions
- No receiving inspection
- Deliver to points of use: first operation for steel and forgings, assembly for bearings

| Commodity | P/N | $/yr. (000) | Vendors | Vendor lead time | Inventory $(000) |
|-----------|-----|-------------|---------|------------------|-------------------|
| Forgings | As per job | 11,000 | 7 | 14-16 wks. | 1,450 |
| Steel rounds | Approx. 30 | 5,500 | 3 | Per mill schedule (up to 16 wks.) | 4,300 |
| Bearings | 12 | 1,200 | 4 | 40-50 wks. | 2,800 |
| | | 17,700 | | | 8,550 (2.1 turns) |

**Exhibit 19-1.** Purchasing Analysis

- One vendor for each commodity
- No lead times in excess of seven working days; five or less days to be the norm
- A target of 5 percent *net* cost reduction for each commodity

---

*Question 1.* Is this a good set of strategies?

---

The action agenda for those goals, along with results realized, differed by commodity.

## Steel Rounds

The purchasing IG felt it necessary, for price reasons, to continue to buy steel rounds directly from the mills. Therefore, cost reductions would have to come from lower freight costs and inventories.

It was the manager of the steel service center (the supplier) who came up with the best opportunities—three of them—for cost reduction:

1. First operation at NAG was sawing the round to size; two saws and one full-time operator performed the operation. The steel service center could cut to size on more efficient equipment at two-thirds of NAG's direct labor alone. The space, saws, and burden savings thus became a "freebie" if NAG chose to take advantage of this plan.

2. NAG's computerized inventory system included a bar-allocation routine and the equivalent of one full-time person to maintain and run it; they would not be needed if NAG no longer cuts bars to size. As a bonus, route/rate would no longer need to determine the cut length; the engineer could set the proper bar length during product design.

3. By leveraging buys of all steel rounds with one steel center, the NAG account would be very attractive to the distributor. Steel centers, especially captive ones, usually buy mill quantity, FOB distribution, at less than consumer mill pricing. A sole steel center could offer NAG a price structure 6 percent below what it was paying.

To summarize the benefits:

— FOB, North American Gear = no freight charges
— Elimination of first operation (sawing) and 12 percent faster throughput time on shop floor

— Headcount reduction of two persons
— Supplier lead time = three days
— Elimination of raw material inventory
— Elimination of one route/rate operation
— Phone release from production planner eliminates purchase-order generation

---

*Question 2.* These strategies depend on sole-sourcing the steel rounds. Is sole-sourcing wise in this case?

---

## Bearings

A profile of bearing demand showed irregular and erratic use at the part-number level. Therefore, the IG was faced with two poor options: continue to inventory bearings or require a power-transmission distributor to stock the items for them.

One member of the IG suggested NAG take advantage of its parent company's position in the market place and survey the distributors that sell Western Engine Company's products. What seemed like a simple task took months and was costly, but it yielded useful information: While the bearings typically used were not commonly stocked by all distributors, there was a reasonably stable national demand for all bearing part numbers.

The IG's plan was for NAG to persuade a national distributor to centralize its nationwide stock of those bearings in the local warehouse. The distributor could then order at the maximum-quantity price break, achieve better inventory turns, and service a valuable account—both customer and supplier (the parent company).

That plan has been carried out: The assembly foreman now releases the required bearings two days prior to need. NAG now pays an average of 4 percent less per bearing than in the previous year.

---

*Question 3.* Presumably most companies have the opportunity to do the sort of thing that NAG did with bearings. Why have companies so rarely taken advantage of those opportunities in the past?

---

## Forgings: Assisting the Supplier

The goal of on-time, short-lead-time acquisition of large (300 to 4,000 pounds) forgings proved to be a challenge for the IG. Size and configuration were rarely repetitive, and forging industry practice was always to work with a backlog. Average lead time was fourteen weeks.

The forging suppliers at first resisted shortened delivery times (three days for manufacture and two days for order entry and transportation). They argued that a backlog was the only way to be assured that billet stock of the proper alloy would be available for forging. Furthermore, they could not assure hammer availability without notice, because forging dimensions varied widely. Finally, no forging supplier wanted to dedicate more than 15 percent of its capacity (roughly 60 percent of NAG's requirements) to a single customer. One forge shop did agree to work with the IG in the detailed analysis phase.

The analysis began with seeing what factors the supplier used in assigning a forging to a specific hammer. The chief factor turned out to be surface size or spread of metal. The IG member from engineering found a way to quantify the factor: inches of maximum spread. The engineer developed a graph (Exhibit 19-2 is a highly simplified version), which went into use at the forging supplier's plant. The graph simplified the planning of capacity requirements on each hammer. Further study showed a mostly even demand for both size ranges of forgings.

The IG suggested that purchasing classify each size range as a subcommodity and then see about splitting the forging business between two suppliers; the purpose was simply to allay the forge shops' concern about accepting more than a 15 percent capacity commitment from any customer.

---

*Question 4.* Is the tendency for suppliers to restrict their business with a given customer likely to persist or change in the next five or ten years (given all the other changes in supplier–customer relations that are going on)?

---

The next analysis was of alloy demand for each subcommodity. Larger forgings were all made of the same alloy. The smaller forgings used two major alloys and three minor ones. It turned out that a

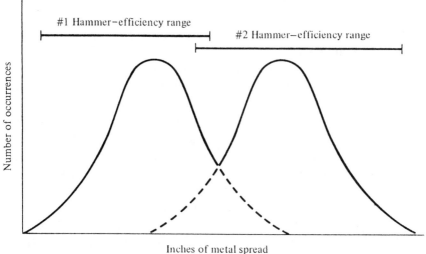

**Exhibit 19-2.** Distribution of Hammer Capacities (Simplified)

single design engineer had consistently specified the three atypical alloys. When asked why, the engineer could reply only that no one had ever challenged him before, and he felt the alloys suited the need. Since no data could be found to support the position, the engineer agreed to go with the two alloys favored by the rest of the design group.

The IG's next concern was with the forge shops. The actual manufacturing cycle was three days: roughly one day each at billet sawing, hammer, and normalize. Shops with the most constrained space had the lowest and most consistent queues.

As was true at NAG, the forge shops' paperwork cycle was longer than the production cycle: two weeks versus three days. All four suppliers released orders to their shops at least a week prior to sawing, and only after the billet stock was allocated. The IG asked why. No reason, other than habit. Order-entry time was also about the same for the four forge shops: about five days. All but a few hours of the order-entry time was devoted to drawing forging prints from the customer's finished print.

The purchasing IG learned that when NAG prepares a proposal for a customer, the design engineer draws a rough sketch of the forging. The sketch is used to estimate the raw material cost and the machining requirements. Thus, NAG has a quasi-acceptable forging print before the forging order even exists. With a little training on the drawing requirements of the forge shops, NAG's engineers could complete the finished forging drawing at the time of proposal. That, in turn, would allow the price to be calculated according to prenegotiated parameters.

The next idea was to transmit the forging drawing (proposal stage, but prepriced and in finish form) via telecopier; that would cut the supplier's order-entry cycle from five days to a few hours of editing and shop-order generation. By agreement with the suppliers, drawings received by 11 A.M. were to be in the shop at the first operation by 7 A.M. the next day. (Note: One of the forge shops persuaded a number of other large customers to adopt the same procedure. It was able to eliminate two of five draftsmen. Half of the savings were voluntarily passed on to NAG.)

Armed with better knowledge of billet and capacity usage patterns, two of the forge shops agreed to allocate resource capacity every other day. Thus, maximum lead time from order to receipt was six days: two days of order entry or scheduling, three days for manufacture, and one day of transportation.

The agreement provided recourse in cases when NAG's sales volume changed: If volume increased, then, with four weeks notification, the allocation frequency could be changed to two of every three days, once a day, etc. If sales were cut within a four-week period, then NAG would pay a penalty. NAG's total penalty in the first year was $650, paid to one of the two forge shops. The IG thought it a small penalty for virtually eliminating raw material ($1,450,000), reducing the lead time from fourteen weeks to six days, and stabilizing the pricing.

---

*Question 5.* Are penalties good ways to deal with the problem of customer volume changes?

---

The 5 percent cost-reduction goal was not met until the next year, when the suppliers realized how much productivity they had gained through the agreements. Then they agreed to hold the pricing formulas, including raw materials, at the same level.

## Order Entry

Exhibit 19–3 shows the pre-JIT order-entry procedure. Customer service (reporting to sales) received the order, sometimes by mail,

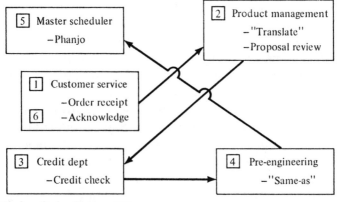

**Exhibit 19-3.** Order Entry—8 Days

more often by phone. It assigned an internal job-order number and set up an order file. Product management (also reporting to sales) pulled the proposal, checked it against the order, and "translated" the customer order into company nomenclature. The rewritten order went to the credit department for approval. Copies of the credit acceptance went back to customer service and product management, and the order flowed onward to production control.

In production control a control clerk, and then the working supervisor, reviewed the order and assigned a phanjo number, which was keyed to a record showing work-center routing and capacity requirements. From that data, the master scheduler—next on the flow path—could calculate backlogs at key work centers, assign a due date, and forward the order to customer service for acknowledgement to the customer. A copy of the order went to engineering for design and detailing.

That procedure averaged eight days. Work sampling showed only two hours of work actually done on the order. The order spent the rest of the time in a queue or in transit. Flow-charting the order-entry process disclosed that only about 15 percent of the operations were actually adding some value to the order. The IG labeled the remaining 85 percent "waste" or, putting it more positively, "targets of opportunity."

---

*Question 6.* What is the ratio of paperwork lead time to actual work content time for the above procedure?

---

The credit manager's desk held the largest pile of orders, because "a credit check took 3-4 days." However, seventy-five repeat customers dominated the order file, and for them there was never a credit hold. A quarterly audit of the seventy-five seemed sufficient. Credit checks could be limited to potential new customers—and could be done in parallel with proposal development.

A study of customer order history showed a strong tendency for repeat orders for the same product type. Since product management was already organized by product type, the IG recommended that paperwork "cells" be established around the product management group. One or more customer service people would be assigned to each cell. Each would assume lead responsibility for propsal development. Each would also receive any credit-hold advice, and credit checking would thus become an exception-only task.

Phanjos were also organized by product type, with each type having fifteen to twenty specific phanjos. With minimal training each customer service representative could assign the phanjo number, thus eliminating the second largest queue, which was at the engineering supervisor's desk.

The IG resisted the temptation to merge master scheduling with product management. However, the master scheduler was physically moved to an area central to all product management groups.

Exhibit 19-4 shows the order-entry procedure after the order-entry IG disbanded. The changes in procedure—centering on organization of paperwork cells—were simple but profound in effect. A few years earlier there had been a cost-reduction program aimed at

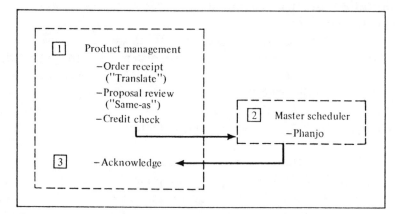

**Exhibit 19-4.** Order Entry—2 Days

the offices. Each department made sacrifices, but no one considered cells. One reason is that each department was analyzed separately.

---

*Question 7.* What are the likely human effects of thrusting the office workers into cells?

---

## Route/Rate

The route/rate activity comes after design engineering completes the job packet. Route/rate throughput time averaged three weeks.

As previously noted, a byproduct of setting up manufacturing cells and cutting out the sawing operation for steel rounds was reduction of throughput time in route/rate. The route/rate IG found that even with no changes, route/rate should not take three weeks. There was rarely any urgency, because the order was usually awaiting receipt of forging or steel rounds anyway. The supervisor explained that three weeks was simply "customary." He suggested dropping it to five working days. The IG thought that was still too long and began detailed study of the function.

An IG member dug into the phanjo files and found that the basic routings were already available; they were just never offered to the route/rate group. A few changes to the phanjo file format permitted their ready use of the file.

Since the cell leader could do the detail routing, little phanjo file maintenance was required. The detail routing, in turn, was needed by industrial engineering in setting standard rates for the piecework incentive system. (Lead-time data in the phanjo were not in standard hours.) The question came down to whether to retain piecework or scuttle it in favor of measured day work. The IG decided not to handle that "hot potato" and instead requested a decision from the improvement task force.

Meanwhile, the IG pressed on. It reviewed job-packet arrivals from engineering; the arrival pattern was highly irregular. While that created a feast-or-famine planning workload in route/rate, the nine professionals in the group kept reasonably busy (or at least looked busy) on other assigned duties: maintain the work-element file, perform check studies on disputed rates, develop new equipment justifications, program NC equipment, and perform most of the tool specification work. (Tool engineering was a separate group—omitted from the study because of the feeling that it did not affect throughput time.)

The IG recommended dedicating three of the professionals to route/rate; the others in the group were available if the flow of job packets was high or for a nasty mix of jobs that took more than usual route/rate work. Basically, however, the IG thought packet arrivals from engineering would smooth out a good deal when the pull system from the shop through engineering was fully functional. It thought that with more even work flow and backup people on hand, the route/rate throughput time should drop to two days. Overall throughput time in the department was projected to drop to three and a half days—from fifteen.

## Overall Results

Most of the IGs' recommendations were put into effect. Within four months the overall average lead time fell from between twenty-eight and thirty-two weeks to ten or eleven weeks (Exhibit 19–5)—and the steering committee had not even started in the plant.

Other gains: Inventories were projected to drop by nearly $8,000,000; net reductions in prices for purchased materials saved a projected $530,000 for the first year; and headcount among the premanufacturing people in the offices fell 29 percent:

|  | Before | After |
|---|---|---|
| Customer service | 6 | 0 |
| Credit | 1 | 1 |
| Product management | 4 | 8 |
| Master scheduler | 1 | 1 |
| Purchasing | 4 | 3 |
| Engineering | 27 | 16 |
| Route/rate | 10 | 10 |
| Planning | 1 | 1 |
| Miscellaneous | 2 | 0 |
|  | 56 | 40 (29%) |

Sales volume remained steady despite a 20 percent decrease in market. One of the three competitors ceased manufacture of engineered products. NAG almost doubled its market share.

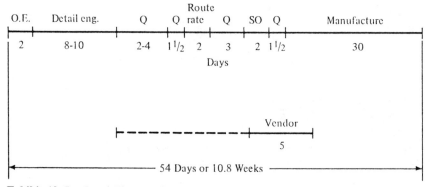

**Exhibit 19–5.** Lead Time—After Improvement

---

*Question 8.* What logically should have happened to total employment at NAG over the time period of the case?

---

# 20

# TQC/JIT
# at Tennant Company

*Case topics:*

Rigid work stations
Make to order vs. make to
  stock
Effect of layout on
  communication
Size of work team
Effect of lot size

Warehouse on wheels
Workers taking initiative
Material review board
Supplier quality
Possible JIT/TQC "turf"
  disputes
Process accounting

Tennant Company manufactures industrial floor sweepers, scrubbers, and scarifiers in two plants in northwest Minneapolis. The smaller plant (170,000 square feet) fabricates metal parts and scrubber brushes; the other plant (276,000 square feet), 3 miles away, houses welding, subassembly, and final assembly, along with certain administrative and support offices. Tennant Company employs in excess of 350 wage-earners: about 250 direct labor and about 120 support people.

**Progressive Management**

Tennant Company is among the first companies in North America to become aware of the potential of both total quality control (TQC) and just-in-time (JIT) production. The emphasis on quality began in 1980 and on JIT in 1981. Tennant Company's early awareness is not surprising in view of its reputation for progressive management. Some examples follow:

• North American manufacturers have led the world in using computers for planning and control, especially the set of computer applications called *material requirements planning* (MRP). Tennant Company has been well known in the MRP community for some twenty years as one of the first to implement each new MRP-related development.

• The quality crusade in North America dates back only to about 1980. Again, Tennant was in on the ground floor. Philip Crosby, a prominent author and teacher in the quality movement, gives Tennant Company credit, along with IBM, for being especially supportive in getting the Crosby Quality College launched.[1]

• Tennant held its second annual Zero Defects Day in May 1983. The Guthrie Theater was rented for the affair, and the company's 1,100 Minneapolis-based employees, plus seventy people from key supplier companies, were invited. A theater group from Bethel College had been hired to create and stage a musical comedy on the ZD theme. The result was a ninety-minute performance with about ten song-and-dance numbers. It featured a mail delivery man who, on stage, visited a succession of work areas in a hypothetical factory. At first the mailman scoffed at the quality-improvement activities he noticed at each stop, but, of course, by the end of the play he had become sold on ZD.

• Tennant Company has been active in the Twin Cities area in spreading the word. For example, Tennant Company arranged to sponsor, jointly with the Japan Management Association (JMA), a Conference on Quality and Productivity. About 500 people, paying a fee to cover costs, attended the conference, which was held in Minneapolis on November 7–8, 1984. (Similar conferences had been held for the five previous years, but audience sizes were more modest.)

## JIT Campaign

Tennant Company's JIT activities gathered steam as a result of reading by key people of the available books on the subject. The facilities

---

[1] Philip B. Crosby, *Quality Without Tears: The Art of Hassle-Free Management* (New York: McGraw-Hill, 1984), p. xi.

WORLD CLASS MANUFACTURING CASEBOOK

planning committee was converted to a JIT committee in 1981, and the committee brought in outside authorities to conduct seminars.

One reason for the early interest in JIT was bloated inventories. Tennant Company has a companywide profit-sharing program, but the amount of profit available for sharing had declined, and dollars tied up in inventory seemed to be an obvious reason. There were hopes that the JIT campaign would hold inventory growth in check and obviate the need for erecting a new building.

The pace of implementation was slow at first, but by the fall of 1984 there were multiple JIT projects. Work-in-process inventory turnover had increased from three to nine, and a sharp further improvement in WIP turns appeared to be just around the corner. JIT implementation began with a pilot project.

## Pilot JIT Projects

The simplest of Tennant's products, the Model 432 walk-behind scrubber, was chosen as the pilot JIT project. The project was begun in the spring of 1983. By the fall of 1984, the 432 was being assembled on an L-shaped production line incorporating a number of JIT concepts:

1. Most subassemblies are produced on-line.
2. Four carts transport major subassemblies through three stages of manufacture. At any given time one cart is in welding, one is in painting, one is in final assembly, and one is on reserve. Each cart holds one day's supply of major parts: four back panels, four frames, and so forth (see Exhibit 20-1).
3. The production line consists of six stations, designed so that materials and tools are positioned in close, dependable locations. Small parts are in shelves and bins around the circumference of some of the work benches (see Exhibit 20-2), and larger parts are just steps away in small racks and carts that hold a day's supply. Several of the stations are work platforms that hydraulically raise up and lower into the floor and rotate for easy access by the assemblers.

---

*Question 1.* What do you think of the hydraulic assembly platforms?

---

**Exhibit 20-1.** Carts for Frame Pieces for 432 Scrubber

4. The 432 is produced to a daily rate that fluctuates between four and eight units. Typically the rate is held stable for two or three weeks between adjustments.

---

*Question 2.* What positive and negative effects would there be if the 432 scrubbers were made in exactly the quantities that were ordered each day instead of to a schedule frozen for two or three weeks?

---

5. All testing, touch-up, and packing are done on the production line.
6. The crating supplier delivers crating materials, used at the end of the line, twice a day.
7. Before the JIT project was begun, the assemble-to-ship time for the 432 was two weeks. By late 1984 the time had been cut to sixty hours.

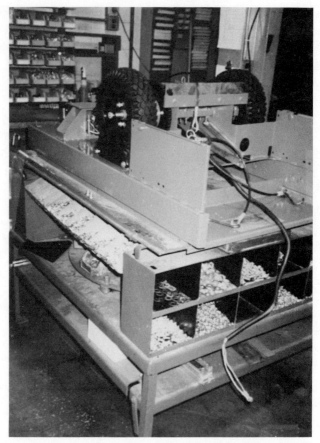

**Exhibit 20-2.**  Positioning of Tools and Parts for Assembly of 432 Scrubber

## Power-Driven Sweeper

The pilot project involved a "vanilla" product. More recently, JIT production was expanded to include products made in a variety of models, such as the 240 sweeper line.

The 240 product line comprises fifteen models of powered-wheel-driven sweepers. A nine-person assembly team had been assembling the 240 on one production line. Assembly lot sizes were sixteen to twenty units. The assembly area was laid out with racks for component parts on one side of the work stations and assembly benches on the other side (see Exhibit 20-3). One manager observed that in this assembly approach there was "no human communication."

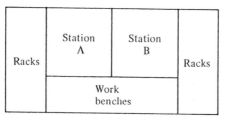

**Exhibit 20-3.** Assembly Area for 240 Sweeper—Before JIT

---

*Question 3.* What did the manager mean by "no human communication"?

---

Tennant implemented a JIT production approach in 1984. It features three assembly teams and areas (see Exhibit 20-4). The teams comprise about four people each, the maximum number of models per team is seven, and assembly lot sizes are from three to nine of a given model. One of the teams assembles small rider and electric rider models. Another assembles larger "low-dump" models. The third team assembles "high-dump" models.

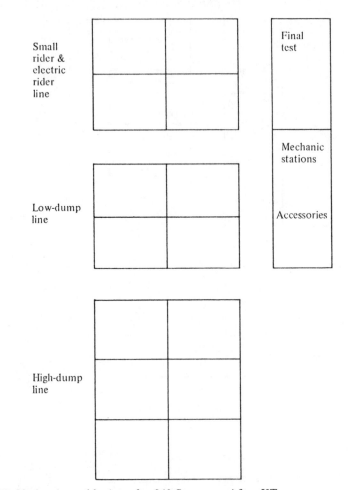

**Exhibit 20–4.** Assembly Area for 240 Sweeper—After JIT

---

*Question 4.* What are the advantages in going from one nine-person line to three small lines?

*Question 5.* Discuss the benefits, along with the likely problems and costs, of cutting from assembly lot sizes of three to nine to lots of one unit.

---

The new layout does not include conventional racks. Instead, assembly stations are surrounded by "WOW carts," WOW meaning warehouse on wheels (see example in Exhibit 20–5). The WOW carts

**Exhibit 20-5.** Two Examples of "WOW Carts"

hold one or two days' supply of parts; a twin cart filled in central stores is exchanged for an empty one on the line. Subassembly benches and tool stations also surround the assembly stations. The tool stations are actually tool display cases in which every tool has a location so definite that it can be found with virtually no search time.

---

*Question 6.* What, if anything, do WOW carts have to do with JIT production? How about carefully positioned tools and small parts?

*Question 7.* Tennant's pilot JIT project involved a vanilla product. Would it have been wiser to have selected a more complicated product to attack first? Discuss.

---

## Fabrication

Some of the greatest JIT opportunities at Tennant lie in the fabricated parts areas, where just a few JIT actions have been implemented so far. One is in fabrication of frames, which involves a good deal of wire-feed welding. The old procedure was to complete sub-weldments (primary operation) and store them in a large rack area. Later, another work order would result in pulling a discrete order quantity of those weldments from storage, sending them to another work center for a boring operation, and returning the completed units to storage. Still another work order caused the welded and bored parts to be pulled from storage and sent out to welding for a secondary welding operation.

There were proposals back in the pre-JIT era (1970s) to combine some of those operations. Making the necessary modifications had been estimated to cost $120,000, and the project was put off.

The project did not get officially resurrected. However, some of the welders figured out a way to make the changes for a modest $2,000, and they carried the project through to completion. They devised a type of cantilevered rack or fixture that properly presented work surfaces for completion of the required operations. They found an I-beam for the rack at a salvage yard, and they appropriated hoists that were not being used from another work area. There was one additional investment: They bought a vertical drill press large enough to do the boring operation.

---

*Question 8.* What does it take to get this kind of initiative from shop floor operators?

---

The result of combining operations was a cut in throughput time from weeks to about a day to make a frame. With the capability to build a frame so quickly, it made sense to release frame orders only as they were needed in final assembly, and so frame orders came to be scheduled by "pull" signals from assembly.

Shortening the throughput time to build frames cut work in process (WIP) to the same extent. The reduction of frame parts in combination with similar planned reductions in other fabricated parts resulted in a plan to eliminate a large rack area—10,000 square feet—in the main building. Elimination of the stock and removal of the racks was slated for the spring of 1985.

A few modest JIT efforts were also under way in the fabrication building. For example, in sheet metal a shear, a punch press, and a press brake will be arranged into a flow line in order to reduce flow time and distance for a family of parts that followed that production sequence.

## Supplier Quality Emphasis

Since purchased parts make up about two-thirds of product cost at Tennant, attention had to be given to performance of the suppliers. Late in 1980 the vice president of manufacturing, the director of materials, and the quality engineering group leader selected fifteen key suppliers as candidates for Supplier Quality Emphasis.[2] Tennant sent each of those suppliers a letter inviting the chief executive, along with the top person in manufacturing, quality engineering, and mar-

---

[2]This section is adapted from Tim K. Sehnert (quality engineering manager at Tennant Company), "Tennant Company's Supplier Quality Improvement Emphasis," unpublished paper, September 1984. Used by permission.

keting, to come to Tennant for a full day of discussions on quality improvement.

The suppliers accepted the invitations: About one supplier per month attended throughout 1981. In the meetings, Tennant's people surprised some of the suppliers by admitting to errors in communicating requirements and specifications and in using materials wrongly. The suppliers' top executive was asked to select an improvement goal to commit to within two or three weeks and to name a single person to serve as quality coordinator with Tennant's quality engineering people. All suppliers agreed to those requests, and in most cases problems with supplier-provided materials dropped, sometimes sharply.

A few other features of Tennant's supplier quality emphasis are:

1. *Supplier reduction so that more time can be spent with fewer suppliers.* The number of suppliers was cut 20 percent between 1981 and 1983.
2. *A "supplier corrective action request" document and procedure.* The documents provide an orderly way for Tennant to communicate requests to suppliers. Tennant people enter the requests into a personal computer, which signals when a response from the supplier is overdue.
3. *Supplier qualification.* Tennant's purchasing and quality engineering departments classify suppliers as qualified, conditionally qualified, or unqualified.
4. *Materials qualification.* Tennant's purchasing and quality engineering departments qualify a supplier's material or process capability.
5. *Data analysis and reporting.* In 1982 Tennant implemented a personal computer system for analyzing and reporting purchased-part nonconformances. A year later the system was processing about 300 records a month.
6. *Quality cost estimates.* Supplier "soft" costs of quality—those other than direct labor, overhead, and scrap—are estimated each year following guidelines supplied by the finance department.
7. *A supplier corrective action team.* Tennant's purchasing manager, quality engineering manager, two quality assurance technicians, and a design engineer meet weekly to make disposition of nonconforming parts, and, more importantly, to take action to ensure that the problem doesn't happen again.

Among the positive results of the supplier quality emphasis are the following:

1. Hydraulic leaks, identified as a major problem in 1979, dropped from two per unit in 1979 to two-tenths per unit in 1984. (The average unit has about 150 hydraulic joints that could leak.) Key actions taken to achieve the improvements include reducing from sixteen suppliers of fittings and hoses to two. Those two suppliers have provided expertise for development of a training course for Tennant assembly people on prevention of hydraulic leaks. One supplier contributed a better way to tighten hydraulic joints, and the suppliers also offered suggestions for Tennant designers to cut the chances of leaks, including some ideas that cut Tennant's product cost.

2. The percentage of purchased parts rejected in incoming inspection dropped from about 7 percent in 1980–81 to 2.9 percent in 1984, about a 60 percent reduction.

3. Beginning in 1983, defective purchased parts found in final assembly were measured as a percentage of standard hours of final assembly and test time. Between 1983 and 1984 the improvement in this measure was 40 percent.

4. The purchased-part cost of quality (hard costs) were reduced 22 percent between 1982 and 1983 (no figures available for 1984).

5. The "cost of quality" recovered from suppliers improved from 7–8 percent in 1981–82 to 33.4 percent in 1984. Those are costs that Tennant bills to suppliers for bad materials. The main reason for the improved cost recovery is the computer data base that tracks purchased-part nonconformances.

*Question 10.* Is the Supplier Quality Emphasis well conceived? For example, does it place top priority on the truly vital aspects of supplier relations?

*Question 11.* Tennant's quality campaign began a bit earlier, and training for it, as well as program development, were apart from its JIT production campaign. This creates the possibility for "turf" disputes between champions of quality and champions of JIT. Would you expect those disputes to be minor or serious? Brief or long-lasting? (In your answer consider whether the quality emphasis should have paved the way or presented obstacles to an effective JIT effort. Also consider whether the JIT effort should have stimulated or hampered the rate of quality improvement?)

## Computer Systems

The computer based reporting and accounting system is geared to job-lot production—separate work orders, weekly time buckets, collection of costs against the work orders, and so forth. Some of that system does not fit well with the greatly reduced fabrication and assembly throughput times. For example, in the 432 scrubber area, the system calls for each scrubber to be treated as a separate work order—for scheduling, labor and materials reporting, and so forth. Shop recorders are used so that assemblers can clock in and out on each unit produced.

Now, under JIT, there are thoughts about simplifying the reporting and accounting—for example, a conversion from job-order to process accounting.

*Question 12.* What is process accounting? How would it probably work for the 432 scrubber, and what advantages would it offer?

# 21

# Goodstone Tire Company: Creating Responsibility Centers

*Case topics:*

Shrinking markets
Size of loads in material
   handling
Flow racks
Supplier delivery of
   nonstandard materials

Merging processes
Eliminating AS/RSes
Cellular manufacturing
Number of cells
Automated handling vs. cells

The Goodstone Tire Company had been hammered by foreign competition—especially Bridgestone of Japan—in the late 1970s and early 1980s. Two inefficient Goodstone plants had been shuttered, and the threat of more plant closings had served as the catalyst to bring management and locals of the United Rubber Workers (URW) together after years of being at each other's throats. The cooperation led to cost reductions and better quality. By 1984 Goodstone had elevated itself to the brink of profitability.

---

The source information for the case is drawn from several real tire plants.

While there were some feelings of relief, there was not much genuine optimism, because all tire companies were basking in surging sales to the booming auto industry. The next general downturn could push Goodstone into another downward slide. Goodstone needed further cost-cutting; the large raw material and in-process inventories in all of Goodstone's tire plants were a natural target.

## South Dakota Plant

Instead of looking at Goodstone as a whole, we shall examine just one of its typical facilities, the South Dakota (SD) plant. The inventory situation at SD had been a target for improvement for more than a year. Martha Smith, materials manager, and her staff had been under the gun to figure out ways to cut inventories. They had achieved some encouraging results: On-hand raw material, which had averaged eighteen days, was cut to thirteen days six months later; work-in-process (WIP) inventory had been cut from twelve days to eight days in the same time period. For about the last six months, however, progress had essentially come to a halt.

Like the other tire makers and like other Goodstone plants, the South Dakota plant is laid out by process and has large inventories of partially built tires between processes. SD is currently producing 22,000 steel-belted radial tires a day in about fifteen different grades and sizes in a 1.3-million-square-foot single building.

Because of the boom in auto sales, SD had just gone to a three-shift, seven-day-a-week schedule (from a five-day schedule) in many of its production departments. There were protests from the URW, but the union ended up agreeing to the extended work week.

Factory employees are on the measured day work (MDW) pay system, except for the operators of first- and third-stage tire-building machines, who are on piece incentive pay. SD's radial tire-building operation, typical of the industry, proceeds as follows.

### Body Ply and Tread

The basic raw material for a tire is bales of natural rubber and some synthetic as well. Fork trucks bring the bales from the raw material stockroom to the first production process, which is mixing baled rubber with other ingredients. SD uses two banbury mixers, one very large and one small.

There are two mix cycles. The first, in the large banbury, mixes the bales with carbon-black oil and pigments to produce a "master batch." Each batch is a weighed amount—perhaps ten bales plus part of another bale, which the operator slices off using a bale-splitter. The operator also weighs the pigments and tosses the weighed bags of pigment into the banbury. Batches come out about every two minutes. Different chemical compounds are mixed for different uses, mainly ply and tread. The master batch comes out in sheets, which are piled on pallets.

After cool-down and aging, fork trucks take the stacked sheets of master batch to the second banbury. The second cycle mixes the "final batch," which includes sulphur and accelerators. Final batch material that is not used right away or is rejected for quality reasons at a later process is called "remill." It gets thrown into the banbury to be remixed. (Remill is also known as TMA: to be milled again.)

Final batch emerges pressed into wide sheets. The sheets flow into festoon-coolers, where the rubber is fan-cooled so that it is not sticky and does not vulcanize too fast. SD has two festoon-coolers, each 180 feet long. The cooled sheet rubber is layered back and forth onto wigwag loaders. The layers stack up about 6 feet high on the loaders.

Fork trucks move the wigwag loads of sheet to warming mills and then feed mills, which mill the sheets down to the desired thickness. One kind of compound from the feed mills diverts to calenders, which produce fabric-reinforced body ply. Another compound goes through a tread-tuber to form the tread.

The tread-tuber weighs out lengths of sheet tread, cools it, and cuts it to length. Different tire sizes require different sizes of sheet tread, and typically there are twelve size changes per shift. Each size change requires a die change taking about four minutes. The lengths of sheet tread go onto a special type of forkliftable rack called a tread booker, where the sheet tread is stacked like pages in a book. Typically there are fifty to sixty "pages" on one of the tread bookers.

---

*Question 1.* What changes in material handling (from raw bales though the tread-booker stages) would be consistent with JIT concepts?

---

The fabric-reinforced body ply is made on SD's inverted "L" four-roll calender. (One mill roll of fabric yields four calender rolls.) Goodstone is currently using Kevlar, a DuPont fabric, as the reinforcing material. Rolls of Kevlar fabric and rubber sheets feed the calenders, which heat-press them together under tension. The product goes back onto rolls interleaved with a reusable liner. The schedule for a calender might call for twenty rolls of one size, then four of another, then ten of another, and so forth.

Calendered rolls must age twelve hours (to reduce "tack") before they can be cut and processed further. At SD, fork trucks take the calendered rolls to an automatic storage/retrieval system (AS/RS), where the rolls are automatically put away in random stock locations for the twelve-hour age cycle. No pallets are necessary, because a shaft protrudes from the center of each side of the large roll. The shaft straddles the forks during fork truck travel and then rests on a cradle in the AS/RS space. The AS/RS has storage spaces for 300 rolls.

Periodically the stock-cutting supervisor at the next process calls a fork truck to fetch a few rolls of a certain size from the AS/RS. The fork truck driver sets the rolls on stands. Then an operator uses a crane to position a roll on one of SD's nine bobtail bias cutters. There is a swivel crane mounted at each of the nine cutters. The cutter splices the calendered material and then cuts it to length at an angle (on the bias) of 35–45 degrees. It takes five to ten minutes to unload/load a roll, and typically there are ten to twelve roll changes per day for each bias cutter. One setup step is to change the bias angle.

Martha Smith, the materials manager, had once been an ardent fan of AS/RSes. Now she was saying, "I'd sure like to get rid of the beast. Maybe flow racks would work."

---

*Question 2.* How could inventories and lead times be reduced for the calendering, aging, and stock cutting stages of manufacture? Could flow racks (Smith's suggestion) work? Explain.

---

Jack Arno, plant manager at SD, has been trying to get corporate approval to buy two Fisher cutters, which cost roughly $150,000 each. The Fisher cutter requires a two-person crew for a setup and takes an hour or more for setup, but it runs much faster than the present cutters.

---

*Question 3.* Should corporate approve the purchase of the Fisher cutters? Explain.

---

## Creels to Bead Hoops

Since the radial tire is to be steel-belted, rubber-coated steel wire is produced at the same time as tread and body ply are made. Purchased creels (spools) of steel wire, the raw material, weighing 40–80 pounds per creel, are mounted on spindles in the creel room; the wire strands are run through eyelets to an organizer roll. Threading the eyelets averages twenty minutes and is done about five times per shift.

Getting the spools of wire ready to be fed into the eyelets takes a good deal longer. At SD there are spindles for about 600 spools. A full crew of eight people takes three to four hours to load the spools onto the spindles and splice to previous spools; it takes longer than that on the occasions when fewer people are on hand. The setup person loads a spool onto a cart, rolls the cart to the spindle, and splices and mounts the spool. Splicing, using a splicer on the cart, takes about twenty minutes.

Uriah Washington, creel-room supervisor, has a head full of ideas for improving his operation. Some of Washington's ideas call for better performance from the wire suppliers. Two of SD's four suppliers deliver spools of varying length. If lengths could be standardized at, say, 11,000 yards, spools would not be running out at different times; with same-length spools, Washington estimates that an hour of splicing time could be cut from the setup time. Also, Washington admits, "We sometimes run out of material from one supplier and have to splice to wire from a different supplier—which technically is not allowed by our specs."

Another problem is that one of the suppliers—one that at least delivers in standard lengths—ships the reels stacked horizontally on pallets. The operator has to pick up each one and turn it vertically on the cart in order to slide it onto a spindle in the wire room. Washington would like to see the supplier stack the spools vertically on the pallets.

---

*Question 4.* What should be done about these problems with the raw material, and how would the operation be improved by resolving the problems?

---

After the wires are organized in a sheet form, they are coated with rubber in a wire calender. The diameter of the coated wire varies from 1 1/2 to 1 7/8 inches; the extruder is undergoing diameter changes about one-fourth of the time, and each change takes twenty minutes. The coated wire feeds into SD's dual wire windup unit. Next, the coated wire is removed from the calender and goes to a cutter. The cut wire is put into metal spool storage containers, or "bead hoops."

## Tire-Building

The radial tire is built from three main components: fabric-reinforced body ply, steel bead hoops, and tread. The materials become a finished tire by going through four steps: first-stage tire-building, third-stage tire-building, press-cure, and final finish (Goodstone does not send its radial tires through the old second-stage process).

SD has seventy-six first-stage tire-building machines, all located in one department. The basic process is bead and ply assembly. Fork truck drivers bring pallets of body ply and pallets of bead hoops. Typically there will be about two shifts' worth of bead stock—roughly 1,200 beads—in a rack before each first-stage machine. There are a few other purchased materials, such as the inner liner and inner-liner splice gum. The machine layers bead hoops between body-ply sheets under pressure and heat, and the result is a tire carcass shaped like a flattish cylinder. There is one operator for each machine, and each operator is able to build in the range of 200 to 250 units a shift. Different sizes are made on each machine, so the operator must spend time—usually an hour and a half to two hours—on machine setup one to three times per shift.

The carcasses go into a rack between the first- and third-stage machines in the tire room. There usually are about 12,000 tires in the rack; that is about one-half day's supply.

There are about forty third-stage machines, and their job is to produce "green" (uncured) tires. It used to take about four hours to set up to run a different tire size, but recently some of SD's third-stage machines had been modified to cut setup time in half.

Fork truck drivers deliver tread and carcasses to the third-stage machines. The racks hold eight tires each, four to a side, and the racks rotate on a stand so that the machine operator does not have to walk around to the other side. The operator applies a dope solution to the inside of the carcass so that it will not stick to the drum, then loads the carcass and tread in the machine. The machine applies heat and pressure, expanding the carcass and stitching down the tread. An operator can produce more than 400 green tires per shift. The green tires go into racks to await curing; typically there are 10,000–12,000 green tires in the racks.

The South Dakota plant has more than 200 press-cure machines each of which cures two tires at a time. Uncured tires go in on the front side and go out the back side, so two more uncured tires are mounted and ready for insertion as pressing/curing is in progress. It takes a whole shift for a crew to set up the machines for a different tire size, which involves inserting two molds. Many of the machines are old and in bad condition; there are always quite a few that are down for repairs. The cure cycle for two tires averages just over fifteen minutes. Cured tires are postinflated at 25 pounds as a test.

Final finish includes inspecting, repairing, checking for uniformity, trimming off vents, and grinding. About two dozen classifiers handle those tasks in a facility comprising a system of conveyors and grading machines—"tire uniformity optimizers" that can grind off excess tread. The classifiers sort the tires by quality grades and put them on a conveyor that carries them to the sort line. Samples are occasionally drawn and taken to X-ray. If bad ones are found, large quantities of tires from the same batch are pulled from the warehouse and become "frozen inventory."

The sort line is a perpetual conveyor. It circulates a mixture of tire types and sizes, and people on the line select the tires needed to fill orders from the warehouse. Those selected are put onto a floor-chain-driven cart and taken to the warehouse.

## Inventory and Handling

Jack Arno was discussing the inventory problem with Martha Smith and Fred Ferrin, an engineer, over coffee at afternoon break. "We are one of the most backward industries in material handling," Smith volunteered. Arno could not help but agree. Ferrin had another view. He had been at a conference and heard a presentation by two managers from a Firestone plant in Canada. The Canadians told about a pilot project to combine first-and third-stage machines into cells, which cut most of the inventory of carcasses between the two machine stages.

Arno and Smith immediately saw the possibilities. One idea led to another, and the coffee break discussion consumed the rest of the shift and on into the evening. The three spent the bulk of their time discussing various cell arrangements, including one proposal to put first-stage, third-stage, press-cure, and final finish stations into a cell.

> *Question 5.* Sketch an idealized JIT cell that would include all four processes. Show numbers of each type of work station that would yield good machine balance. On your sketch specify the units of WIP inventory that would be likely at each work station in the cell. Compare the present ratio of pieces (tires) to work stations with the ratio in your proposed plan. (Some WIP data are given: you may guess at the figures where not given.) What other benefits, besides WIP reduction, would be gained?

The other proposals seriously discussed by Arno, Smith, and Ferrin are:

- Other cell arrangements:
  — First- and third-stage only, as at Firestone, Canada
  — First- and third-stage, plus press-cure
- No cells (no machines moved); instead, automate the handling by one of the following means:
  — Overhead and floor-chain conveyor
  — Belt conveyor
  — Automatic guided vehicle (AGV) systems.

> *Question 6.* If one of the plans for cells is adopted, how many cells should there be? That is, should all machines be immediately moved into cells, or only some of them? Suggest in general a time-phased plan for conversion to cells.
>
> *Question 7.* What's best, cells or automated handling? Explain.

# 22

# Land and Sky
# Waterbed Company

*Case topics:*

Self-discovery of JIT

Make-to order JIT

Off-line subassembly

Pay for knowledge/multifunctional employees

Pay incentive for quality

Frequency of deliveries from key suppliers

Evolving from a small to a large business

As of October 1982, Land and Sky Waterbed Company of Lincoln, Nebraska, was the fourth largest waterbed company in the United States and the largest in the Midwest. Land and Sky (L&S) was founded in 1972 by two brothers, Ron and Lynn Larson. The brothers remain as co-owner/managers. One of the brothers is responsible for research and development. (Outside R&D consultants are called upon for assistance sometimes.)

The total work force, including office staff, is sixty-seven. The oldest employee is the vice president, Jim Wood, a psychology graduate in his mid-thirties. Wood has played a major role in developing the scheduling, inventory, quality, and employee payment system at L&S.

## The Product Line

L&S produces two lines of waterbed mattresses and liners in standard sizes (king, queen, double, super single, and twin). L&S also manufactures special made-to-order mattresses for other frame manufacturers. The Land and Sky label goes on the higher-quality gold and bronze bed sold exclusively to franchised dealers. L&S produces another brand called the Daymaker. It is sold without advertising as a "commodity" product. The Daymaker is available to any dealer.

There is a trade group for the waterbed industry, but the group has not yet achieved consensus on standard dimensions for king size, queen size, and so forth for the soft-sided foam frame. Therefore, more than sixty sizes must be built to order. Also, some customers make beds to their own dimensions before checking to see what mattress sizes they can readily obtain. L&S will accept special orders for such unusual sizes, but the price will be high and the order will take thirty days to be filled.

L&S also makes two kinds of soft-sided frames, which make a waterbed look like a conventional bed with box spring and ordinary mattress ("a waterbed that appeals to older people," according to Jim Wood). One kind is made of rigid foam and is cheap and easy to make. The other kind, L&S's own unique design, has a plastic rim built in and is called Naturalizer 2000; the rim keeps the foam from breaking down.

## Competitive Climate

Since waterbed manufacturing is not highly technical and is quite labor-intensive, competitors spring up all over. Low-wage countries like Taiwan are becoming tough competitors.

L&S markets its product line throughout the United States and Canada. An Australian producer makes to L&S's specifications under a licensing agreement. (Jim Wood now wishes that L&S had set up its own Australian subsidiary, rather than licensing the Australian manufacturer.) The European market for waterbeds is still too small to bother with.

There are two main market outlets. The older outlet is the small waterbed retailer, many of whom tend to be less experienced in the ways of the business world and therefore unstable. Recently waterbeds have become popular enough for a second major market outlet to emerge: old-line furniture stores. The two market types place very different demands on the waterbed manufacturer. The small waterbed retailer wants "instant" delivery response. The old-line furniture store plans orders carefully in advance and does not expect delivery right away, but does drive a hard bargain on price. L&S has developed a quick-response production system aimed at filling orders faster than the competition. Most orders can be shipped within forty-eight hours, and same-day production and shipment is possible (but not cost effectively). With the emergence of price-conscious furniture stores as a second major market, L&S has instituted procedures that tightly control material storage costs, labor costs, and costs of scrap and defects.

One complicating factor is that a few retailers are unsophisticated in their ordering. For example, one retailer phoned in a large order specifying the quantity but not which models he wanted. When asked which models, he said, "Just send about what I have ordered before." That was not of much help, because prior orders had come in at different times for different models.

Some inventory of finished waterbeds is kept in bonded public warehouses in different regions of the country so orders in those regions may be filled quickly.

## The Plant

L&S is in an industrial park, housed in three noncustom metal buildings arranged in a U-shaped configuration. Building 1—at one leg of the U—houses the sales and administrative offices with a shipping and receiving warehouse in the back. Building 2, forming the bottom of the U, is the main manufacturing and quality-check area. Building 3—the other leg of the U—is for fiber baffle production and assembly, liner production, and injection-molding and assembly of soft-sided frames. A parking lot in the center of the U is also used for vinyl storage.

## Assembly

### Producing the Waterbed

*Vinyl processes.* The waterbed begins as a roll of vinyl. It is cut to size by hand. (A $20,000 cutting machine had been used, but it broke down often and also yielded too much scrap.) The next steps are to install valves and corner seam panels using special machines. Then the vinyl sheets go to machines that fuse the corners together by high-frequency radio waves. Last, the ends and sides are sealed (see Exhibit 22–1).

*Baffle installation.* High-quality waterbeds contain a fiber baffle that keeps the water from "making waves" when in use. Research and development at L&S has come up with a baffle made of polyurethane fiber that reduces the "wave time" from twenty-five to three seconds. L&S considers fusing of the side and end seams on the mattress especially important, and the best operators are assigned that operation. One outside observer watching the job estimated that the two operators were working at about 140 percent of normal pace.

## Responsiveness

Total throughput time for these steps in making the waterbed is thirty-five minutes. The daily output is about 450 waterbed units.

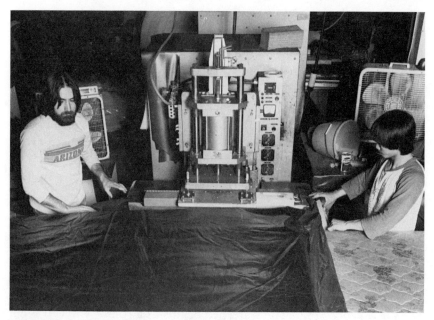

**Exhibit 22–1.** Sealing Ends and Sides

One way that L&S holds down production lead time is by performing early stages of manufacture—such as cutting the vinyl, installing valves, and fusing corners—before knowing exactly what the model mix is. Later the same day, late-arriving orders are totaled by product type, and final model-mix instructions go out to the shop floor. Some of the options that are determined "at the last minute" are (1) the number that are to be top-of-the line beds with fiber baffles and (2) the number that are to have the L&S label or the Daymaker commodity label.

---

*Question 1.* In what sense do the assembly operations sound like just-in-time production? (No one at L&S had ever heard of JIT at the time of the case.) What JIT improvements do you suggest for assembly?

---

## Subassemblies and Accessories

Baffles (a subassembly) and frames and liners (accessories) are scheduled to avoid stockouts. The items are made as follows:

*Fiber baffles.* Baffles are machine-cut—on the cutting machine originally bought for $20,000 to cut vinyl. Then holes are drilled around the edges of a stack of fiber sheets, and vinyl ties are threaded through the holes to hold the stack together for storage and transport (the idea for vinyl ties was developed after glue and plastic hooks failed).

*Soft-sided frames.* Frames are injection-molded and assembled. L&S has patented a plastic rim insert, for which it spent $250,000 on research and development; the insert lends support and adds life to the foam in the frame.

*Cardboard-reinforced bottom liner.* The bottom liners were developed by L&S to make it faster and easier for the customer to set up the waterbed (it cuts setup time by about 20 percent). The liners have been on the market for about seven months. Retailers love this feature, because the liner is reusable—a good sales point; the bottom liners sell for $16 to $20 at retail.

---

*Question 2.* What could be done about subassembly and accessories manufacture to mold

---

them into more of a JIT relationship with their "customers" (assembly and final pack and ship)?

---

## Pay System

In July 1982, L&S converted from a straight hourly pay plan to a piece-rate system having the following features:

*Base piece rate.* The base piece rate depends on the assigned job, e.g., $0.20 per bed.

*Achievement raise.* An operator gets a 5 percent bonus on top of base rate for each additional machine that the operator learns to run. A few operators have learned to run ten or twelve machines and therefore get 50–60 percent more than the base piece rate. The bonus buys flexibility for the company. Typically an operator who can run just two or three machines averages $5–$7 per hour, while one who can run twelve machines might earn $9–$11 per hour. Jim Wood stated that other companies send people home when a machine is down; here "we put them on another machine."

*Quality bonus.* Operators get a bonus of 25 percent of total pay per period for zero errors. The bonus decreases for each error found: one or two errors, 20 percent; three errors, 15 percent; four errors, 10 percent; five errors, 5 percent; and six or more errors, 0 percent. The owners were initially dubious about the 25 percent bonus (Jim Wood's idea). Previously the bonus was 15 percent. Their feeling was, "Why pay a large bonus for what the employees are supposed to do anyway?" But they agreed to give the plan a try and were very pleased with the results. The error rate had been about 5 percent (five out of 100 beds). It was down to about 0.5 percent by October. Some of the better operators were achieving zero error rates.

*Error penalty.* The operator has to pay a penalty of $0.65 for every error discovered by quality control inspectors. Errors are easily traced back to the operator responsible, because each operator has an employee number that is attached to the bed when the operator is working on it. If the operator notifies quality control of an error by marking it, then the penalty is only $0.25. Plans are in motion to make the penalty zero for an admitted error; that way there will be no temptation to try to sneak one by the inspector. Inspection is much more efficient and valid when operators mark their own errors.

Quality control does the bookkeeping for the entire piece-rate and quality incentive system. QC people record daily production and quality performance data for each employee. All information is maintained on the computer.

## Labor Policies

Waterbeds are a somewhat seasonal product, which makes staffing difficult. The peak seasons are March–April–May and August–September–October. L&S will not build inventory just to keep operators busy. Competition from other waterbed manufacturers is fierce, especially the Taiwanese manufacturers of liners. A low-inventory policy is a competitive necessity. Therefore, in the slack season operators are laid off. Layoffs are strictly by productivity, not seniority.

Since bed materials are too large for one person to handle easily, operators usually work in pairs; pairings are generally by comparable skill levels. If one operator is tardy or absent, the partner must keep busy on lower-pay work and forgo the chance for piece-rate bonuses—a sacrifice that the opeator is sure to complain about. Therefore, policies on absenteeism and tardiness are rigid: Absenteeism usually means automatic termination.

> *Question 3.* In what ways does the pay and labor system stand in the way of, or further, JIT aims?

## Quality Control and Warranties

Quality control visually inspects each bed. Inspectors check surfaces for blemishes, check seams, check valves, and so forth. Once in a while the inspector will blow up a bed with air like a balloon in a more thorough leak check. Water is not used to test beds, because it leaves a residual odor.

If no blemishes or defects are found, L&S ships the bed to the retailer with a five-year warranty. Beds with a flaw are sold as blems at a lower cost and with a three-year warranty.

> *Question 4.* Critique the L&S approach to quality control.

## Purchasing and Inventory Control

In the waterbed business, material costs are a good deal higher than payroll costs. Thus materials are tightly controlled.

There are rather few manufacturers of vinyl, a key raw material, and vinyl suppliers require a thirty-day lead time. Vinyl suppliers ship to L&S by a regular purchase-order schedule, and any schedule changes require about thirty to sixty days' advance notice. Therefore demand forecasting is important for L&S. One of the owners does the forecasting, which is based on seasonal factors and past sales.

Other materials are reordered by a visual reorder-point method: When stock looks low based on the projected manufacturing schedule, an order is placed. The safety stock is typically about two and a half days' supply.

Average raw material inventory is typically two to three weeks' worth. In other words, inventory turns twenty times a year or more. That is partly a matter of necessity. Fiber must be stored indoors, but since it is bulky and there simply is not space to store more, it is maintained at a two-and-a-half-day inventory level. Fiber orders are delivered twice a week in semitrailer loads of 8,000 pounds.

The main purchased material is vinyl in large rolls. Since vinyl is waterproof and may be stored cheaply outdoors, L&S orders larger lots of vinyl than it does for other materials. Vinyl is received about three times a month, 40,000 pounds at a time.

Purchasing and traffic (shipping) are under the management of a single individual, Mr. Bergman. Purchasing buys from at least two sources, which provides protection in case one supplier should shut down—a serious matter, since L&S's inventories are kept so low. On occasion, purchased parts have been delayed to the point where vinyl rolls are gone; then the operators do what they can with scrap materials, after which they perform other duties or shut down and go home.

Finished goods are stored in the warehouse for a short time prior to loading onto an outbound truck.

A complete physical inventory of finished goods and raw materials is taken every four weeks.

---

*Question 5.* What are some ways to improve purchasing procedures?

*Question 6.* How can L&S protect itself from the miseries that plague most Western companies as they grow large?

---

# 23

# Lincoln Electric Company

*Case topics:*

| | |
|---|---|
| Flow-through production | Flat organization structure |
| Factory-within-a-factory | Pay for performance |
| Multimachine operation | Worker flexibility |
| Competitive strategies | Strong supervision |
| Employee benefits, bonuses, | Blended staff support |
| and piecework pay | Technical competence |

The Lincoln Electric Company is the world's largest manufacturer of welding machines and electrodes. Lincoln employs 2,400 workers in two U.S. factories near Cleveland and about 600 in three factories in other countries. That does not include the field sales force of more than 200 persons.

The main plant is in Euclid, Ohio, a suburb on Cleveland's east side. The layout of the plant is shown in Exhibit 23–1. There are no warehouses. Materials flow from the half-mile-long dock on the north side of the plant through the production lines to a very limited storage and loading area on the south. Materials used at each work station are stored as close as possible to the work station.

Condensed and adapted by Richard J. Schonberger from A. D. Sharplin's "Case 20: Lincoln Electric Company," in George A. Steiner and John B. Miner, *Management Policy and Strategy: Text, Readings, and Cases* (New York: Macmillan, 1982), 2d ed., pp. 958–80. Used with permission of Arthur Sharplin, Sharplin Associates, Monroe, LA.

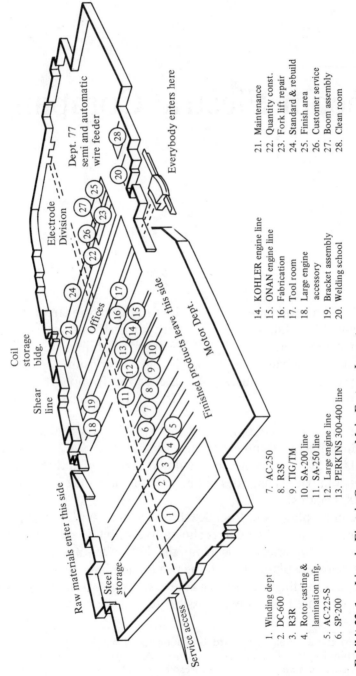

Raw materials enter this side

Steel storage

Service access

Shear line

Coil storage bldg.

Offices

Finished products leave this side

Electrode Division

Motor Dept.

Dept. 77 semi and automatic wire feeder

Everybody enters here

1. Winding dept
2. DC-600
3. R3R
4. Rotor casting & lamination mfg.
5. AC-225-S
6. SP-200
7. AC-250
8. R3S
9. TIG/TM
10. SA-200 line
11. SA-250 line
12. Large engine line
13. PERKINS 300-400 line
14. KOHLER engine line
15. ONAN engine line
16. Fabrication
17. Tool room
18. Large engine accessory
19. Bracket assembly
20. Welding school
21. Maintenance
22. Quantity const.
23. Fork lift repair
24. Standard & rebuild
25. Finish area
26. Customer service
27. Boom assembly
28. Clean room

**Exhibit 23–1.** Lincoln Electric Company Main Factory Layout

The new plant, just opened in Mentor, Ohio, houses some of the electrode production operations, which were moved from the main plant. The main plant is currently being enlarged by 100,000 square feet, and several innovative changes are being made in the manufacturing layout.

## Production and Market Information

The company's main products are electric welding machines and metal electrodes used in arc welding. Lincoln also produces electric motors ranging from 1 to 200 horsepower. Motors constitute about 8 to 10 percent of total sales.

The electric welding machines consist of a transformer or motor and generator arrangement powered by commercial electricity or by an internal combustion engine and generator. They are designed to produce from 130 to more than 1,000 amperes of current.

Welding electrodes are of two basic types: (1) coated "stick" electrodes, usually 14 inches long and smaller than a pencil in diameter, which are packaged in 6- to 50-pound boxes, and (2) coiled wire, ranging in diameter from 0.035 to 0.219 inch. The wire is designed to be fed continuously to the welding arc through a "gun" held by the operator or positioned by automatic positioning equipment. The wire is packaged in coils, reels, and drums weighing from 14 to 1,000 pounds.

### Manufacturing Processes

Electrode manufacturing is highly capital-intensive. Metal rods bought from steel producers are drawn or extruded down to smaller diameters. Then they are cut to length and coated with pressed-powder "flex" for stick electrodes or plated with copper (for conductivity) and spun into coils or spools for wire. Some of Lincoln's wire, called Innershield, is hollow and filled with a material similar to that used to coat stick electrodes. Lincoln is highly secretive about its electrode production processes.

Lincoln produces welding machines and electric motors on a series of assembly lines. It purchases gasoline and diesel engines partially assembled, but it makes practically all other components from basic industrial products, for example, steel bars and sheets and bare copper conductor wire.

Lincoln makes individual components, such as gasoline tanks for engine-driven welders and steel shafts for motors and generators, in numerous small "factories with a factory." For example, one operator uses five large machines, all running continuously, to make the shaft for a certain generator out of a raw steel bar. A saw cuts the bar to length, a digital lathe machines different sections to varying diameters, a special milling machine cuts a slot for a keyway, and so forth, until a finished shaft is produced.

The operator moves the shafts from machine to machine and makes necessary adjustments. Another operator punches, shapes, and paints sheet metal cowling parts. One assembles steel laminations on a rotor shaft, then winds, insulates, and tests the rotors. Crane operators move finished components to nearby assembly lines.

---

*Question 1.* Is the plant layout good? Any suggestions for improving it?

---

## Market Information

Although advances in welding technology have been frequent, arc-welding products, in the main, have hardly changed over the last thirty years. The most popular Lincoln electrode, the Fleetweld 5P, has been virtually the same since the 1930s. The most popular engine-driven welder in the world for at least three decades has been the Lincoln SA–200, a gray-painted assembly that includes a four-cylinder Continental "Red Seal" engine and a 200-ampere direct-current generator with two current-control knobs. A 1980 model SA–200 even weighs almost the same as the 1950 model, and it certainly is little changed in appearance. It also seems likely that changes in the machines and techniques used in arc welding will be evolutionary rather than revolutionary.

Lincoln and its competitors now market a wide range of general-purpose and specialty electrodes for welding mild steel, aluminum, cast iron, and stainless and special steels. Most of those electrodes are designed to meet the standards of the American Welding Society, a trade association. They are thus about the same as to size and composition from one manufacturer to any other. Every electrode manufacturer has a few unique products, but they typically constitute only a small percentage of total sales.

Lincoln's research and development expenditures have recently been less than 0.2 percent of sales. There is evidence that others spend several times as much as a percentage of sales.

Lincoln's share of the market has been between 30 and 40 percent for many years, and the welding products market has grown somewhat faster than industry in general. The market is highly price-competitive. Variations in prices of standard products normally amount to only 1 or 2 percent. Lincoln's products are sold directly by its engineering-oriented sales force and indirectly through its distributor organization. Advertising expenditures amount to less than 0.25 percent of sales, one third as much as a leading Lincoln competitor with whom the casewriter checked.

---

*Question 2.* What do you think of Lincoln's competitive strategies?

---

In order to understand how Lincoln achieved its position of strength in its markets, we must look briefly at the company's beginnings and historical roots.

## A Historical Sketch

In 1895 John C. Lincoln, after being "frozen out" of the depression-ravaged Elliott-Lincoln Company, a maker of electric motors he himself had designed, took out his second patent and began to manufacture his improved motor. He opened his new business, then unincorporated, with $200 he had earned redesigning a motor for young Herbert Henry Dow, who later founded the Dow Chemical Company.

Started during an economic depression and badly damaged by a fire after only one year in business, Lincoln's company grew but hardly prospered through its first quarter-century. In 1906 Lincoln incorporated his company and moved from his one-room, fourth-floor factory to a new three-story building he erected in East Cleveland. In his new factory he expanded his work force to thirty, and sales grew to more than $50,000 a year. John Lincoln was more an

185

engineer and inventor than he was a manager, though, and it was to be left to another Lincoln to manage the company through its years of success.

James F. Lincoln, John's younger brother, joined the fledgling company in 1907, after a bout with typhoid forced him to leave Ohio State University in his senior year. In 1914, with the company still small and in poor financial condition, he became the active head of the firm, with the titles of general manager and vice president. John Lincoln remained president of the company for some years but became more involved in other business ventures and in his work as an inventor.

One of James Lincoln's early actions as head of the firm was to ask the employees to elect representatives to a committee that would advise him on company operations. The first year the advisory board was in existence, working hours were reduced from the fifty-five per week then standard to fifty hours a week. In 1915, the company gave each employee a paid-up life insurance policy. A welding school, which continues today, was begun in 1917. In 1918, an employee bonus plan was attempted. It was not continued, but the idea would resurface and become the backbone of the Lincoln management system.

The Lincoln Electric Employees' Association was formed in 1919 to provide health benefits and social activities. The organization continues today and has assumed several more functions over the years. By 1923, a piecework pay system was in effect, employees got two-week paid vacations each year, and wages were adjusted for changes in the consumer price index. Approximately 30 percent of Lincoln's stock was set aside for key employees in 1914, when James F. Lincoln became general manager, and a stock purchase plan for all employees was begun in 1925.

The board of directors voted to start a suggestion system in 1929. The program is still in effect, but cash awards, a part of the early program, were discontinued several years ago. Now suggestions are acknowledged by additional "points," which affect year-end bonuses.

In 1934 the advisory board proposed the now legendary Lincoln bonus plan, which James Lincoln accepted on a trial basis. The first annual bonus amounted to about 25 percent of wages. There has been a bonus every year since then.

By 1944, Lincoln employees enjoyed a pension plan, a policy of promotion from within, and continuous employment. Base pay rates were determined by formal job evaluation, and a merit rating system was in effect.

Lincoln has had a medical plan and a company-paid retirement program in effect for many years. A plant cafeteria, operated on a break-even basis, serves meals at about 60 percent of usual costs. An employee association, to which the company does not contribute, provides disability insurance and social and athletic activities. An employee stock ownership program, instituted about 1925, and regular stock purchases have resulted in employee ownership of about 50 percent of Lincoln's stock.

As to executive perquisites, there are none. Instead there are crowded, uncarpeted, austere offices, no executive washrooms or lunchrooms, and no reserved parking spaces. Even the company president pays for his own meals and eats in the cafeteria.

By the start of World War II, Lincoln Electric was the world's largest manufacturer of arc-welding products. Sales of about $4,000,000 in 1934 had grown to $24,000,000 by 1941. Output per employee more than doubled during the same period.

During the war, Lincoln Electric prospered as never before. Despite challenges to Lincoln's profitability by the Navy's Price Review Board and to the tax deductibility of employee bonuses by the Internal Revenue Service, the company increased its profits and paid huge bonuses.

Certainly since 1935 and probably for several years before that, Lincoln productivity has been well above the average for similar companies. Lincoln claims levels of productivity more than twice those for other manufacturers from 1945 onward. Lincoln's total inventory turnover, at between four and six turns per year, is also better than industry averages. (In 1982, average inventory was about $38 million, and cost of sales was $213 million, which yields a turnover of 5.6.)

James Lincoln died in 1965, and there was some concern that the Lincoln system would fall into disarray, profits would decline, and year-end bonuses might be discontinued. Quite the contrary: Fifteen years after Lincoln's death, the company appears stronger than ever. Each year since 1965 has seen higher profits and bonuses. Employee morale and productivity remain high; employee turnover is almost nonexistent except for retirements; and Lincoln's market share is stable.

## Company Philosophy

James Lincoln was the son of a Congregational minister, and Christian principles were at the center of his business philosophy. There is no indication that Lincoln attempted to evangelize his employees or customers—or the general public, for that matter. The current board chairman, Mr. Irrgang, and the president, Mr. Willis, do not even mention the Christian gospel in their recent speeches and interviews.

### Attitude Toward the Customer

James Lincoln saw the customer's needs above all else. "When any company has achieved success so that it is attractive as an investment," he wrote, "all money usually needed for expansion is supplied by the customer in retained earnings. It is obvious that the customer's interests, not the stockholder's, should come first."[1] In 1947 he said, "Care should be taken . . . not to rivet attention on profit. Between 'How much do I get?' and 'How do I make this better, cheaper, more useful?' the difference is fundamental and decisive."[2] Mr. Willis still ranks the customer as Lincoln's most important constituency.

Certainly Lincoln customers have fared well over the years. Lincoln prices for welding machines and welding electrodes are acknowledged to be the lowest in the market place. Lincoln quality consistently has been so high that Lincoln Fleetweld electrodes and Lincoln SA–200 welders have been the standard in the pipeline and refinery construction industry, where price was hardly a criterion, for decades. The cost of field failures for Lincoln products was an amazing 0.04 percent in 1979. A Lincoln distributor in Monroe, Louisiana, says that he has sold several hundred of the popular AC–225 welders and, though the machine is only warranted for one year, he has never handled a warranty claim.

[1]James F. Lincoln, *A New Approach to Industrial Economics* (The Devin-Adair Company, 1961), p. 119.
[2]"You Can't Tell What a Man Can Do—Until He Has the Chance," *Reader's Digest,* January 1947, pp. 93–95.

## Attitude Toward Stockholders

Stockholders are given last priority at Lincoln. This is a continuation of James Lincoln's philosophy: "The last group to be considered is the stockholders who own stock because they think it will be more profitable than investing money in any other way."[3] Concerning division of the largess produced by incentive management, Lincoln wrote: "The absentee stockholder also will get his share, even if undeserved, out of the greatly increased profit that the efficiency produces."[4]

## Attitude Toward Unionism

There has never been a serious effort to organize Lincoln employees. Although James Lincoln criticized the labor movement for "selfishly attempting to better its position at the expense of the people it must serve,"[5] he excused abuses of union power as "the natural reactions of human beings to the abuses to which management has subjected them."[6] Lincoln's view on the correct relationship between workers and managers is: "Labor and management are properly not warring camps; they are parts of one organization in which they must and should cooperate fully and happily."[7]

## Beliefs and Assumptions About Employees

If fulfilling customer needs is the desired goal of business, then employee performance and productivity are the means by which that goal can best be achieved. The Lincoln attitude toward employees is reflected in the following quotations:

> The greatest fear of the worker, which is the same as the greatest fear of the industrialist in operating a company, is lack of income. . . . The industrial manager is very conscious of his company's need of unin-

[3]Lincoln, *New Approach*, p. 38.
[4]*Ibid.*, p. 122.
[5]Ibid., p. 18.
[6]*Ibid.*, p. 76.
[7]*Ibid.*, p. 72.

terrupted income. He is completely oblivious, evidently, of the fact that the worker has the same need.[8]

If money is to be used as an incentive, the program must provide that what is paid to the worker is what he has earned. The earnings of each must be in accordance with accomplishment.[9]

Status is of great importance in all human relationships. The greatest incentive that money has, usually, is that it is a symbol of success. . . . The resulting status is the real incentive. . . . Money alone can be an incentive to the miser only.[10]

## Organization Structure

Lincoln has never had a formal organization chart. Managers throughout the company practice an open-door policy, and personnel are encouraged to take problems to the person most capable of resolving them. Perhaps because of the quality and enthusiasm of the Lincoln work force, routine supervision is almost nonexistent. A typical production foreman, for example, supervises as many as one hundred workers, a span of control that allows only infrequent worker–supervisor interaction.

Position titles and flows of authority do imply something of an organizational structure. For example, the vice president for sales and the vice president for electrode division report to the president, as do various staff assistants such as the personnel director and the director of purchasing. Using such implied structure, it appears that production workers have two or, at most, three levels of supervision between themselves and the president.

## Financial Management

James Lincoln felt strongly that financing for company growth should come from within the company—through initial cash invest-

[8]*Ibid.*, p. 36.
[9]*Ibid.*, p. 98.
[10]*Ibid.*, p. 92.

ment by the founders, retention of earnings, and stock purchases by those who work in the business.

Lincoln does not rely at all on borrowing, and debt is limited to current payables. Even the new $20,000,000 plant in Mentor, Ohio, was financed totally from earnings.

The pricing policy at Lincoln is succinctly stated by President Willis: "At all times price on the basis of cost and at all times keep pressure on our cost." The SA–200 Welder, Lincoln's largest-selling portable machine, decreased in price from 1958 through 1965. According to Dr. C. Jackson Grayson of the American Productivity Center, Lincoln's prices have increased only one-fifth as fast as the Consumer Price Index since 1934. As a result, Lincoln is the undisputed price leader for the products it manufactures. Not even the largest Japanese manufacturers, such as Nippon Steel for welding electrodes and Osaka Transformer for welding machines, have been able to penetrate the U.S. market.

## Managerial Performance

It is easy to believe that the reason for Lincoln's success is the excellent attitude of Lincoln employees and their willingness to work harder, faster, and more intelligently than other industrial workers. However, Mr. Sabo gives credit to Lincoln executives, who, he says, carry out the following policies:

1. Management has limited research, development, and manufacturing to a standard product line designed to meet the principal needs of the welding industry.
2. New products must be reviewed by manufacturing and all production costs verified before being approved by management.
3. Management challenges purchasing not only to procure materials at the lowest cost, but also to work closely with engineering and manufacturing to ensure that the latest innovations are implemented.
4. Manufacturing supervision and all personnel are held accountable for reduction of scrap, energy conservation, and maintenance of product quality.
5. Top management closely supervises production control, material handling, and methods engineering.

6. Material and finished goods control, accurate cost accounting, and attention to sales costs, credit and other financial areas have constantly reduced overhead and led to excellent profitability.
7. Management has made cost reduction a way of life at Lincoln and has established definite programs in many areas, including traffic and shipping, where tremendous savings can result.
8. Management has established a sales department that is technically trained to reduce customer welding costs. This, along with other real customer services, has eliminated nonessential frills and resulted in long-term benefits to all concerned.
9. Management has encouraged education, technical publishing, and long-range programs that have resulted in industry growth, thereby ensuring market potential for the Lincoln Electric Company.

---

*Question 3.* For each of these "management strengths," designate whether it is consistent or inconsistent with today's notions about world-class manufacturing? Explain your designations.

---

## Personnel Policies

Every job opening at Lincoln is advertised internally on company bulletin boards, and any employee can apply for any job so advertised. Lincoln hires externally only for entry-level positions. They select people for those jobs through personal interviews: there is no aptitude or psychological testing. Not even a high school diploma is required, except for engineering and sales positions, which are filled by graduate engineers. A committee of vice presidents and superintendents interviews candidates initially cleared by the personnel department. The supervisor who has a job opening makes the final selection. In 1979, out of about 3,500 applicants interviewed by personnel, fewer than 300 were hired.

After one year, each employee is guaranteed not to be discharged except for misconduct. Each is guaranteed at least thirty hours of work each week. There have been no layoffs at Lincoln since 1949.

## *Performance and Pay*

Each supervisor formally evaluates all subordinates twice a year on quality, dependability, ideas, cooperation, and output. Employees who offer suggestions for improvements tend to receive high evaluations. Supervisors discuss individual performance marks with the employees concerned.

Lincoln determines basic wage levels for jobs at Lincoln by a wage survey of similar jobs in the Cleveland area. Those rates are adjusted quarterly with changes in the Cleveland Area Consumer Price Index. Insofar as possible, base wage rates are translated into piece rates. Practically all production workers and many others—for example, some fork truck drivers—are paid by piece rate. Once established, piece rates are never changed unless a substantive change in the way a job is done results from a source other than the worker doing the job.

In December of each year, a portion of annual profits goes to employees as bonuses. Incentive bonuses since 1934 have averaged about the same as annual wages and somewhat more than after-tax profits. Total bonuses in 1979 were $46,000,000, and the average bonus was about $17,000. Individual bonuses are exactly proportional to merit-rating scores. For example, a person with a score of 110 would receive 110 percent of the standard bonus as applied to his regular earnings.

Exceptional worker performance at Lincoln is a matter of record. The typical Lincoln employee earns about twice as much as other factory workers in the Cleveland area. Yet the labor cost per sales dollar at Lincoln, currently 23.5 cents, is well below industry averages.

Sales per Lincoln factory employee currently exceed $157,000. An observer at the factory quickly sees why the figure is so high. Each worker is proceeding busily and thoughtfully about his task. There is no idle chatter. Most workers take no coffee breaks. Many operate several machines and make a substantial component unaided. The supervisors, some with as many as a hundred subordinates, are busy with planning and record-keeping duties with hardly a glance at the people they supervise. The manufacturing procedures appear efficient—no unnecessary steps, no wasted motions, no wasted materials. Finished components move smoothly to their next work stations, and crane operators keep materials close at hand.

## Supervision and Employee Responsibilities

Management has authority to transfer workers and to switch between overtime and short time as required. Supervisors have undisputed authority to assign production of specific parts to individual workmen, who may have their own preferences because of variations in piece rates. "We're very authoritarian around here," says Mr. Willis. James Lincoln placed a good deal of stress on protecting management's authority. "Management in all successful departments of industry must have complete power," he said. "Management is the coach who must be obeyed. The men, however, are the players who alone can win the games."[11] Despite this attitude, employees at Lincoln participate in management in several ways.

Richard Sabo, manager of public relations, says, "The most important participative technique that we use is giving more responsibility to employees. . . . We give a high school graduate more responsibility than other companies give their foremen."

---

*Question 4.* What JIT concepts are there that could strengthen Lincoln's already impressive levels of employee involvement?

---

### Employee Interviews

During the late summer of 1980, the casewriter, A. D. Sharplin, conducted numerous interviews with Lincoln employees. Typical questions and answers from those interviews are presented below. In order to maintain each employee's personal privacy, the names are disguised.

I

Interview with Jimmy Roberts, a forty-seven-year-old high school graduate who had been with Lincoln seventeen years and who was working as a multiple drill press operator at the time of the interview.

Q:   What jobs have you had at Lincoln?
A:   I started out cleaning the men's locker room in 1963. After

[11]*Ibid.,* p. 228.

about a year I got a job in the flux department, where we make the coating for welding rods. I worked there for seven or eight years and then got my present job.

*Q:* Do you make one particular part?

*A:* No, there are a variety of parts I make—at least twenty-five.

*Q:* Each one has a different piece rate attached to it?

*A:* Yes.

*Q:* Are some piece rates better than others?

*A:* Yes.

*Q:* How do you determine which ones you are going to do?

*A:* You don't. Your supervisor assigns them.

*Q:* How much money did you make last year?

*A:* $47,000.

*Q:* Have you ever received any kind of award or citation?

*A:* No.

*Q:* What was your merit rating last year?

*A:* I don't know.

*Q:* Did you supervisor have to send a letter—was your rating over 110?

*A:* Yes. For the past five years, probably, I made over 110 points.

*Q:* Is there any attempt to let others know . . . ?

*A:* The kind of points I get? No.

*Q:* Do you know what they are making?

*A:* No. There are some who might not be too happy with their points and they might make it known. The majority, though, do not make it a point of telling other employees.

*Q:* Would you be just as happy earning a little less money and working a little slower?

*A:* I don't think I would—not at this point. I have done piece-work all these years and the fast pace doesn't really bother me.

*Q:* Why do you think Lincoln productivity is so high?

*A:* The incentive thing—the bonus distribution. I think that would be the main reason. The paycheck you get every two weeks is important too.

*Q:* Do you think Lincoln employees would ever join a union?

*A:* I don't think so. I have never heard anyone mention it.

*Q:* What is the most important advantage of working here?

*A:* Amount of money you make. I don't think I could make

this type of money anywhere else, especially with only a high school education.

*Q:* As a black person, do you feel that Lincoln discriminates, in any way, against blacks?

*A:* No, I don't think any more so than any other job. Naturally, there is a certain amount of discrimination, regardless of where you are.

---

*Question 5.* How important is labor flexibility in the way that Lincoln operates?

---

## II

Interview with Ed Sanderson, twenty-three-year old high school graduate who had been with Lincoln four years and who was a machine operator in the electrode division at the time of the interview.

*Q:* How did you happen to get this job?

*A:* My wife was pregnant and I was making three bucks an hour and one day I came here and applied. That was it. I kept calling to let them know I was still interested.

*Q:* Roughly what were your earnings last year, including your bonus?

*A:* $37,000.

*Q:* What have you done with your money since you have been here?

*A:* Well, we've lived pretty well and we bought a condominium.

*Q:* Have you paid for the condominium?

*A:* No, but I could.

*Q:* Have you bought your Lincoln stock this year?

*A:* No, I haven't bought any Lincoln stock yet.

*Q:* Do you get the feeling that the executives here are pretty well thought of?

*A:* I think they are. To get where they are today they had to really work.

*Q:* Wouldn't that be true anywhere?

*A:* I think more so here, because seniority really doesn't mean anything. If you work with a guy who has twenty years here and you have two months and you're doing a better job, you will get advanced before he will.

*Q:* Are you paid on a piece-rate basis?

*A:* My gang does. There are nine of us who make the bare electrode and the whole group get paid based on how much electrode we make.

*Q:* Do you think you work harder than workers in other factories in the Cleveland area?

*A:* Yes, I would say I probably work harder.

*Q:* Do you think it hurts anybody?

*A:* No, a little hard work never hurts anybody.

*Q:* If you could choose, do you think you would be as happy earning a little less money and being able to slow down a little?

*A:* No, it doesn't bother me. If it bothered me I wouldn't do it.

*Q:* What would you say is the biggest disadvantage of working at Lincoln, as opposed to working somewhere else?

*A:* Probably having to work shift work.

*Q:* Why do you think Lincoln employees produce more than workers in other plants?

*A:* That's the way the company is set up. The more you put out, the more you're going to make.

*Q:* Do you think it's the piece rate and bonus together?

*A:* I don't think people would work here if they didn't know that they would be rewarded at the end of the year.

*Q:* Do you think Lincoln employees will ever join a union?

*A:* No.

*Q:* What are the major advantages of working for Lincoln?

*A:* Money.

*Q:* Are there any other advantages?

*A:* Yes, we don't have a union shop. I don't think I could work in a union shop.

*Q:* Do you think you are a career man with Lincoln at this time?

*A:* Yes.

### III

Interview with Roger Lewis, twenty-three-year old Purdue graduate in mechanical engineering who had been in the Lincoln sales program for fifteen months and who was working in the Cleveland sales office at the time of the interview.

*Q:* How did you get your job at Lincoln?

*A:* I saw that Lincoln was interviewing on campus at Purdue and I went by. I later came to Cleveland for a plant tour and was offered a job.

*Q:* Do you know any of the senior executives? Would they know you by name?

*A:* Yes, I know all of them—Mr. Irrgang, Mr. Willis, Mr. Manross.

*Q:* Do you think Lincoln salesmen work harder than those in other companies?

*A:* Yes. I don't think there are many salesmen for other companies who are putting in fifty- to sixty-hour weeks. Everybody here works harder. You can go out in the plant or you can go upstairs and there's nobody sitting around.

*Q:* Do you see any real disadvantage of working at Lincoln?

*A:* I don't know if it's a disadvantage, but Lincoln is a Spartan company, a very thrifty company. I like that. The sales offices are functional, not fancy.

*Q:* Why do you think Lincoln employees have such high productivity?

*A:* Piecework has a lot to do with it. Lincoln is smaller than many plants, too; you can stand in one place and see the materials come in one side and the product go out the other. You feel a part of the company. The chance to get ahead is important, too. They have a strict policy of promoting from within, so you know you have a chance. I think in a lot of other places you may not get as fair a shake as you do here. The sales offices are on a smaller scale, too. I like that. I tell someone that we have two people in the Baltimore office and they say "You've got to be kidding." It's smaller and more personal. Pay is the most important thing. I have heard that this is the highest-paying factory in the world.

---

*Question 6.* While Lincoln Electric has much in common with some of the best leading JIT manufacturing companies, it is generally believed that piece rates (extra pay for extra output) do not fit well with JIT. Are piece rates a vital part of Lincoln's success? Discuss.

*Question 7.* What is the most glaring weakness at Lincoln Electric (or are none apparent), and what are your recommendations?

---

# 24

# JIT Beginnings—Hewlett-Packard, Greeley Division

*Case topics:*

Plant-level organization for JIT

Computer-generated kanban signals

Prepack and kitting

Low-cost, flexible insert equipment

Limiting work between processes

Linearity index

"H-P way"

B for "bulky" (in ABC analysis)

Vendor day

Skit: "Stockless Production"

Group technology cells

Autonomous versus progressive assembly

The Greeley Division of Hewlett-Packard manufactures small disc drives (3½-, 5¼-, and 8-inch) for desk-top or other small computers. It is a product line appealing to more of a mass market than H-P, best known for its advanced electronics, is accustomed to.

The Greeley Division is currently crammed into space shared with other H-P divisions in Fort Collins, Colorado. A new building is going up in Greeley, 25 miles away. It will be ready for occupancy

Adapted from Richard J. Schonberger's "Case Study: Hewlett-Packard—Greeley Division," in his book *Operations Management: Productivity and Quality* (Plano, TX: Business Publications, Inc., 1985), pp. 307–15, by permission.

in four months. Wiring for phones, electrical outlets, and so forth must be final in three months. A first-draft floor plan has been prepared by industrial engineering.

A JIT project was kicked off one and a half months ago. A JIT core group consisting of four people has been meeting every day, trying to make decisions that could be built into the floor plan at the new Greeley plant site. The core group includes Dave Taylor, materials manager; Gus Winfield, process engineering manager; Doug McCord, production manager; and Mark Oman, a production section manager. Gary Flack, manufacturing manager, is the group's boss and an enthusiastic backer of the JIT project. About forty more people, including line supervisors and support staff, have been meeting in various JIT project task forces to make recommendations to the core group. For example, there was one task force for measurement, one for containerization, and one for scheduling.

---

*Question 1.* Was the JIT effort well organized? Explain.

---

## Plant Tour

It is now December 29, 1982, and John Richards, a JIT consultant, has just spent two days at the plant. Richards spent his first morning touring the Fort Collins operation, which is housed in three connected buildings—Buildings 1, 2, and 3—plus one warehouse for incoming materials a mile away. The tour followed the natural process flow to manufacture a disc drive: in the warehouse building, receiving, quality check, prepack, and storage; and in the main building complex, kitting, printed circuit (PC) board processing, final assembly, and shipping. Here are some of the things that Richards found out:

### Quality Check

Receiving inspection is a dominant activity of the quality assurance department. The defect rate on a key purchased item, the mechanical disc drive units, ranges from 5 percent for one supplier to 20 and 30 percent for two others. It takes three hours to inspect fifty drive units. The hope of doing away with most receiving inspection, as mature JIT operations in Japan do, does not seem near at hand.


## Prepack

Goods such as transistors, diodes, and memory chips do not arrive counted out in packages in the same quantities as are being used in production. Therefore, a number of people work full time opening cartons, counting pieces (sometimes by weighing) and inserting them into packages.


## Storage

Bulk storage consists of three long rows of racks served by two semiautomatic stock-picking vehicles, which allow the driver to pick by hand and also have forks for picking a whole pallet load. A card file keeps track of all storage locations.

A small-parts storage area is equipped with four long horizontal carousel storage units, which are something like those used in dry cleaning businesses to hang cleaned clothes. Cardboard boxes holding hundreds of small electronic components and hardware are on trays hung from the carousel's frame. Across from one end of the carousel units are several inclined roller conveyors.

An order is filled as follows: One person keys in a stock number at a computer terminal, which rotates the carousel so that the right bin is facing the stock-picking area, and puts the selected parts into sacks, which go into tote boxes, which move down the roller conveyors. A person at the other side of the flow racks puts delivery labels on the tote boxes to note where they are to be delivered, and the boxes are put on pallets for later delivery to the main production complex in Buildings 1 and 3.

Computers drive the put-away and order-filling activities in the bulk and carousel storage area (and also a third storage area consisting of ordinary shelving). The computers are linked to on-line terminals in all production areas. Material requirements planning (MRP) issues lists of parts needed, and storage has four days to deliver.

An "electric kanban" system conveys a message (by computer) when a using work center needs material sooner. Delivery is within twenty-four hours for electric kanban items. Fifty (of 4,000) parts presently are covered by the kanban system, and fifty more will soon be put on it. Connie Weichel, the supervisor in bulk storage, told the touring group that "we will never be able to handle fifty more." The kanban procedure dates back to August 1981, and it went on line ("electric") in October 1982.

---

*Question 2.* What do you think of the electric kanban approach? Discuss.

---

The storage area is up to date but also, by JIT standards, elaborate and containing a large quantity of materials. Examples of items kept in particularly large amounts are:

1. Printed circuit boards. An eight-month supply is on hand, partly because PC board suppliers require long purchase lead times.
2. Aluminum top covers. Almost a three-month supply is on hand right now, and it has been four or five times greater than that, even though the supplier is only 2 miles away.
3. Packing materials and manuals. Of some 600 pallet loads of material in bulk storage, about 100 hold cardboard used in packing, and 100–200 hold manuals sent out in final product cartons.

## Kitting

A kit is a set of parts that goes into one unit of product. The division prepares kits of diodes, resistors, and so forth for later insertion into printed circuit boards. The kitting is done in Building 1. Mostly the kits consist of trays or circular racks of parts used in semiautomatic insertion machines. The concept, according to Doug McCord, is to "prearrange and predevelop locations where assemblers will not need to search." Kitting has become very efficient, going from a staff of four three or four months ago to about one worker now.

---

*Question 3.* What should be done about prepack? About kitting?

---

## PC Process

The printed circuit process, in Building 1, comprises eight operations, each located in a separate area with its own crew:

1. *Silk screening.* Place dots of solder-resist on the PC board at places where solder is not intended.
2. *Preform.* Tapes of resistors and other components are fed through a machine that cuts wire ends to length and bends them so they will fit into PC board holes.
3. *Insertion.* Insert components into circuit board holes—either using a Royonic machine, which aids in hand loading, or a semiautomatic machine that inserts parts from a plastic carousel tray.

One factor that slows down insertion is the large number of different board designs, including much variation in spacing of holes in the different circuit board models. Richards asked about product standardization. He was told that H-P engineers are used to a lot of freedom to innovate and follow their own inclinations; however, there are some process engineers who work with design engineers.

4. *Wave soldering.* A wave of molten solder passes under the circuit board to connect the ends of the wires. The single large, expensive wave-soldering machine, in the middle of Building 1, can run mixed models, but only if boards are all the same thickness; the different models now come in several thicknesses.

Richards noted that the machine seemed very well vented so that no fumes or heat was noticeable.

5. *Wash.* Wash foreign matter off the circuit board.
6. *Add on.* Add various nonwashable components to the circuit board.
7. *Test.* Place each board on an H-P designed electronic testing machine, called a "bed of nails"; "nail" points make contact with various circuit locations, and a sequence of tests is run.

There are several of these machines, each set for a different size board. It takes less than a minute to key in the proper instructions to test a different model of CB.

8. *Board age.* Plug in each board for up to twenty-four hours of "burn in."

The PC process is not as automated as it is in various other large electronics companies. One reason is that H-P's volumes are small and variety of designs is large. So cheaper, more flexible machines are used. For example, H-P's semiautomatic insert machines (step 3 above) cost about $20,000, as compared with $100,000–$150,000 for highly automated machines available on the market. The core group is pleased with the low-cost equipment, since it gives them the kind of flexibility that JIT plants normally need to keep going without cushions of inventory.

---

*Question 4. How* can the low-cost equipment hold down inventory?

*Question 5.* Is there any alternative to locating each of the PC assembly steps in its own separate area? (Remember that several different products require circuit boards.)

---

## Assembly

Assembly includes a small subassembly step, making line filters, and then final assembly, in which a circuit board, filters, memory devices, drive units, and so forth are assembled and installed into a metal and/or plastic case. Assembly is not paced, that is, not regulated by the pace of a powered conveyor. Instead, each assembler has a collection of tasks leading to a tangible product that the assembler can take some personal pride in.

In the assembly area for one of the higher-volume disc drives, assemblers sit at stations along a roller conveyor. A material handler feeds drive units, circuit boards, and other component parts down the conveyor; assemblers pick the components off the conveyor, perform the assembly, set completed units aside for transport to packing, and grab more parts. Before the JIT project began, the conveyor was always crammed with components awaiting assembly. Mark Oman, the section manager, had changed the procedures so that just enough work is on the conveyor to keep the assemblers going. The idea is to cut the in-process inventory so that it piles up at an earlier stage of production—then cut it there, and so on, which results in more of a just-in-time process from start to finish.

The JIT core group has picked a low-volume line of disc drives called the Sparrow as a JIT pilot product. Gail Johnson, a production worker in Sparrow assembly, showed Richards the results of an initial JIT effort: a prominently displayed chart of the number of units produced per day for about the past month. The goal is to make exactly the same number every day, so that all stages of manufacture and purchase connected with the Sparrow line can depend on the number needed. The chart showed almost perfect "linearity"—H-P's term for meeting the fixed daily production rate (it is fixed until marketing changes it, which happens every few weeks).

The core group devised a linearity index. It is simply the number of units short or over the daily schedule; for example, if ten units were scheduled but only eight were made, that is 80 percent linearity for the day. In order to make it possible to achieve linearity on a regular basis, Mark Oman, the section manager, has instituted Toyota's concept of less-than-full-capacity scheduling of labor for the Sparrow operation. Meeting a daily schedule had not even been conceived of in the pre-JIT era, which featured the well-known "end of month push."

## Packing

Cathy Cameron, packing supervisor, told the touring group that her three largest-volume products were currently being shipped in quantities of 800, 700, and 250 per month. An "instapack" machine is central to the packing operation. The machine operator's tasks are to place a cardboard box on a stand, put a disc drive wrapped in clear plastic into the box, and squirt a liquid into the space between the wrapped drive and the box. The liquid is stored under high pressure in a tank; when it is released, it expands and quickly hardens into a lightweight rigid foam, molded around the plastic-wrapped drive. Then the box is closed and sent to taping and stenciling. One concern about instapack is that it can yield an odor. Another is that the high-pressure vessels containing the liquid could be a safety hazard. Those matters are of concern partly because of being inconsistent with "the H-P way," discussed next.

## "The H-P Way"

During the morning tour, John Richards learned that some H-P employees refer to the company rather affectionately as the "H-P Land

and Building Co.'' On seeing the main building complex for the first time, Richards had thought he was probably seeing a modern part of the Colorado State University campus. The buildings and land-scaping are quite lovely and unlike a factory. The inside is immac-ulately clean, light, airy, open, quiet, and full of plants. Richards learned that H-P spends far more on buildings than the average for the industry and that such expenditures are another element of ''the H-P way,'' which is the name for a humanistic corporate culture molded over the years by Hewlett and Packard, the founders. One concern that Richards expressed was that the present buildings did not have much dock space, which can mean a good deal of conges-tion and extra handling to unload frequent JIT deliveries.

Labor policies also reflect the H-P way. All employees are cov-ered by flex-time, in which workers receive a liberal number of flex-days off per year, based on seniority. There is no separate allowance for sick leave. The flex-days are used for everything. They may be taken an hour at a time, a day at a time, or any way desired, as the employee chooses. Employees may pick their own hours of the day to work. H-P plants are not unionized, and H-P has never had a layoff.

## Presentations

During the rest of the day and at dinner that evening, Richards met with the core group, Gary Flack, and the task forces. Plans, hopes, strategies, and concerns were presented and discussed. A few of the topics covered are as follows.

### ABC

Dave Taylor explained to Richards that all inventory items in the computer data base had been sorted out by traditional ABC analysis. They found that, instead of the usual smooth Pareto curve, H-P has a rather small number of high-dollar-usage (class A) items and a very large number of small-dollar-usage (class C) items—but hardly any in-between (class B) items. Included in the class C group, however, are a number of items that are very bulky, mainly cardboard boxes and packing materials. These were upgraded to class B, where B is for "bulky."

Taylor and Jim Heckel, the purchasing manager, feel that the ABC results provide special advantages in moving toward JIT. They may focus their JIT energies on the very modest number of class A and B items; class C items can be left largely uncontrolled at little expense.

The present ABC policy guidelines are to order and deliver class A items weekly, class B items monthly, and class C items semiannually. The core group wants the new policies under JIT to be daily for classes A and B, and quarterly for class C.

---

*Question 6.* Is the proposed ABC policy a good one? Why should bulky items get special attention? Discuss.

---

## Purchasing

Getting suppliers to convert to small, frequent lots is a central concern of the core group and Heckel. The problem is that H-P's order quantities are a drop in the bucket for most of its suppliers. H-P, Greeley, does not have the clout to get special treatment from suppliers. One hope is that other users will also begin demanding JIT deliveries from the same suppliers; also, some of the suppliers will probably get involved in just-in-time programs of their own.

Heckel's plans include bringing in some of the key suppliers for a group meeting to explain what H-P is trying to do and why. Richards mentioned that Kawasaki in Nebraska did exactly that early in its own JIT program. Like Kawasaki, H-P is calling it a "vendor day."

Richards also noted that a few other companies that have started JIT programs have elected to make a daily truck circuit to pick up small quantities of boxing and packing materials from their suppliers of those items instead of their former practice of getting separate, large, infrequent deliveries from each. Dave and Jim could see no reason why the Greeley Division couldn't do the same thing.

Heckel said paper towels, cups, napkins, and so forth were class B items that would be reduced to one-day supplies, delivered every day.

## Inventory Control

Being in the computer business, H-P has been partial toward extensive use of computers for manufacturing control. Material requirements planning (MRP) is used in most H-P plants, and use of on-line terminals to track the flow of WIP inventory is widespread. The core group's objective is to move products through the plant so fast that there is no need to track WIP—and the same goes for labor, which could simply be allocated over the total number of circuit boards at month's end. One core group member speculated that "accounting and Price-Waterhouse will tear their hair out when we start doing that." The irony of a computer company's reducing its use of computer controls also was not lost on the group.

Taylor noted during the morning plant tour, and reiterated in the afternoon, the existence of many "stockroom U's" throughout the plant. "Stockroom U" is a term sometimes used by MRP people to describe stock on the production floor treated by the MRP system as if it were in a stockroom—that is, the computer logs all flows of stock into and out of that shop floor area stockroom. The stockroom U's and ther inventory are prime candidates for reduction in the JIT project.

Gary Flack participated in part of the presentations to Richards. Flack stated that the plant currently had an average of 2.8 months' inventory on hand; his goal or edict is to reduce it to 1.9 months' worth by the end of the fiscal year (October 31). (Taylor later noted that his own target was a more ambitious 1.5 months' supply.) Flack also noted that in his division material costs account for 25 percent of end product costs, whereas labor accounts for only eight-tenths of 1 percent. Flack feels strongly that far too much attention has been paid in the past to controlling labor costs and far too little to controlling material costs. Just-in-time control seems to be just what is needed.

Flack also suggested a way to reduce the huge stock of manuals in bulk storage. H-P has state-of-art laser printing facilities in the plant, and Flack thought that perhaps it could print its own manuals, a few every day, "just in time."

## Training

The core group considered training and understanding to be keys to JIT project success. They had prepared a demonstration of the ef-

208

fects of job-lot versus JIT production. The demonstration was partially captured on slides, which were shown at an afternoon meeting attended by many of the task forces and Richards. The slides showed the four core-group members around a U-shaped mock production line made up of tables in a conference room. They were making a "product" out of styrofoam packing materials and cardboard packers. The first slides showed tables heaped with materials and production in lots of six. The next slides showed somewhat less material for a lot size of three; but a quality defect introduced toward the end caused an inventory buildup at that point. Next, slides showed nearly clear tables, achieved by one-piece lots and full JIT production. The final slides summarized results, which were based on careful counts and timing: dramatic reductions in space, lot size, cycle time, and WIP. Also, quality and rework problems that had been buried in inventory were shown to be immediately visible under JIT.

## Redundant Tasks

Gus Winfield, core group member and head of a containerization task force, felt that too much counting and prepacking is done—that the suppliers should do it as much as possible. Also, there was debate about the need for kitting and prepacking everything to improve production line efficiency. One suggestion was to have certain purchased items delivered right to the using work center with as little handling by material control as possible. Gail Johnson (Sparrow line) thought this might create a lot of packing litter that would present disposal problems.

## Plant Layout

The liveliest discussions centered on plant layout. In one of the afternoon meetings blueprints of the proposed floor plans were laid out on the table. The prints showed a more logical arrangement of processes than was possible in the present shared buildings. Everything, including storage, would be in one building. Instapack, with its potential fumes and safety problem, would be isolated somewhat in a separate room on an outer wall. Although the design of the new building does not provide for an appreciable increase in dock space for JIT deliveries, Flack observed that a wall could be knocked out if necessary.

Richards was asked for his impressions on the layout. He replied that an alternative would be to abandon totally the process-oriented layout. Instead of putting all kitting in one location, all assembly in another, and so forth, separate production lines could be developed for each product. The underlying concept is known as group technology (GT), with which the core group was familiar but had not had time to consider fully. For a given product, one long production line could be planned from receiving to shipping, with work stations so close together that work could be handed from one station to another. Alternatively, one product, say the Sparrow, could be made in two or three GT cells, perhaps U-shaped for maximum staffing flexibility. A natural separation might be wave soldering: Since there is only one wave machine, GT cells for each product could end at the wave machine; then, more GT cells could complete the production process for each product. There was some discussion about the feasibility of small, simple tabletop alternatives to the large wave machine so that each product could have its own wave process capability.

One option discussed was doing a pilot test of the GT-cell concept—probably for the Sparrow. The results could then be used to decide whether to extend GT cells or production lines to all products.

---

*Question 7.* What decision should be made on plant layout, and why?

---

Another point of controversy was whether to break up assembly jobs so that each assembler has a few operations to perform in a GT cell. At present each assembler works rather independently and is self-paced, an approach called "autonomous build." There was some sentiment for going to divided tasks in GT cells in order to get the benefits of teamwork and mutual dependency.

---

*Question 8.* Should assembly stay as it is—in mostly self-contained jobs? Or should jobs be divided up and apportioned to a mutually dependent assembly team?

---

The implications of going to GT cells were considerable. The core group members, especially the material manager, Dave Taylor, could see their jobs being eliminated or significantly altered. For example, if work stations are butted up against each other with no handling in between, the material handling staff could be reduced to almost nothing; if the production line receives, inspects, and unpacks its own materials, there go several other functions now under material control. The storage area shrinks to the point where the need for semiautomatic stock pickers, carousel storage systems, and computer-based planning may be greatly reduced. There was a lot of good-natured joking about all this and a surprisingly cavalier attitude about the prospect of eliminating one's own job.

## *Consultant's Presentation*

After lunch on December 29, Richards gave a one-hour presentation to a group of about forty—the core group, Gary Flack, and many of the task force people. Richards gave his views on the advantages of JIT, told about other Japanese and American companies doing it, and detailed a few of the alternative ways to proceed in the Greeley Division, especially focusing on the provocative issues of plant layout by processes or by GT cells. After the meeting broke up, Richards was saying goodbye and getting ready to catch a plane, and Taylor and Winfield were marveling at the groups of task force members out in the halls buzzing about the issues before them and the hard decisions that had to be made.

# 25

# JIT in Purchasing at GE, Erie

*Case topics:*

Reducing number of suppliers
Rejuvenating a sick business
JIT purchasing in a large job shop
Measures of performance in purchasing
Centralized purchasing by commodity group
Visitations to suppliers
Codestiny with suppliers
Late and early deliveries
Pushing inventory back on makers
MRP as a precurser to JIT
Selecting items for JIT purchasing
Terms of a sole-source contract
Pace of implementing JIT purchasing

In mid-1982 John Yates, manager of purchasing at General Electric Company's Transportation Systems Business Operations (TSBO) in Erie, Pennsylvania, was facing several crucial decisions. GE, Erie, was expanding its JIT program, and full implementation of JIT in purchasing would require a sharp break with traditional purchasing

Adapted from Edward W. Davis's case UVA-OM-484, "General Electric Company—Transportation Systems Business Operations." Copyright © 1983 by the Colgate Darden Graduate Business School Sponsors, University of Virginia, Charlottesville, VA. Reproduced as adapted by permission.

policies. One of those policies was to strive for multiple competing suppliers for each purchased part. TSBO has pursued that policy with renewed vigor in recent years, and had gained significant cost savings in the process. However, JIT seemed to call for fewer, not more, suppliers.

One immediate decision facing Yates involved a critical diesel engine part. He was reviewing a proposal to negotiate a long-term supply contract with a single supplier, which would replace short-term contracts with two suppliers currently supplying the part. Yates knew that following that philosophy on a broader scale would lead to a large reduction in the number of TSBO suppliers, possibly as much as a 50 or 60 percent reduction. The prospect was troubling, and Yates was unsure to what degree the just-in-time approach should be attempted, if at all, in purchasing.

## Background: Pre-JIT Era

TSBO in Erie produced complete railway locomotives and electric drive motors for use in off-highway vehicles and in oil and other drilling equipment. TSBO produced many different types of railway locomotives, including diesel-electric, electric, switching, and mining locomotives for both the domestic U.S. and export markets. The Erie facility is shown in Exhibit 25–1.

The manufacture of locomotives was complex and time-consuming. Each locomotive was built to the unique specifications of the customer. The variety of end products was large relative to the total number of units produced each year. Manufacturing took place in ten separate buildings, as is illustrated in Exhibit 25–2. Parts, materials, and semifinished components moved among and within these buildings.

The period from 1970 through 1976 was one of severe decline for the Erie operation. General Motors' locomotive manufacturing division in LaGrange, Illinois, had long dominated the domestic U.S. market for rail locomotives. For example, of the 28,000 rail locomotives estimated to be operating in the United States in 1976, approximately 24,000 were built by GM and only 4,000 by GE. In the 1970–76 period GE's share of new locomotive sales was extremely low. According to one top GE manager, "We didn't even deserve that." He agreed with other observers that GE's locomotive product image in the market place presented a picture of generally low quality

213

**Exhibit 25-1.** TSBO Erie Facility

and high operating costs. The chief users were reported to be giving GE small orders to maintain a second source of supply, "just in case" of need. The absolute low point was reached in 1976, when TSBO received not a single new order for domestic locomotives.

In 1977 C. J. Schlemmer appointed M. S. (Rick) Richardson general manager of locomotive operations. With the support of other members of the Erie top management team, the two convinced corporate management that TSBO could be a viable, successful business. Corporate management authorized a $300-million expansion program. That represented the first large-scale "retrofit" of an existing GE operation in a mature industry in the Northeast. TSBO began new programs to upgrade product quality, improve productivity, and reduce costs. Automation was a principal component of the programs. Plans called for introducing robotics and numerically controlled equipment in the welding and metal fabrication shops, a flexible machining center in motor frame manufacturing, and several computer-controlled storage-retrieval systems for raw material and work in process. GE also planned a highly automated facility for the manufacture of locomotive diesel engines, to be built 60 miles away in Grove City, Pennsylvania.

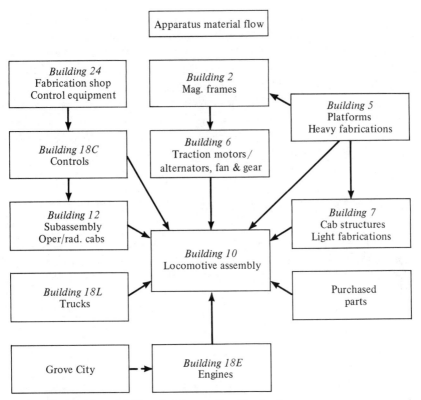

**Exhibit 25–2.** Material Flow in Locomotive Production

## Purchasing at TSBO

Purchasing at TSBO was a sizable support function, involving about 6,000 suppliers, 50,000 parts, more than 100,000 drawing numbers, and approximately $300 million in annual procurement value. Until 1978 purchasing operations were divided into four independent product-oriented units: locomotive and diesel, propulsion, control, and transit cars. About forty buyers and forty expediters handled purchases.

TSBO was an enormous job-shop complex, with great variety in day-to-day activities, and purchasing reflected that variety. The number of purchase orders, mostly small-lot "buys" of five to ten parts, was in the tens of thousands per year. Lead times on those orders were often short, and the purchasing staff worked on tight deadlines. As one purchasing manager noted, "Running a purchasing operation in a business like TSBO is a high-pressure affair. Thirty percent of our items are needed in two weeks or less from order placement. Manufacturing is pushing us to get the parts in so they can meet their delivery deadlines." Many of the buyers and expediters cited a normal fifty- to sixty-hour work week as proof of the rigors of the job, and they also expressed pride in their ability to meet manufacturing's deadlines. As a manager in contract administration noted, "I don't think the locomotive line has ever been stopped due to lack of purchased parts; that's rule number one around here; we will never knowingly hold up the line."

## Materials Management Improvements, 1977–79

In the period 1977–79 TSBO initiated a number of cost reduction and productivity improvement efforts in the materials management area. Edward R. Woods, manager of materials, who came to the Erie operation in 1975, commented on the situation that existed prior to 1977:

> Materials management was out of control. The sales forecasts given to us were insufficient; we had no capacity planning; production schedules were revised every month and we couldn't react fast enough; the number of new parts, products, and engineering changes were driving us crazy; and there were continual delays in new product introductions. We had tried MRP [material requirements planning] a couple of times, but it failed because we didn't involve the work force and they didn't support it.
>
> Every building had its own separate purchasing and materials staff. Some buildings reported to the production control manager, some to the materials manager. The business was so fragmented; everyone was looking out for his piece of the total. There was no overall plan. Oh, we had a systems plan, but it wasn't integrated across the whole business. We left it up to finance [TSBO's systems people] to implement things. There was no one in manufacturing to coordinate materials systems with other functions.

In 1979 Ed Woods was given total responsibility for materials in all buildings. Under Woods, the department drew up the first-ever materials operating plan and a total system plan. Woods appointed a new production control manager to coordinate the plans. Over the next two years materials management started a number of projects, including a new MRP education program for the work force; established building-by-building inventory reduction plans; and improved

216

inventory record accuracy and stockroom discipline. It also launched a manufacturing cycle analysis to aid in setting inventory goals. A dominant product, the locomotive diesel engine, was selected for this study. As Woods noted,

> This was a massive effort. There were so many different possible engine variations. We knew what we wanted to do, but the job was immense. So we got some help from corporate consulting. We did a generic engine manufacturing and procurement cycle analysis for each of the basic model families we had: about eight to ten different models [Exhibit 25-3 provides an illustrative chart]. We formed study teams for every line on the chart and went in and asked, "How can we reduce the cycle? How can we reduce the buffer inventories?" We found out what really went into each of the products, and how to manage them, how to cut cycle times. It took us two years to do it all, but we knew we had to have those facts.

By December 1979, the MRP system was operating, with a high degree of employee support, and significant improvements in materials operating performance were beginning to be realized. For example, from 1977 to 1979 locomotive material availability increased from 60 to 85 percent, and stockroom accuracy for locomotive parts increased from 75 to 85 percent. Commenting on those improvements, George Sauerwine, manager of inventory programs, said that "the most important step for us was first understanding the manufacturing cycle. You have to understand the cycle before any big adjustments to inventory can be made." He also credited people's acceptance of the new inventory goals to the careful analysis of manufacturing cycles.

---

*Question 1.* Are those levels of material availability and stockroom accuracy high? Are they good measures of performance? Discuss.

---

## Purchasing Improvements, 1980–81

In 1980, TSBO implemented the first of a series of important reorganization and consolidation steps in purchasing. Plans for the changes had been formulated during the previous two years, along with the restructuring of the materials management function. One step was to create an advanced materials organization, which con-

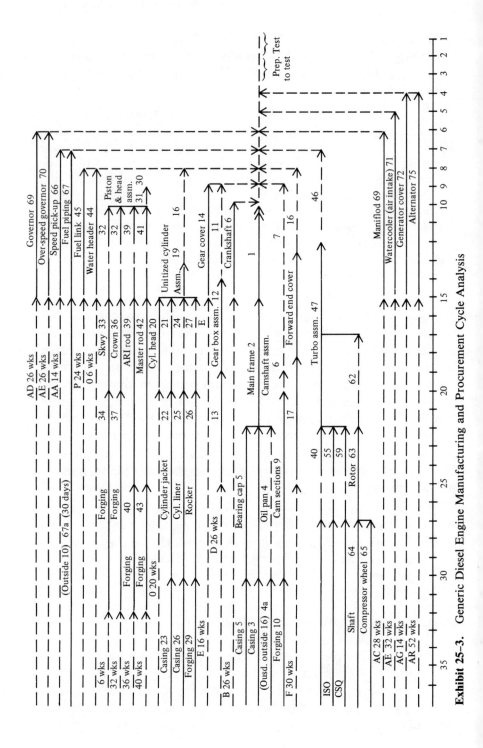

**Exhibit 25-3.** Generic Diesel Engine Manufacturing and Procurement Cycle Analysis

218

solidated three of the four independent purchasing operations. Over a one-year period propulsion was combined with locomotive and diesel. The transit car operation was dissolved because of declining sales. The previous duplication of buyers, expediters, and other personnel, which existed with the separate organizations, was eliminated. The new organization used only one head buyer for each major commodity group (steel, rubber, and so on), with specialty buyers for subgroups such as steel castings and plastic injection moldings. Because of those and similar efficiencies, manpower was reduced from eighty to about fifty-five, and the new ratio of buyers to expediters was on the order of 2 to 1. Exhibit 25-4, showing the material management organization under Woods, includes the purchasing changes.

The reorganization was part of what some people termed a "new era" for purchasing at TSBO. That era had its origins in the new directions set by the Richardson management team in 1977. As Woods noted,

> Up through the mid 1970s our cost containment and productivity improvement concerns here, like most other U.S. manufacturers, were primarily focused on direct labor. But after we backed off and looked at it from a fresh perspective, we began to see the increased importance of purchased materials. The purchased parts content of our end product was up to over 50 percent, and our inventory carrying charges alone were about equal to the direct labor content of the product. So that motivated us to look harder at purchasing, to intensively examine everything we were doing.

Along with the appointment of Yates as manager of purchasing, the new efforts included creating three new programs for improving the quality and reducing the cost of purchased materials. Exhibit 25-5 contains excerpts from a brochure distributed to suppliers, including summary descriptions of two of those programs.

One of the programs was called PACE: Product Application and Cost Evaluation. Focusing on TSBO's principal dollar-volume suppliers, PACE called for new levels of cooperation between TSBO and the suppliers. Also, PACE was intended to offer the suppliers more than the traditional cost-cutting "philosophies and platitudes," as Yates put it. Yates noted further:

> In the past, whenever there was a big push on controlling purchased parts, TSBO would rent a conference room, invite a hundred to two hundred suppliers in, and lecture to them. But that was essentially a one-way conversation. PACE was something entirely different; it involved our bringing the suppliers in one at a time. First, Richardson

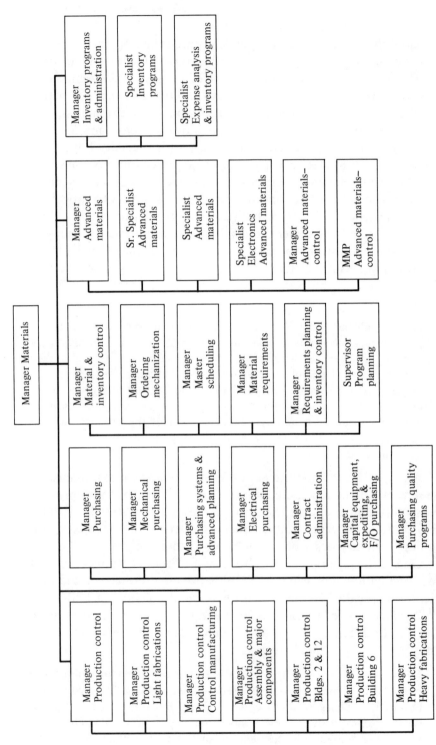

**Exhibit 25–4.** TSBO Materials Management Organization

Manager Materials

Manager Production control
- Manager Production control Light fabrications
- Manager Production control Control manufacturing
- Manager Production control Assembly & major components
- Manager Production control Bldgs. 2 & 12
- Manager Production control Building 6
- Manager Production control Heavy fabrications

Manager Purchasing
- Manager Mechanical purchasing
- Manager Purchasing systems & advanced planning
- Manager Electrical purchasing
- Manager Contract administration
- Manager Capital equipment, expediting, & F/O purchasing
- Manager Purchasing quality programs

Manager Material & inventory control
- Manager Ordering mechanization
- Manager Master scheduling
- Manager Material requirements
- Manager Requirements planning & inventory control
- Supervisor Program planning

Manager Advanced materials
- Sr. Specialist Advanced materials
- Specialist Advanced materials
- Specialist Electronics Advanced materials
- Manager Advanced materials–control
- MMP Advanced materials–control

Manager Inventory programs & administration
- Specialist Inventory programs
- Specialist Expense analysis & inventory programs

# The GE Locomotive Operations Material Procurement Story

- Product Application and Cost Evaluation — P.A.C.E.
- Supplier Originated Savings — S.O.S.

**Excellence Thru Productivity**

The **QUALITY** MAKERS

Locomotive Operations

---

**GENERAL ⊛ ELECTRIC**

# Our material productivity program . . . the best materials to build today's best locomotives, motorized wheels, drilling motors, transit equipment and control units.

**Keeping management informed.**

We call it our Productivity Improvement Program. It's a detailed plan that lets top management know just what Materials Procurement sees in the future and how we've done so far.

Through monthly forecasts we tell management what they can expect in material cost reductions during the coming year.

Each buyer constantly tracks his personal performance to assure monthly predicted cost reduction goals are met.

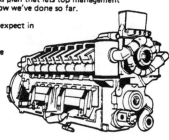

**Exhibit 25-5.** Excerpts from Vendor Brochure

or C. M. Watland [general manager of manufacturing] would have breakfast with them, then we'd give them a complete tour, show them what we were doing, ask their opinions on how we could make improvements, cut costs. After they visited Erie, we'd send a team into their facility, which often included people from engineering and manufacturing, in addition to purchasing. We'd work with the supplier's

**Product Application and Cost Evaluation. P.A.C.E.**

The more we save on material costs, the more competitive we make General Electric products. Through our P.A.C.E. Program, we're challenging our suppliers to help us achieve a 6% material productivity goal.

Participation in our P.A.C.E. Program provides our major dollar suppliers the opportunity to help us value engineer our products. Beneficial material substitutions, design changes and process modifications are just a few ways we can achieve material productivity.

The program gives the suppliers a lot more than our cost cutting philosophy. A GE team actually works with the supplier to recommend new equipment, improved manufacturing techniques and more effective quality control. The team determines whether a long-term GE contract will help the supplier lower his prices and strengthen his position as a strong competitive business.

**A GE Team that helps our suppliers meet our needs.**

Locomotive Operations will put a special General Electric task force to work for its suppliers. Experts in engineering, manufacturing, quality control and finance. Professionals who can help our suppliers meet our rigorous quality and cost needs.

# Our Supplier Originated Savings program . . .

■ **Objective**
Provide opportunity to our suppliers to earn increased share in the locomotive business and reduce our costs by 6%.

■ **Procedure**
Suppliers are encouraged to submit cost saving recommendations to the buyer they normally call on. The dollar magnitude of accepted recommendations will be considered in evaluating the overall price of their products. Suppliers can earn a greater share of our business by submitting innovative recommendations that save dollars anywhere in locomotive operations.

- Each and every cost savings recommendation will be dispositioned within 60 days after receipt.
- All recommendations will be reviewed for adoption and dispositioned by our cognizant productivity team chairman. A formal letter will be forwarded to the supplier advising of our evaluation.
- Quality and reliability will not be compromised.

■ **Recognition**
Based on results, a vendor of the month and year will be selected.

**Exhibit 25-5**—*Continued*

people on ways to improve their business: new manufacturing techniques, new equipment, better financial controls, new quality control procedures. Sometimes both Ed Woods and I would go on these visits, which could last one or two days.

Another goal of PACE was to see if our better suppliers might be able to increase the number of products they supplied to us. We thought

**Keeping our suppliers competitive.**

We're always trying to develop new suppliers. Why? Because the more suppliers we have, the more competitive each supplier has to be to get our orders. They have to keep their price in line and quality high. Also, we want to create a blend/mix buy on critical parts and a second source for every item. We always want to have a source we can depend on.

How are we developing new sources? For one thing, we're looking off-shore, as we also sell off-shore. And we're using some new techniques and helping our major suppliers find more economical sources of their own. We're using General Electric overseas operations to develop new suppliers.

# General Electric's material productivity objectives . . .

- **Reduce costs** — We must find better ways to build the products manufactured at Locomotive Operations at lower cost.
- **Improve quality** — No matter how good our products, we can not afford to rest on our reputation.
- **Improve customer service** — There's a lot more to our program than the right product at the right price. Like meeting deadlines, and bending over backward to provide the customer the kind of service he needs.

These are our Operations goals. In the next few pages you'll see how Locomotive Procurement is doing its share.

**Exhibit 25-5**—*Continued*

this could result in a higher-quality product and also reduce the total number of suppliers we had to deal with. We were at 6,000 suppliers in 1979 and increasing. So when we took them through our business we didn't just talk about what they were already doing with us; we'd show them other parts, other applications of their own products, and encourage bids on them, too. We were after quality improvements with PACE as much as after cost savings. But we also got cost savings, sometimes in unexpected ways. For example, one of our suppliers of a precision-machined part asked, after he saw how we were using the part, "Why do you require those polished surface finish tolerances in these noninterfacing areas?" We didn't really know; our engineering department said, "That's always been our spec for that type of part." It turned out we didn't need that finish, so we eliminated the spec and saved money with absolutely no loss in performance quality.

There were many examples like that. Right from the beginning one of our main rules was, never criticize a supplier's idea, no matter how silly is seems at first. And it paid off for us. Another reason the PACE program was so effective was that for the first time the suppliers heard right from the top of our organization what our problems and concerns were, and we heard from their top people the same kinds of things . . . and everybody involved heard it all at the same time; they all heard the same thing. Before this, whatever was said often got twisted up in being passed around.

According to Yates, a key factor in the success of PACE was the direct support of top management. He noted that over a two-year period Richardson or Watland never missed a PACE meeting at Erie. Yates felt such support was responsible for the steady growth of the program; it grew in spite of the amount of time and effort spent working with each supplier, which effectively limited participation to fewer than fifty suppliers a year. By the middle of 1982 more than ninety suppliers had been involved. They accounted for more than 60 percent of the annual dollar value of purchased parts, and estimated total savings to GE were in the neighborhood of $4 million.

Another program, the SOS (Supplier Originated Savings), was established in mid-1981 to involve the remaining suppliers—providers of lower-dollar-volume parts. Based on a similar earlier program at the Ford Motor Company, SOS provided incentive bonus awards, prizes, and added business to suppliers for their worthy suggestions and ideas. The program had an announced goal of reducing TSBO purchase costs by 6 percent. To initiate SOS, special announcements went out to approximately 4,500 suppliers. Exhibit 25–6 shows an enclosure from the announcement, and Exhibit 25–5 gives a summary of the SOS program from a brochure distributed to suppliers. TSBO people met with individual suppliers as the need arose, but not on the same scale as with the PACE program. The SOS program was well received, and by mid-1982 savings were estimated to be in the neighborhood of $1 million.

Another improvement program undertaken in 1980–81 was the Dual Source Savings (DSS) program. In 1979, competitively sourced parts accounted for about 51 percent of purchased parts dollar volume. When parts were single-sourced, it was usually because of stringent engineering specifications/approvals and supplier tooling limitations. The DSS program sought to reduce both the number and dollar volume of single-sourced items by opening as many as possible to competitive bidding. Some of the rationale for DSS was traditional purchasing doctrine, calling for multiple sources of supply, with the expectation of lower costs.

The DSS program also provided for cost-functional review teams. The teams analyzed purchasing performance measurements, set sup-

# GENERAL <img_ge> ELECTRIC
## LOCOMOTIVE OPERATIONS

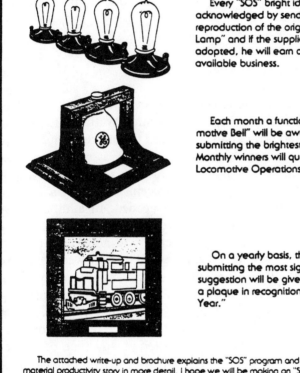

Locomotive Operations has been searching for new and innovative ways to enhance our productivity. Today we are introducing a new program which we are calling SUPPLIER ORIGINATED SAVINGS - SOS. We believe our suppliers have ingenious ideas to help enhance our productivity. Every supplier can participate and we will recognize viable recommendations by awarding additional business for adopted suggestions.

Every "SOS" bright idea submitted will be acknowledged by sending the recommender a reproduction of the original "Edison Mazda Lamp" and if the supplier's suggestion is adopted, he will earn a greater share of our available business.

Each month a functional mounted "Locomotive Bell" will be awarded to the supplier submitting the brightest idea during the month. Monthly winners will qualify for consideration as Locomotive Operations Supplier of the Year.

On a yearly basis, the supplier selected for submitting the most significant productivity suggestion will be given a locomotive ride and a plaque in recognition as our "Supplier of the Year."

The attached write-up and brochure explains the "SOS" program and Locomotive Operations material productivity story in more detail. I hope we will be making an "SOS" award to your firm in the near future.

Manager of Purchasing

**Exhibit 25-6.** Excerpt from SOS Program Announcement

plier evaluation criteria, and established budgets for tooling, samples, and prototypes from suppliers. The program encouraged competition by requesting bids from new suppliers, evaluating and approving multiple suppliers, and actually placing orders with new suppliers. Purchasing undertook those changes, realizing there were

some risks, including possibly higher prices (if the current single supplier turned out to have been supplying the part at an unrealistically
low price), increased tooling costs, more supplier startup problems,
and additional engineering costs.

Savings from the Dual Source Savings program were slow at first
but grew to be quite large. Cumulative total savings in the third full
year after program inception were estimated to be about $3 million.
As a result of the program, suppliers became increasingly competitive; sourcing changes were frequent as first one supplier, then another, reduced prices.

## Just-in-Time Movement: 1982

Application of just-in-time concepts began as an effort to reduce
inventory carrying costs. In early 1981 Chuck Watland, the general
manager of manufacturing, had challenged the entire manufacturing
team to optimize inventories, purchased as well as work-in-process.
TSBO typically ordered raw material and parts on a monthly, quarterly, or even semiannual basis; upon receipt at Erie, the material
was placed in inventory and held until needed. In addition to the
usual problems of occasional late deliveries, material was often delivered earlier then required; that practice had gone unopposed at
Erie for years, for a variety of reasons. JIT, with weekly or even
daily deliveries, would theoretically minimize unneeded inventory,
including deliveries arriving too early. TSBO production control and
purchasing people discussed the delivery problems and agreed on the
need for improvement, but there was great uncertainty about how.
There was also general reluctance to attempt any type of JIT approach without first gaining better control of delivery timeliness.

### Shifting Viewpoints

In October 1981, Woods participated in a GE management seminar
that included a trip to manufacturing companies in Japan. The visits
caused him to rethink the JIT concept. He began to consider seriously applying JIT not only to purchased parts but also to the flow
of materials and components among TSBO's ten locomotive manufacturing buildings. Such an extended application of JIT would require that all work in process (WIP) not required for a particular

days' use at a particular work center be returned to the location from whence it came. If all of that excess WIP were pushed farther upstream in the manufacturing process, all excess material eventually would be returned to raw material inventory or fabricated and purchased parts storage. As inventory built up at those storage locations, it would in turn be pushed back on the supplier. Ideally that process would eliminate all excess raw material and purchased parts inventory held at TSBO.

---

*Question 2.* Is pushing inventory back on the makers likely to do any good? Explain.

---

When those JIT ideas were presented to the shop foremen and production control supervisors in early 1982, there were strong but not unexpected concerns and doubts. The general feeling was that if JIT worked in Japan, it was because of unique conditions there, but it was not suitable for the TSBO environment. There was some agreement among the group that WIP inventories had in the past been too high. They also acknowledged that shop floors were often cluttered with parts and material awaiting work—to the point of confusion. But, the foremen and production control supervisors noted, those problems were already being attacked with the new MRP system and other programs, with good results. The dominant concerns about JIT were not having sufficient stocks on hand to keep lines operating and workers active. Under JIT, buffer stocks would be nearly eliminated, with much higher risks of a long work stoppage if problems occurred.

---

*Question 3.* Are the foremen's and supervisors' views valid? Explain.

---

As the group studied JIT concepts more closely over the next few months, other constraints surfaced. For example, they learned that the MRP system, which had been operating successfully for only a couple of years, would have to be redesigned to permit scheduling in daily intervals of time rather than the weekly periods used. They judged that much higher levels of MRP data accuracy would be required, and higher service levels on all parts would have to be provided, if manufacturing schedules were to be maintained. There would also be much shorter intervals of time for correcting problems and essentially no room for error in quantities or schedules. Another problem they recognized was the more severe impact of poor quality. As one foreman commented, "What good does it do to get the material in right on time if it's no good, and we don't have any buffers to cover our tails?" The proponents of JIT argued that, for fabricated parts, the quality problem could be addressed by intensive educational and motivational programs oriented toward the unionized hourly work force. For purchased parts they felt that the infrastructures established by the PACE and SOS programs could be directed, as another goal, toward still higher quality levels.

In spite of those initial concerns, the implementation of JIT in the shops moved forward in the early months of 1982, primarily through intensive discussions and study sessions by teams of supervisory and middle management personnel. The diesel engine was selected as a test case, with results to be evaluated by the study teams. If the results were favorable, JIT would then be applied at the new, highly automated engine plant under construction at Grove City. Exhibit 25-7 provides some facts about the diesel engines produced at TSBO, including an exploded view showing key components.

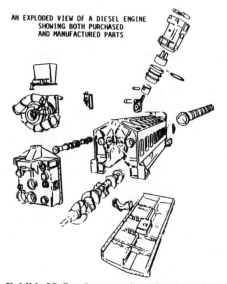

AN EXPLODED VIEW OF A DIESEL ENGINE SHOWING BOTH PURCHASED AND MANUFACTURED PARTS

THE GENERAL ELECTRIC 16-CYLINDER DIESEL ENGINE WEIGHS 43,300 POUNDS AND IS USED IN APPLICATIONS OTHER THAN LOCOMOTIVE POWER. IN THE LAST FEW YEARS, THE DIESEL ENGINE HAS SHOWN ITS ADAPTABILITY IN APPLICATIONS SUCH AS STATIONARY MODULES FOR BACK-UP POWER GENERATION, BOTH ON LAND AND SEA, THE LATTER BEING USED ABOARD OIL RIGS LOCATED OFF-SHORE. OTHER DIESEL ENGINE USES INCLUDE MOTIVE POWER FOR TUG BOATS AND OCEAN-GOING VESSELS.

- 1500 TO 4000 HORSEPOWER

- CURRENTLY APPROXIMATELY 7800 ENGINES IN FLEET

- MINIMUM LIFE 15 YEARS
    - MILLION MILES AVERAGE

- CONSUMES AN AVERAGE OF $9000 PER YEAR IN RENEWAL PARTS AND REBUILD SALES

- RENEWAL PARTS EQUALS 30% OF DIESEL ENGINE SHOP OUTPUT

- MOST PARTS INTERCHANGEABLE AMONG 8, 12 AND 16-CYLINDER MODELS

**Exhibit 25-7.** Locomotive Diesel Engine (Sample Facts)

## JIT in Purchasing

The initial actions in purchasing followed Watland's original ideas about delivery frequency. In view of the broad geographic distribution of TSBO suppliers and the distances involved (see Exhibit 25–8), there was a good deal of skepticism about the feasibility of those ideas. However, with some diligent effort the purchasing study team was able to identify 300 of about 1,000 purchased diesel engine parts that were currently on monthly or quarterly deliveries but were potential candidates for weekly deliveries. They qualified because of proximity, method of delivery, size, weight, or other factors. The total dollar value of those 300 parts was more than 75 percent of the total. It was hard to estimate how many of them could be converted to weekly deliveries. Furthermore the question, noted earlier, of how to gain better control over the timing of deliveries had yet to be answered.

As Yates and his management team dug deeper into the issues, they discovered that much more was involved than simply requesting more frequent deliveries from the suppliers. They found, for example, that Japanese companies had far fewer suppliers than similar North American companies. A partial reason was the Japanese con-

**Exhibit 25–8.** Distribution of TSBO Suppliers

cept of "codestiny," which treated the supplier as an extension of the company. Relations between supplier and user companies were much closer than was common in North America. Sharing of such information as production schedules, long-term demand forecasts, and engineering and design information apparently were factors in the JIT approach that contributed to the very high reliability of supplier deliveries as well as extremely high quality levels.

---

*Question 4.* Is "codestiny" motivated by self-interest, by some finer value, or by cultural conventions? Explain. How can Yates's team develop "co-destiny" relationships with suppliers? Or can they?

---

In reviewing those facts, Yates's team saw that serious pursuit of JIT would require possibly large reductions in the total number of suppliers and an increase in the number of single-source suppliers. The latter prospect was particularly troubling, since it ran directly counter to traditional purchasing doctrine in general and the Dual Source Savings program in particular.

To many on the TSBO study team, the idea of single-sourcing critical engine components was a great concern. After much discussion they decided to select one test case for thorough evaluation before drawing conclusions or making recommendations to higher management. They chose the diesel engine crankshaft, one of the locomotive's highest-priced parts.

## Single-Sourcing: The Crankshaft Decision

Supplier A, TSBO's primary supplier of the crankshaft, was a few hours' drive away in another part of the state. A had a record for prompt deliveries and excellent quality. TSBO's second source, Supplier B, had slightly lower prices than A, but with B there had been problems of missed delivery dates and occasional below-spec quality. The two companies were the only ones considered for supplying the crankshafts, which required many intricate machining operations and expensive special-purpose machinery to manufacture.

Supplier A had already participated in the PACE program because of the importance of the product it supplied. That, plus its past performance record, made A a logical candidate for single-source supply. Yates and Woods requested a meeting with A's top management to discuss the possibility. Along with that initial meeting, the TSBO team visited A's plant to investigate its manufacturing capabilities and fabrication processes and to determine the "critical path" for crankshaft manufacturing.

Supplier A was eager to become the single-source supplier. In addition to increased business the TSBO, A would realize other benefits. For example, A's management pointed out that by being a single source with a long-term contract, A could better plan its capital investments for all crankshaft manufacturing, including non-GE business. The equipment used in A's operations was custom-built, with a two-and-a-half-year lead time. With knowledge of its crankshaft requirements two to three years down the road, A would be more likely to invest in equipment to reduce its costs of operations and lower its prices to TSBO. A's management stated that the investment would not occur if current TSBO purchasing procedures were continued.

With A as the single source of crankshafts, it was likely that the overall quality level and reliability of deliveries would be improved. On the other hand, if crankshafts were not available or were defective, manufacturing of the engine would be stopped in its second work center, upsetting the entire manufacturing operation. Proponents of single-sourcing at TSBO felt there was little chance of such a calamity. They pointed out that A's record showed it to be essentially riskless as a source of supply, the quality of the crankshaft was nearly 100 percent perfect, and deliveries were reportedly always on time. A also had its own steelmaking capabilities in the event the raw material supply was interrupted, while down time of its equipment was negligible. Furthermore, although A was unionized, the union was an independent one, and it had had only one strike in its history; the strike occurred during contract negotiations just at the time President Nixon came out with his wage-price freeze.

In addition to questions of risk and safety of supply there were also issues relating to contract terms and pricing. For example, if TSBO decided to single-source crankshafts at Supplier A, a contract explicitly stating all terms and conditions of the agreement was needed. An important question was, how long should the contract extend? Clearly, A wanted as long-term a commitment as possible (for equipment purchasing and the like), while TSBO wanted a shorter-period commitment as a hedge if single sourcing did not work out. Another contract issue was whether single sourcing of crank-shafts should be explicit or implied. Also to be resolved was the pro-cedure for setting prices.

Finally, the TSBO group was concerned about how much fin-ished goods inventory A would carry. Typically, each TSBO order constituted about an eighteen-week supply. A would usually produce that amount, with a few extra crankshafts as safety stock, shortly before the required delivery time. Thus A typically carried very little finished goods inventory for TSBO. The issue was what level of in-ventory would be appropriate for the new long-term single-source contract? TSBO's purchasing staff felt that at least twelve weeks' supply should be retained at all times, while A's management thought this would be excessive.

The single-sourcing issue generated fierce controversy at TSBO. Some argued that, for lack of price competition, the crankshaft would become overpriced very quickly. Also, with smaller order lots under the JIT approach, quantity discounts would be lost. And there was concern that, given its criticality, the crankshaft was simply not the correct part with which to attempt single sourcing. Finally, there were fears that the supplier would take advantage of the situation and "put it to GE," since suppliers had been played off against one another in the past.

## Other Unresolved Issues

In addition to the single-sourcing issue, the problem of supplier de-livery schedules needed to be addressed. Because of the emphasis given in purchasing to meeting manufacturing deadlines and the skills built up in the expediting group, late deliveries had become a small problem. However, the practice of accepting early deliveries had gone unopposed for years and had slowly been increasing in the past year or so. There were several alternatives, none of them attractive to everyone involved. TSBO could, for example, (1) return the nonre-quired material to the supplier and either charge the supplier for freight or absorb it, (2) keep the excess material on a consignment basis and either hold the supplier's invoice without payment or rein-voice the supplier for the nonrequired portion, or (3) find another supplier who would stick to delivery schedules.

*Question 5.* What is the best answer to the early-delivery problem? Discuss.

Finally, there were important quality management issues that had not yet been resolved. As noted earlier, quality was a greater concern under the JIT approach than before. Finding suppliers who could consistently meet the new quality standards was a sizable task for the TSBO purchasing organization. Also, even if suitable suppliers could be found, the tighter discipline imposed upon them could lead to higher prices for the material supplied. Under JIT, suppliers could be expected to experience higher costs due to additional setups, packaging, freight, and financing, while GE, Erie, would realize savings in such areas as inventory carrying costs, material handling, storage space, and insurance. While it could be argued that it was unrealistic to expect the suppliers to absorb all of the extra costs, there was unfortunately no previous experience to use as a guide.

It was clear to Yates as he considered those issues that the JIT approach, if implemented fully, would greatly alter his purchasing operations. It was also clear that his handling of the issues could influence the success of the entire JIT program at Erie.

*Question 6.* Yates is very tentative and cautious. Is he unreasonably so? Explain.

*Question 7.* In 1980 purchasing at TSBO was centralized. Should it stay that way? Discuss.

# 26

# St. E's Hospital

*Case topics:*

Production-line food service

Automated material handling in
a hospital

Fail-safing (pokayoke)

Loss of technicians trained in
apprentice program

Equipment maintenance

Standardized facilities and
equipment

Needs for buffer stock

Extra machine capacity

Quality and cost performance
of a supplier

Twin-cart system

Volunteer labor versus
automated stock handling

Lot sizes/production intervals

Size of raw material stocks

St. Elizabeth Hospital ("St. E's") existed for years at a site a few miles south of downtown in Lincoln, Nebraska. In the early 1960s, because of fire codes and various other reasons, it became clear that the hospital would have to be either remodeled or completely rebuilt elsewhere. Finding that remodeling costs were higher than the construction of a completely new structure, the officers and board decided to build. They chose a new site in the direction of recent population shifts. The structure, completed in 1970, has a 208-patient bed capacity. Some of the innovative features of that hospital are an

---

The author was assisted in the writing of this case by several of his operations management students at the University of Nebraska.

in-house power generation system with a back-up cooling water supply, a technologically advanced food preparation system, and an automated materials handling system.

St. E's made several operational changes in conjunction with the new hospital's construction. On advice from a consulting firm, Friesen and Associates, the hospital abandoned certain traditional ideas, such as nursing stations. A new concept of health care was adopted.


## SPD (Monorail) System

Mr. Friesen, the consultant, began his career in 1929 and served as a hospital administrator for three hospitals in Canada before planning a chain of United Mineworkers hospitals in the United States. In 1954 Friesen founded a hospital consulting firm in Washington, D.C. Many of Friesen's innovations were incorporated into the new St. E's hospital. They include:

1. Standardization of the size of nursing units and zones and elimination of nurses' stations to encourage more attendance at patients' bedsides
2. Multipurpose private room for the care of any patient regardless of age, sex, diagnosis, or severity of illness
3. Compact nursing alcove in each patient room
4. Nurservor unit that contains a "clean" section and a "soiled" section for medications (The unit is in the wall between the patient's room and the corridor, where technicians remove soiled and used supplies and insert clean and new supplies.)
5. Automated, integrated supply processing and distribution (SPD) system; some of its features:
   a. Twin-cart system for distributing and maintaining inventories of supplies
   b. Adaptation of industrial transportation devices to a health-care facility (The devices include a monorail automatic cart transportation system and an automatic tray ejection device for tray conveyors.)
   c. Nurservor
   d. Innovations in processing reusable supplies, such as double-door washers (in the laundry), double-door sterilizers, and automatic washer-decontaminators
   e. A pneumatic-tube system

    f. Surgical-delivery suite
    g. Concentrated care center located next to surgical-delivery suite
    h. "Ready foods" system—frozen foods heated by microwave ovens just before consumption by patient
    i. Integration of communications systems

## SPD Operations

The centralized materials handling and processing system is the first of its kind to be used in a hospital anywhere in the world. The heart of the system is an interconnected monorail carrier network. The system is capable of conveying unmanned carts throughout the hospital and depositing them at the desired location. Mr. Harsh, director of the SPD Department, describes the system as a huge circular pipeline carrying needed supplies of food to the proper location and returning soiled items to the service area of the hospital.

The monorail's hook and trolly track originates on the first level of the building. Branches of the system are located in food processing, the pharmacy, and the receiving and supply area. Carts or large wire baskets fitted with overhead clamps are lifted and carried by the monorail to a specially designed elevator. The elevator raises the containers to the right floor, where they are ejected into a "clean-hold" room. From there, floor personnel handle the carts. In the same manner carts filled with dirty dishes, floor laundry, and refuse are sent via a separate elevator from a "soil-hold" room on each floor to the soiled-item receiving room on the first level. Most items begin to be processed there. The carts and hooks pass through a steam sterilizer before returning to the supply area to be refilled.

The monorail carts (or baskets) are programmed to exit at the proper location. A set of switches located throughout the hospital is tripped when a cart, with three manually set bars, moves through them. The bars contain a code for any location.

The system is set up to handle different functions at certain times of the day. The normal schedule is as follows:

Laundry: 8:30–10:30 A.M.
Food Service: 7:00–8:30 A.M., 11:00 A.M.–noon, 4:30–5:30 P.M.
Pharmacy: intermittent, giving way to food
Supply: integrated with other functions

In case of emergency, such as a special need in an operating room or emergency room, a direct line is used to phone the control supervisor, who locks out the regular function and directs the system to carry the needed supplies to the right place.

One problem is that people sometimes misset the codes. Then carts are lost, which is an inconvenience and could lead to a patient-care failure. Carelessness and horseplay are thought to be the main cause of lost carts. A training course for persons using the system helped heighten worker awareness, but problems still arose.

---

*Question 1.* Suggest ways to "fail-safe" or "foolproof" (the well-known Japanese word is *pokayoke*) the cart-delivery system.

---

Another problem is with the automatic elevators, which often get hung up on the floors until manually cleared. Although a monitoring system is available to inform supervisors of a jam, the controls are not always properly monitored, so that elevators may be hung up for extended periods of time. Those current problems are modest compared with the early SPD problems.

## Early SPD Problems

When the SPD system was initiated, employees felt a certain amount of "technology shock." Sometimes they would not use the monorail system, and at other times they misused and abused it—dirty dishes to the operating room, laundry to the kitchen, carts to the basement, and so forth.

Part of the reason appears to be that little or no training accompanied the move from the old hospital building to the new one. The employees were merely told to go to work. Besides having normal fears of change, employees were intimidated or fascinated by the machinery, to the neglect of the total system. They didn't seem to realize that food trays still had to get to patients and sterile instruments to the operating room; they lost sight of the goal—delivery—not just loading the monorail.

Lack of training and early misuse of the system led to a lack of confidence, which was aggravated by equipment failures. Making the physical system work was easy compared with restoring the lost confidence.

237

It was obvious that the SPD system was in serious trouble. Friesen and Associates was called back. The Friesen group identified the main problem as a "complete lack of top-level management control in the SPD area." They cited these related problems:

- No scheduled work assignments
- No enforced work descriptions
- Poor staff flexibility
- Poor communication into both the sterile and general processing areas
- Nonuse of monorail
- No accountability of personnel
- Overspecialization of jobs
- Poor control of cart dispatching
- Lack of documented formal systems and procedures for entire area
- No formal review of carts, levels, requests from floors, and so forth

The Friesen group developed a program of improvement with these objectives:

1. Reestablishing confidence in the system
2. Improving management control of the system
3. Enforcing use of the system

To implement the objectives, the consultants recommended establishing a permanent director of SPD. The director was to have two full-time managers. The director and managers were to set up a cohesive organization with defined responsibilities and lines of authority, job descriptions, training programs, and work schedules. A periodic management audit was to be performed with a goal of identifying problems while they still were minor.

## Current Problems

One problem with the monorail is the cost of maintaining and eventually replacing it. Last year alone the SPD department spent $20,000 replacing worn cables. Also, the monorail has an expected life of fifteen years, and SPD estimates that the cost of replacing it will be triple the original cost. (The current monorail system is heavy-steel industrial grade, which had been the only type available. Now lighter-weight monorail is marketed.)

## Maintenance

Besides the SPD system, Friesen also introduced the idea of a total energy plant, which would enable the hospital to supply all its own power and at one-eighth the cost charged by a utility. The power plant is run by a skeleton crew of two key personnel and a supporting staff. One man, a diesel mechanic, was specially trained on the plant's power producing engine. The other was a former small-town electrical generator man, who was responsible for training the rest of the staff. St. E's has not had a power loss in eight years.

The maintenance department is in charge of the power plant and four other divisions as well: (1) general maintenance, (2) security, (3) housekeeping, and (4) building and grounds. All departments are under the supervision of Mr. Wunderlich, an architectural engineer.

General maintenance employs twelve people, the most critical being an electrician, a cart mechanic, a plumber, and an air handler. An apprentice program was developed so that transitions would be smooth when key personnel left St. E's. That has proved unsuccessful, because apprentices are lured away from the hospital to higher-paying jobs before they have a chance to move into the key position.

---

*Question 2:* Some people say the limited technical training and lack of apprentice programs in North America (as compared with the excellent programs in Germany, for example) are a serious obstacle to industrial improvement. Is it really that much of a problem, and, if so, is there anything St. E's can do about it?

---

One of the main responsibilities of the maintenance department is continuous upkeep of the monorail system. Parts for the monorail and other machinery had been supplied by the machine manufacturers only. As a result, St. E's had to stock a costly inventory of spare parts. A search for cheaper alternatives revealed that many parts were interchangeable, and some were supplied by local companies with same-day service. St. E's switched to local sources for those parts.

In addition, St. E's began to require all manufacturers who supplied machines to the hospital also to provide an operations manual, wiring diagrams, a parts list, and training.

Maintenance also has its own biomedical shops, which provide patient instruments. This service began six years ago, when the hospital decided it would be less espensive to handle the service internally than to contract for it.

Several other maintenance services are contracted out on a seven-day, twenty-four-hour basis. Those include (1) elevators, (2) heating and air-conditioning, (3) clock system, (4) fire alarm system, and (5) 1,000 television sets. Housekeeping is also contracted out.

Two other maintenance units at St. E's operate without any particular problems. They are the security division and building and grounds.

## Laundry

The laundry department is the primary user of the SPD system. A description of the laundy flow follows, beginning with laundry on the "floor," that is, being used by the patients and doctors.

A closet in each patient's room has two doors, one leading directly into the room and the other opening into the hall. The closets hold one day's supply of laundry for the room (sheets, towels, etc.). The two top shelves of the closet hold clean laundry, while the dirty laundry goes on the two bottom shelves.

Fourteen people handle laundry pickup and delivery. Once a day they visit each room and stock the closet with the correct items as shown on their preset lists for the given room. After stocking an entire floor, they return to pick up the dirty laundry from each closet. They sort the dirty laundry into color-coded plastic bags. Yellow bags are for general-use laundry; blue bags indicate dirty laundry from operating rooms; and red bags, which are filled by the nurses (who have already been in contact with the laundry and handle the dirty laundry with gloves), are for laundry that is contaminated. The carts are hydraulically raised and placed on the monorail and go automatically, via one of two laundry elevators, to the laundry floor.

When the dirty laundry arrives at the laundry floor, it reenters the monorail system. Laundry workers take the dirty laundry from the carts. If it is in a red bag, workers place the laundry in a pressurized gas sterilization chamber before it is touched by human hands. The carts, made of stainless steel, go to be sterilized in the adjoining room.

If the laundry is in a yellow or blue bag or not in a bag, workers put it on an overhead conveyor that takes it to the sorting room, where it accumulates in an overhead chute. The sorter pulls a cord to allow a certain amount of laundry to drop. The laundry is sorted (towels, sheets, uniforms, etc.) into green carts. The sorting acts to avoid imbalances in the washing process and allows drying times to be standardized by type. The sorter rolls the carts to the washing area and dumps the laundry into large white canvas bags hung from the ceiling. An attendant then loads the laundry from the canvas bags into the washers.

There are two washing machines, each with a 400-pound capacity. A partition separates the clean side from the dirty side, and the washing machines sit in the middle with openings on both sides. After a one-hour wash cycle, the attendant unloads the clean laundry on the clean side and then loads the clean laundry into dryers. There are three dryers, one with a 100-pound capacity and the other two dryers with 50 pounds of capacity each. Maximum drying time per load is fifteen minutes.

Dried laundry is emptied into carts and later folded and shelved. Any pieces that look worn are taken out of inventory to be used as rags by cleaning and maintenance crews. Also, at this point any stained items are separated from the regular inventory, dyed, and used only in special-care units.

Total laundry inventory is about $75,000 worth. That inventory includes four times the amount of linen needed per patient. It is enough for one day on the floor, one day in backup, one day on the shelf, and one day in processing. Annual replacement costs approximately $40,000.

Each patient uses an average of 4 to 5 pounds of laundry per day, and each surgery uses from 35 to 40 pounds. To keep up with that volume, the laundry is operated seven days a week by fourteen full-time employees. The washing shift is ten hours, while the remaining laundry duties are run on eight-hour shifts.

The age of the equipment is the chief concern. All washing and drying machines are seven years old, with an expected ten-year life. St. E's bought the machines from a manufacturer in Louisiana. Machines have been breaking down at an increasing rate over the last several years. For example, on the date that Mr. Harsh was being interviewed, the large washing machine was down, and there were problems with one of the dryers. Because of the distance to the manufacturer, parts could take as long as a month to arrive at the hospital after they were ordered.

Harsh got approval to buy a new 450-pound capacity washing machine in January 1978 from the Louisiana manufacturer. The plan was gradually to phase out the old machines. St. E's would buy from the same manufacturer to keep down the inventory of parts and maintenance training.

---

*Question 3:* Standardized machines—same manufacturer—sometimes is cited as a principle of just-in-time production. What JIT benefits, if any, apply in this case?

---

When St. E's washing machines broke down, the laundry still did get done, but at higher cost. When one machine was down, the extra cost was for overtime wages to run the other machine extra hours. When both were down, the extra cost was to subcontract to an outside laundry service; that cost was about $1,100 a day, as against $825 a day to do it inside.

---

*Question 4:* Is the one day of backup laundry needed? If so, what conditions justify the need, and what could be done about those conditions?

---

## Food Service

Food service at St. E's Hospital is operated by ARA Company, a nationwide food service provider headquartered in Philadelphia. ARA has held the contract at St. E's since 1970, and it provides food service to other hospitals in the immediate area as well. ATA corporate headquarters negotiates the contract with St. E's on a fee basis.

St. E's employs a new process called reconstituted food. It involves precooking, freezing for indefinite time periods, and reheating the food when it is ready to be served. The food service operation is also unique in that it uses the monorail conveyor system to transport food from the main kitchen to the patient, which avoids the usual manual carrying of food trays.

Bill Warren is the food service manager. Also on the ARA payroll are an assistant manager, a unit clerk, and two dieticians. Warren also supervises fifty-five part-time and full-time employees (forty-four full-time equivalents), who are on the hospital payroll.

ARA prepares meals for contract and outside delivery, for the cafeteria, and for patient service. The equivalent of two and a half full-time employees work on outside contracts, seven work in the cafeteria, and the remainder are about evenly divided between the main kitchen and patient service. There are five full-time cooks in the main kitchen, as well as porters and salad and storeroom workers. The patient-service employees are either diet clerks or galley technicians.

Food service employees are on three different work cycles:

1. Salad and cafeteria people are on a three-week cycle with odd days off and working two out of three weekends.
2. Main kitchen workers produce the food on an eight-hour day, five-day-a-week schedule. Part-time workers do porter and storeroom work during the weekend.
3. Patient-service employees work a two-week cycle of four ten-hour days.

There also are a dietician and a diet cook for weekends.

Food service provides 1,200 meals a day. Of that total, 450 are "Title 7" government-contract meals, which are delivered to three local sites daily and five rural cities once a week. Other contract meals, for special diets only, go to the state penal complex. (See Exhibit 26–1.)

## Purchasing and Control

Peglar and Company is St. E's supplier of foodstuffs. ARA calls upon a secondary supplier when Pegler cannot supply the needed food item.

The ARA inventory clerk orders meat daily and items such as canned goods, produce, and baked goods once a week. Food is stored by food groupings, and the inventory clerk keeps track of the dollar

| | | |
|---|---|---|
| *Meals served per day* | | 1,200 daily |
| Patients | | 600 |
| Employees & guests (cafeteria) | about | 130 |
| Elderly clients [1] | | 450 |
| Special orders [2] | about | 20 |

*Variety of meals served*
Salads:
    15 entree salads
    10 smaller salads
Main dishes:   40 entrees
Desserts and beverages

*Diets prepared*
Regular diet – 65 percent
Special diets (ordered by doctor) – 35 percent

*Charge for meals* (does not vary according to selection)
80 cents per meal materials + 45 cents labor = $1.25
Guests – $2.00 main meals – $1.00 breakfast

---

[1] Meals to elderly in surrounding areas–City Council on Aging.

[2] Special diets to inmates at penal complex, etc.

**Exhibit 26-1.** Meals Served/Cost of Meals Served

investment of goods on hand, along with a log book by item. The inventory clerk estimates needed purchases based on upcoming orders for food preparation.

Bill Warren states that ARA is very pleased with the service and prices from its supplier, Pegler and Co. Warren states that it is rare in the food service business to find a supplier who provides both the best service and the lowest price.

---

*Question 5:* Should good service normally mean higher prices? Answer the question for Warren's food service operation and also for any type of production. Be specific, e.g., *what* extra costs would there be, if any?

---

Upon receipt, the purchased items are checked, dated, and put into storage alphabetically, moving the old items forward and placing the new inventory in the back.

To minimize shortages in inventory, (1) the doors of the storeroom within the work area are kept closed, (2) the remote-area storeroom is under lock and key, and (3) all inventory removed for preparation of food is measured (weighed or counted) and recorded in the inventory log as to quantity and use.

## Packaging and Storage

Packaging includes loading a dish with predetermined portions of meat, vegetables, and a starch; in the case of special diet foods, the "dish" is an individual pouch. After the main dish is assembled, it is plastic-wrapped and passed through a shrink tunnel to remove the excess air, then placed in baskets—nine dishes, twenty cups, or twenty-five pouches to a basket.

After packaging, food service people place the baskets on separated racks in the blast freezer, where the temperature is dropped to minus 40 degrees F. for three hours. When the air is circulated in the blast freezer, the chill factor is equivalent to minus 120 degrees F. The food is then moved to another freezer, where the temperature is maintained at 0 degrees F. The food can be stored up to three years. The storage freezer has space for enough meals to take care of the hospital for two weeks. All meals (in-house and Title 7 meals) go through the packaging line, but only the in-house meals are put into cold storage.

## Food Service

The cooking area is equipped with a floor mixer, a cabinet mixer, three mixing basins, two large convection ovens, two conventional ovens, a cabinet-top stove or grill, a deep-fat frier, and a charbroiler. (See Exhibit 26–2). Only two or three main dishes are prepared and completed in the eight-hour day worked by the cooks.

The day's production schedule of main dishes is determined by taking a physical inventory of meals in storage and comparing with a minimum storage list.

Preparation of a main dish is done in portions of tens and hundreds. All the ingredients for the batch are removed from inventory by weight per the recipes, which indicate the number of scoops and the scoop size for the batch.

---

*Question 6:* Are the lot sizes and frequencies of "production" right for the situation? Explain.

---

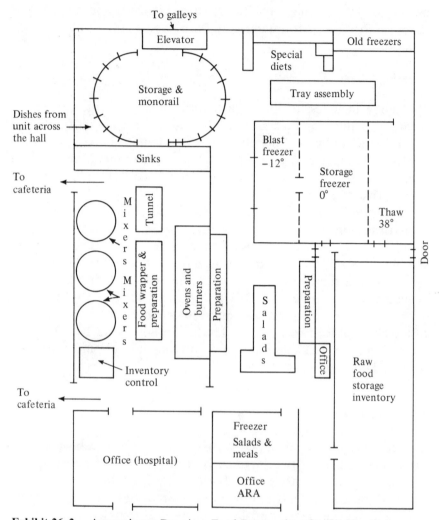

**Exhibit 26-2.** Approximate Drawing: Food Preparation, St. E's Hospital

Each evening, after receiving the following day's patients' orders from nursing services, food service people remove the meals from the storage freezer and place them in a cooler kept at 38 degrees F. Average time in the cooler is eleven to twelve hours. When the meals are removed from storage, they are marked with the microwave oven setting and dates, as they have a five-day life after removal.

Prior to meal time, food service assembles the "house" meals and the individual patients' meals. Meals, on trays, are assembled by floor and by quadrant on each floor, which makes it easier to avoid error in programming the carts to move by monorail to the proper floor and quadrant galley.

The tray assembly line has eight stations staffed by eight galley technicians. Galley techs work on meal assembly for forty-five minutes, then go by elevators to the galleys to prepare and heat the food. Additional duties include maintaining the cleanliness of the galleys.

---

*Question 7:* Many hospitals rely on volunteers to move trays and fetch things. Is St. E's solution—automated movement—better? In answering, keep in mind the appropriate principles of world-class manufacturing.

---

The dietician measures, prepares, and assembles special diets requested by a doctor: bland, low fat, weight-reduction, and salt-free diets. The special-diet meals are marked with special instructions and placed on the appropriate cart for delivery to the galley and then the patient.

The eight galleys are each equipped with two microwave ovens, three small refrigerators, two large refrigerators, a coffee pot, and tray-area storage at 38 degrees F. The galley tech prepares each of the thirty or so meals for the quadrant and presents the meals to nursing service for delivery. It takes about thirty minutes to serve all the meals. (See Exhibit 26–3.)

If a patient is not ready for a meal at serving time, the meal stays in galley storage until the patient is ready. Then a nurse heats and serves the meal.

Patients who enter the hospital after orders are placed are served stock meals until they are able to order their own choice of food. Warren pointed out that with the four- or five-day life of items in the thawing freezer, meals are not wasted when a patient is dismissed from the hospital after ordering a meal. The meal is simply given to another patient who orders the meal within a four- or five-day period.

Patient contact with the nurses when taking food orders provides ARA with feedback as to patient complaints. The most common complaints were cold food and lack of variety in food choices. ARA staff also attempt to survey patients to determine their complaints, but not on a daily basis.

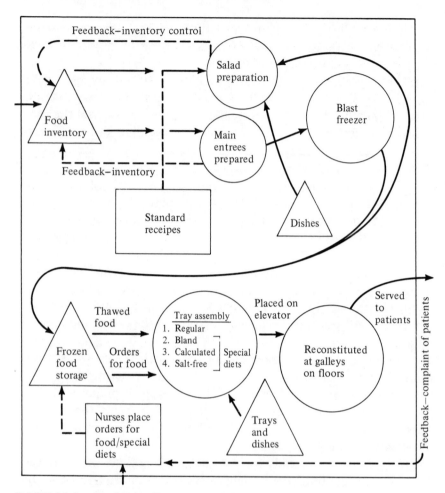

**Exhibit 26-3.** Production Process, Food Service, St. E's

## Food Director's Evaluation

Warren stated that the following were the most severe problems in food service:

1. Lack of counter space and poor design in the food preparation area (No one asked a cook about how the kitchen should be laid out.)
2. Mechanical breakdowns of the monorail and the microwave ovens
3. System of determining unit cost: Hospital Association Stan-

dard system versus Medicare system (HAS is used with some meals, whereas the Medicare System is used for meals served to Council-for-Aging clients.)

4. Dish breakage: expensive, but not billed to ARA
5. Communication problems between nurses and food service workers (Often a meal might be hot when it leaves the galley but cold by the time a nurse serves it.)

Warren's overall evaluation was based on service to the patients, which he ranked as the number one priority. He felt that the system did a good job, especially in providing patients with a variety of food selections. As to cost, he said he thought the transer of labor costs from cooks (high cost) to galley technicians (low cost) saved money. Further, portions have been accurately predetermined to hold down waste. Besides, food utilization is better than in other food-service systems, because food has a five-day life after its removal from frozen storage. It is also easier to hire cooks since they are able to work five- to eight-hour days.

Warren had not checked the ARA accounting books and had no idea whether the reconstituted food service actually saved money. He thought that an HAS survey ranked its food service operation second or third out of a field of ten hospitals.

## Other Services

The SPD system has an impact on the operating methods of three other service areas: warehouse, pharmacy, and operating rooms.

### *Warehouse*

The warehouse comprises the receiving, supply room, and supermarket areas. Goods received are stored according to their assigned computer number. The supply room carries a 90- to 180-day stock of items. Goods are transferred daily from the supply room to the supermarket area, which carries a forty-eight-hour inventory of carts for various hospital areas. Floor supply carts, filled with each floor's supply requirements for the two days, roll out each morning. When the new supply cart (called a sister cart) arrives in clean hold, the previous day's supply cart (a twin cart), which is now partially empty, is returned to the supermarket area and replenished for the next day.

---

*Question 8:* Suggest improvements in inventory
management.

---

The supply carts are parked in clean hold for access by the nursing staff. Server carts are loaded from the supply carts and used to replenish the nurservors for each room.

## Pharmacy

The pharmacy usually sends supplies to the floors in wire baskets by the monorail system; the nursing staff then transfers the supplies to the pharmaceutical stations. Special orders can reach the elevators in minutes through the emergency interrupt system. Also, the pharmacy may send small items throughout the hospital via the pneumatic tube system.

## Operating Rooms

Sterile, wrapped instruments and other items are collected on an individual-patient basis, either from a list filled out by the operating room nurse or from a list generated by the computer. The list comes from a case card containing surgeon numbers, case type, and instrument preferences. These items are placed on carts and then wrapped in plastic for their trip to the operating room on the second level.

After the instruments have been used, they and other reusable items are returned on a "soil" cart to soil-receiving, where they are washed and sterilized. A belt conveyor then moves the instruments into the instrument washer receiver room, where they are rewashed, resterilized, and stored for future use.

---

*Question 9:* What should St. E's do about its
aging SPD equipment?

---

# Bibliography

**Books**

Deming, W. Edwards. *Quality, Productivity, and Competitive Position.* Cambridge: Massachusetts Institute of Technology, Center for Advanced Engineering Study, 1982.

Fukuda, Ryuji. *Managerial Engineering: Techniques for Improving Quality and Productivity in the Workplace.* Stamford, Conn.: Productivity Press, 1984.

Hall, Robert W. *Zero Inventories.* Homewood, Ill.: Dow Jones–Irwin, 1983.

Hayes, Robert H., and Steven C. Wheelwright. *Restoring Our Competitive Edge: Competing Through Manufacturing.* New York: John Wiley, 1984.

Ishikawa, Kaoru. *Guide to Quality Control.* Tokyo: Asian Productivity Organization, 1972.

———. *What Is Total Quality Control? The Japanese Way.* Englewood Cliffs, N.J.: Prentice-Hall, 1985.

Monden, Yasuhiro. *Toyota Production System.* Norcross, Georgia: Institute of Industrial Engineers, 1982.

Schonberger, Richard J. *Japanese Manufacturing Techniques: Nine Hidden Lessons in Simplicity.* New York: The Free Press, 1982.

———. *World Class Manufacturing: The Lessons of Simplicity Applied.* New York: The Free Press, 1986.

251

Shingo, Shigeo. *A Revolution in Manufacturing: The SMED System.* Stamford, Conn.: Productivity Press, 1985.

――. *Study of Toyota Production System from Industrial Engineering Viewpoint.* Tokyo: Japan Management Association, 1981.


**Selected Articles**


Ashburn, Anderson. "Toyota's 'Famous Ohno System.'" *American Machinist,* July 1977, pp. 120–23.

Hayes, Robert H. "Why Japanese Factories Work." *Harvard Business Review,* July–August 1981, pp. 57–66.

Hunt, Rick; Linda Garrett; and C. Mike Merz. "Direct Labor Cost Not Always Relevant at H-P." *Management Accounting,* February 1985, pp. 58–62.

Kaplan, Robert S. "Measuring Manufacturing Performance: A New Challenge for Managerial Accounting Research." *The Accounting Review,* 58, No. 4 (October 1983): 686–705.

――. "Yesterday's Accounting Undermines Production". *Harvard Business Review,* July–August 1984, pp. 95–101.

Leonard, Frank S., and W. Earl Sasser. "The Incline of Quality." *Harvard Business Review,* 60, No. 5 (September–October 1982): 161–71.

Miller, Jeffrey G., and Thomas E. Vollmann. "The Hidden Factory." *Harvard Business Review,* September–October 1985, pp. 142–50.

Schonberger, Richard J. "Integration of Cellular Manufacturing with Just-in-Time Production." *Industrial Engineering,* November 1983, pp. 78–83.

――. "Production Workers Bear Major Responsibility in Japanese Industry." *Industrial Engineering,* December 1982, pp. 34–40.

――. "Rationalizing the Workplace: First Step in Implementing Robotics." *Robot-X News,* February 15, 1983, p. 15.

――. "A Revolutionary Way to Streamline the Factory." *The Wall Street Journal,* November 15, 1982.

――. "The Quality Dividend of Just-in-Time Production." *Quality Progress,* October 1984, pp. 22–24.

――. "Work Improvement Programs: Quality Control Circles Compared with Traditional and Evolving Western Approaches." *International Journal of Operations and Production Management,* 3, No. 2 (1983): 18–32.

Schonberger, Richard J., and James Gilbert. "Just-in-Time Purchasing: A

Challenge for U.S. Industry.'' *California Management Review,* Fall 1983, pp. 54–68.

Schonberger, Richard J., and Marc Schniederjans. ''Reinventing Inventory Control.'' *Interfaces,* 14, No. 3 (May–June 1984): 76–83.

Suzaki, Kiyoshi. ''Work-in-Process Management: An Illustrated Guide to Productivity Improvement.'' *Production and Inventory Management,* Third Quarter 1985, pp. 101–11.

Walleigh, Richard C. ''What's Your Excuse for Not Using JIT?'' *Harvard Business Review,* March–April 1986, pp. 38–54.